P9-EDZ-644

AMERICAN RELIGIOUS VALUES
AND THE
FUTURE OF AMERICA

AMERICAN RELIGIOUS VALUES
AND THE
FUTURE OF AMERICA

edited by
RODGER VAN ALLEN

with contributions by

Sydney E. Ahlstrom	Michael Novak
Martin E. Marty	David J. O'Brien
Benjamin E. Mays	Rosemary Radford Ruether

Marc H. Tanenbaum

FORTRESS PRESS Philadelphia

CAMROSE LUTHERAN COLLEGE
LIBRARY

BL
2530
U6
A46
/ 30,271

Biblical quotations from the Revised Standard Version of the Bible, copyright
1946, 1952, © 1971, 1973 by the Division of Christian Education of the National Council of the Churches of Christ in the U.S.A., are used by permission.

COPYRIGHT © BY FORTRESS PRESS 1978

All rights reserved. No part of this publication may be reproduced, stored in a retrieval
system, or transmitted in any form or by any means, electronic, mechanical, photocopying,
recording, or otherwise, without the prior permission of the copyright owner.

Library of Congress Catalog Card Number 76-15894
ISBN 0-8006-0486-5

5776L77   Printed in the United States of America   1-486

Contents

Editor's Foreword

The pages which follow had their beginning in 1974 with a conversation I had with Norman Hjelm, director of Fortress Press, concerning the American Bicentennial and the occasion that it presented to the religious community for doing what it should be periodically doing anyway: critically assessing the past that the present might be better understood, and the future more positively and creatively charted. The conversation concerned the qualities of the desired reflective process.

The next step was dialogue with colleagues in the Religious Studies Department of Villanova University. A theme was agreed on: American Religious Values and the Future of America. It was decided that the Religious Studies Department would sponsor a series of lectures with particular perspectives on this theme reflecting the experience of Protestants, Catholics, Jews, blacks, and women, in addition to a keynote and concluding lecturer. The participating lecturers were those whose essays you will have the pleasure of reading in the pages that follow: Sydney E. Ahlstrom, Martin E. Marty, David J. O'Brien, Marc H. Tanenbaum, Benjamin E. Mays, Rosemary Radford Ruether, and Michael Novak. The essays are somewhat revised versions of the papers presented during the 1975–76 academic year at Villanova.

Participants did not gather as a group at any one time, but desired dialogue was achieved by the format of this volume. Each participant in addition to writing a major paper also wrote an introduction to one colleague's paper and a response to another's, and the results are lively, direct, and clearly worthwhile. This process was completed during the 1976–77 school year. Occasioned by the Bicentennial the book is thus a product of reflections that both preceded and assessed it. The idea of rushing the book into print during the Bicentennial year was dismissed as unworthy of the seriousness and quality of content of the book desired.

A volume such as this, however, is presented with humility. History, Reinhold Niebuhr has observed, is "essentially unpredictable." A bit more than a decade ago a noted symposium on religion in America saw the clergy to be "preeminently activists," and communities to be intent

Rodger Van Allen is Professor of Religious Studies at Villanova University. He is author of *The Commonweal and American Catholicism* (Philadelphia: Fortress, 1974) and co-editor of *Horizons,* the Journal of the College Theology Society.

upon de-ethnicization as "the ability to rise above Old World provincialisms."[1] While that symposium produced notable and worthwhile insights, it was carried on as a rather self-consciously narrow intellectual enterprise. Today, what activist clergy there are get little notice; recapturing one's ethnic identity is a serious affair; and intellectuals are taking considerable pains to be in broad community dialogue. (It was instructive to see the respect for broad exchange which several contributors showed by revisions they undertook following questions from and dialogue with the large, diverse audience attending the Villanova lectures.)

But, however shifting and difficult the terrain beneath us might be, we need to keep moving forward. We cannot simply stand still and wait for "essentially unpredictable" history to occur, for we are not only witnesses, we are participants, indeed, important creators of that which comes about. With this in mind, each contributor was asked "to reflect on the values, events, and features in our American religious experience that need to be called to mind if we are to meet our present and future challenges both resourcefully and effectively."

In a brilliantly sweeping historical overview which begins and situates our discussion, Sydney Ahlstrom concludes his presentation by pointing to the egalitarian principle which is the major premise of the Declaration of Independence and stresses the need to restore the ideal of equality to its proper place in the dialectics of freedom. Martin Marty in an impressive survey of Protestants in the United States (see the helpful map enclosed inside the back cover) gives a long list of the positive features of various Protestant church communities, and suggests that there is wisdom in sharing and working with one's best qualities. David O'Brien exhorts Catholics to use their post-Vatican II freedom in creative communal forms of social concern that will help reshape their own identity and the world in which they live. One may be grateful that both Catholics and Protestants are beyond the time when their identity was established merely over-against one another. More positive and creative identities are now needed.

Marc Tanenbaum, Benjamin Mays, and Rosemary Ruether, speaking from the experience of a Jew, a black, and a woman, inform us, to use Rabbi Tanenbaum's words, "that after two centuries there is no such thing as a single monochromatic 'official' American history, but that America makes no sense unless the nation knows the histories of all its

1. Cf. William G. McLoughlin and Robert N. Bellah, eds., *Religion in America* (Boston: Beacon, 1968), pp. xi, xiii.

constituent parts." Unlike some, the groups these writers discuss have not been tempted by nationalistic millennialism, and instead have frequently represented, as Benjamin Mays states, "hope in the midst of suffering, confidence in the ultimate goodness of God in the face of massive evil, and certainty that his sovereignty over time and eternity is unimpaired by the human misuse of freedom."

Michael Novak's contribution identifies Catholics as a pivotal religious group in America and celebrates their caution of moral rhetoric and practical concern with family, neighborhood, and foreign policy. His views are challenged as are those of all contributors in the comments which precede and follow their essays.

Grateful thanks are extended to the following members of the Villanova academic community who in various crucial ways supported this project: Rev. Edward J. McCarthy, O.S.A.; Rev. John M. Driscoll, O.S.A.; Dr. James J. Cleary; Rev. Richard D. Breslin, O.S.A.; Rev. Francis A. Eigo, O.S.A.; Rev. Hugh J. Cronin, O.S.A.; Dr. John Custis; Rev. Edward Hamel, O.S.A.; and Rev. Bernard Lazor, O.S.A. The patience and cooperation of each of the contributors and of the staff of Fortress Press have been most appreciated. Finally I wish to thank my wife, Judy, and our children, Rodger, Katie, Tom, Paul, and Peter, for the support they give in many ways.

Villanova University　　　　　　　　　　　　　　　RODGER VAN ALLEN
Villanova, Pennsylvania
Fall 1977

Acknowledgments

Acknowledgment is gratefully extended for quotations from the following:

Jürgen Moltmann, "The American Dream," *Commonweal* (August 5, 1977), New York: Commonweal Publishing Co.

Clinton Rossiter, *Seedtime of the Republic*, New York: Harcourt Brace Jovanovich, Inc., 1953.

American Religious Values
and the
Future of America

Introduction

Sydney E. Ahlstrom has written widely on the history of religious, and especially Protestant, thought in the United States. In 1972 his magnum opus, *A Religious History of the American People,* was published by Yale University Press. This massive volume was immediately acclaimed as the outstanding scholarly achievement of this generation in the field of American religious history. The book is a unique blend of exhaustive scholarship and creative and profound interpretation. Its author is a man of energy, imagination, and integrity who has provided Americans with a sweeping interpretation, not of their religious life alone, but of their historic self-understanding. For this reason, Ahlstrom's work is a contribution not only to our knowledge of the American past but to our continuing national effort to renew and revitalize both our public and private lives.

In his essay introducing our analysis of "American Religious Values and the Future of America" Ahlstrom draws upon his enormous knowledge of Christian history to provide a challenging context for the discussion. Like all great historians, Ahlstrom provides a dramatic structure to his descriptions of religious change and development. In this essay he places American history in the broad sweep of Western civilization. In the long history of the West, religious values and visions have been central to human experience. These values changed through the Middle Ages, producing tensions which burst forth in the Protestant Reformation. For Ahlstrom, the great movements for reform provide the fundamental starting point for America. It was Protestantism, and Puritanism in particular, which shaped the foundations of the English colonies and the formation of the American national consciousness.

To begin a discussion of American religious values, then, we must first deal with the religious values of Western culture, of which America is a part. Then we must, as Ahlstrom sees it, look to the core ideas of the Reformation, that revolution in Western history which, with Weber, he feels, provided the formative energies for modernity. Finally we must look to English Puritanism; its understanding of God and man, fate and freedom, provided the central images, and the central problems, for American national life. Once settled into the American landscape, the drama unfolds over three and a half centuries, as evangelical Protestantism struggles to legitimate the nation and its institutions, and adapt to the forces of change set loose by its own dynamics in America's spaces. And it is into that drama that we come with our questions of values and futures.

The discussion has been a central concern of Professor Ahlstrom's for some years. His informed judgment is that the Puritan and evangelical traditions have formed national consciousness. He criticizes the manner in which they have reinforced certain disastrous features of national culture, particularly rampant individualism and an exploitative approach to nature. The results are seen, he feels, in the declining faith in human equality and in the economic, military, and political disasters of the contemporary era. "Serious and thorough ideological reconstruction" is needed, and it should begin with the critical reassessment of the American religious tradition. Without that recovery and reevaluation, Americans will suffer a deepening sense of fatalism, and drift, willy-nilly, toward an ever greater loss of social morale and coherence.

He displays here both his erudition and his insight as he seeks to balance the distinctiveness of the American experience and its commonalities with the experience of the entire Western world. Like most American historians, he wishes to help empower Americans by recovering a sense of their unique tradition, but he also wishes to avoid the self-righteous nationalism which is the inevitable companion of an overemphasis on the distinctive features of American culture. For the Christian historian this problem is particularly acute.

Christianity has always attempted to incarnate faith in life, and thus to respect the distinctive features of disparate cultures. In its ideal form, it blends the many cultures of mankind into a unity of faith. Too often in reality it imposes the forms of one culture in the very acts of conversion and community formation. In America preachers wanted to celebrate the unique values and virtues of America, both from self-interest and conviction, but at the same time they tried to remind Americans of their dependence upon the one God and their debt to the age-old tradition of Christ's peoples. To be Christian was to be part of a wider and older stream of historical experience which both preceded and encompassed America. To be a Christian in America was to attempt to preserve and extend faith within a society which knew it was different, which understood itself most precisely as "new." It was not an easy task in the past, as Ahlstrom's work demonstrates; neither will it be easy in the future, as the current debates on civil religion make equally clear.

Finally, there is the problem of Americans' debt to evangelical Protestantism. Without apology Ahlstrom emphasizes the Puritan origins of American culture, and the power of evangelical Protestantism to bend others to its symbols. For Catholics and Jews and Indians, the argument is a hard one to accept—which is not to say it is not true. Today, many groups, black and white ethnic and native American, are seeking a sense of their distinct identity within American society. We live amidst a revolt against the melting pot as theory and practice. It is difficult to deal with Ahlstrom's argument about the centrality of English and American Protestantism. Yet, the revival of group identity would be badly damaged if it was based on a refusal to deal with the formidable case Ahlstrom makes. The dominant symbols have touched the lives of all groups; so has the way of life those symbols shaped and validated. So deep and profound has been the impact that many of us do not even recognize how our rebellion is often fired by those same symbols and experiences. Ahlstrom, sympathetic to the revival of group awareness, nevertheless insists upon recognition of the significance of common, Protestant American symbols and experiences. He insists that they be dealt with critically, and that they be taken seriously. It will be difficult to do so; but it may also be indispensable to the tasks of liberation and growth, and of national renewal, which remain the common goal.

DAVID J. O'BRIEN

American Religious Values and the Future of America

SYDNEY E. AHLSTROM

In his posthumously published book, *The Responsible Self,* H. Richard Niebuhr described his religious position in a rather startling passage. "I call myself a Christian," he said,

> simply because I am a follower of Jesus Christ, though I travel at a great distance from him not only in time but in the spirit of my traveling; [and] because I believe that my way of thinking about life, myself, my human companions and our destiny has been so modified by his presence in our history that I cannot get away from his influence. . . . In one sense I must call myself a Christian in the same way that I call myself a twentieth-century man. To be a Christian is simply part of my fate, as it is the fate of another to be a Muslim or a Jew. In this sense a very large part of mankind is today Christian; it has come under the influence of Jesus Christ so that even its Judaism or Mohammedanism bears witness to the fact that Jesus Christ has been among us.

In this same spirit Niebuhr identified himself with the "cause" of Christ, which he defined as "the establishment of friendship between the power by which all things are and this human race of ours."

This brooding emphasis on the shaping power of history, however, was by no means only a concern of Niebuhr's last years. It functions powerfully in his *Social Sources of Denominationalism* (1929) wherein he

Sydney E. Ahlstrom is Professor of American History and Modern Religious History at Yale University. His special field of interest is American religious and intellectual history, and its European background. He teaches in the Divinity School, the Department of History, the Department of Religious Studies, and the American Studies Program. He has served as Chairman of Yale's American Studies Program, and as Director of Graduate Studies in its Department of Religious Studies. He has been President of the American Society of Church History, and the Chairman of the Consulting Committee on the National Bicentenary of the Lutheran Church in America. He received his B.A. in 1941 from Gustavus Adolphus College, his M.A. in 1946 from the University of Minnesota, and his Ph.D. from Harvard University in 1952. His publications include four books and many articles on American religious and intellectual history. *A Religious History of the American People* was published by the Yale University Press in 1972. It received the National Book Award for 1973 in the category of Philosophy and Religion, and in 1974 the Brotherhood Award of the National Conference of Christians and Jews.

emphasizes how large impersonal movements condition the beliefs and decisions, even the doctrinal positions, of ecclesiastical institutions. One notes the same tendency in his debate with his more activistic brother in 1932. Questioning the wisdom of Reinhold's advocacy of aid for the China of Chiang Kai-shek and doubtful of our power in any case to alter the main course of world history or China's fate, he invoked Hegel's famous dictum: *Weltgeschichte ist Weltgericht* (world history is the world's court of judgment). He spoke of "the grace of doing nothing."

And then again in *Christ and Culture* (1951) he stressed even more sharply the historical context of human choices.

> Though we choose in freedom, we are not independent, for we exercise our freedom in the midst of values and powers we have not chosen but by which we are bound. Before we choose to live we have been chosen into existence, . . . have been elected members of humanity. We did not choose to be rational rather than instinctive beings; we reason because we must. We have not chosen the time and place of our present, but we have been selected to stand at this post at this hour of watch or of battle. We have not chosen our culture . . . there has always been a choice prior to our own, and we live in dependence on it. . . . The history of culture illustrates in myriad ways this dependence of our freedom on consequences we do not choose.[1]

My purpose in quoting these passages is not to clarify the thought processes of an important American thinker, but to underline the importance of giving sufficient scope and depth to a general view of our religious situation as well as to the value structures which condition our existence. In any general survey of American religious values we do well to identify ourselves with Richard Niebuhr's insistence on the power of our heritage. We must see, too, that the momentum of that tradition owes much to the great expanse of time over which it has been gathering force.

We must ask, therefore, what *is* our common fate as participants in that vast fellowship which we call Western civilization. We may or may not share Niebuhr's concern for reconciliation of humankind and the universe, but we must see that there are doctrines woven into the very fabric of our life and thought. There are beliefs or dispositions of mind and modes of response which we hold—even religious doctrines we half-consciously affirm—simply because it has been our common fate to come into existence in that vast geocultural context which we call the West. It

1. H. Richard Niebuhr, *The Responsible Self* (New York: Harper & Row, 1963), pp. 44–45; "The Grace of Doing Nothing," *Christian Century* (March 23, 1932), pp. 379–80; *Christ and Culture* (Harper & Row, 1951), pp. 249–51.

makes relatively little difference whether we were born along the banks of the Wabash or the Rhine but it would make literally all the difference in the world if we had received our nurture along the Ganges or the Yangtze.

In my own most extensive effort to describe the American religious experience, I have already said something about these larger considerations. I argued in fact that "basic to the effective fulfillment of my aims as an historian is the recognition of the degree to which American civilization is a New World extension of Christendom." I also said, however, that "one must forswear the temptation to make American religious history a pretext for writing the history of Western civilization."[2] And that pretext is still being resisted in this essay.

On the other hand the present obligation to make the opening presentation on American religious values in a discussion designed to have other participants deal with several of the major separate traditions has made it particularly appropriate to reflect upon our fate as citizens of the Occident. After considering certain particularly important elements of that heritage, we can then move to a closer consideration of our fate as Americans. We may thus come to see that our own culture is an extreme form of all that makes the West most distinctive. Yet it must be said that I do not undertake this task reluctantly, since my agreement with Richard Niebuhr is at this point almost complete. Acknowledging the nature of our heritage and retracing the history of the culture which shapes our options are ways in which we not only increase the credibility of our interpretations but enlarge our own moral and religious freedom.

The West has its origins in what we call the Middle East where about three millennia ago a group of people calling themselves Hebrews began to differentiate themselves from other peoples of the region, some Semitic, others not. One major way by which they became known as distinct was by their intense commitment to the god Yahweh. And we hear of this first in the so-called Song of (or to) Deborah in the Book of Judges. What we read about there bears the fairly unmistakable attributes of a storm god.

> O Yahweh, when thou camest forth from Seir,
> When thou marchedst from the steppes of Edom,
> The earth quaked, and the heavens also shook,

2. Sydney E. Ahlstrom, *A Religious History of the American People* (New Haven: Yale University Press, 1972), p. 13; 2 vols. (Doubleday Image Edition, 1975), vol. 1, p. 41.

> The mountains rocked at the presence of Yahweh,
> At the presence of Yahweh, the God of Israel. (Judg. 5:4–5)[3]

Of this most early history very little is known, but as certain of these tribes further differentiated themselves and then as still later they clarified their commitment to the one transcendent God during the seventh and sixth centuries, the faith of this people becomes better known. Indeed, it shapes our very conception of reality.

The Hebrew Scriptures are filled with word of God's dealing with this chosen people, and with their hymns to his power and thanksgiving for his mercy. We also hear of their duties and obligations to the Lord God. Gradually we gain a very clear picture indeed of their sense of being a covenanted people.

> Moses went up to God, and the Lord called him out of the mountain, saying, "Thus you shall say to the house of Jacob, and tell the people of Israel: . . . Now therefore, if you will obey my voice and keep my covenant, you shall be my own possession among all peoples; for all the earth is mine, and you shall be to me a kingdom of priests and a holy nation. . . ." (Exod. 19:3–6)

And, as it came to pass, Israel did become a nation whose chronicles, as set forth in Scripture, would make it a model of Western statehood. In the fullness of time various peoples of Christendom would demand and gain their independence as sovereign nations. When this happened, some of these new nations, remembering Israel's exalted status in God's eye, would also see their national history as part of *Heilsgeschichte*, as sacred, holy, or salvation history. In post-Reformation times, moreover, they would be encouraged in this matter by the New Testament's affirmation that the Christian Church was God's New Israel, a royal priesthood that God had called into existence (1 Pet. 2:1–10). In this light it is not inappropriate to see in these developments a major source of modern nationalism.[4]

Even more fundamental to Western thought and belief is the closely related development of Israel's prophetic monotheism, its commitment to one God whose will is sovereign, and to whom therefore unconditional obedience and faithfulness is due. Covenantal obedience to God can, of course, become degraded into various forms of "henotheism" (group worship, or worship of the group), and again we may see Western

---

3. See Theophile James Meek, *Hebrew Origins* (New York: Harper & Row, 1960), *passim*; verse, p. 99.

4. Jacob J. Finkelstein, "The Goring Ox: Some Historical Reflections . . . ," *Temple Law Quarterly*, vol. 46, no. 2 (Winter 1973), pp. 229, 253.

nationalism and certain Christian ecclesiologies as examples of this. But far more important and pervasive in the West is the way in which Israel's fierce rejection of polytheism and syncretism leads to an extraordinarily strong sense of orthodoxy, and therefore also of heterodoxy, especially in matters of religion, ethics, and ideology. Tolerance for alternative views of religion or ethical behavior, or the idea of multiple solutions of the attendant problems, tends to be excluded. In the more or less independent realms of science and philosophy, moreover, the effects of this attitude are particularly consequential since almost instinctive human inclinations to rationality and curiosity about nature are denied full expression. Scientific inquiry into the ways of nature or human nature tends to be hindered or forbidden. God's word in Holy Scripture becomes definitive.

These were prominent features of Israel's faith even while its people were confined to their ancient lands and context; and both the Bible and secular history record the resultant forms of conflict. But this attitude became vastly more significant for Western history when Hellenistic and Roman conquests gradually brought Israel onto a larger political and cultural stage, for these attitudes now began to have a significant impact on Greco-Roman civilization, with results that the ancient lovers of that tradition regarded as catastrophic. Most momentous in this regard is the fact (already alluded to above) that a messianic (Christian) movement that erupted first in Rome's Palestinian provinces began to establish itself in various places throughout the empire. As this Christian Church continued to expand, many of the most characteristic attitudes and doctrines of Israel became equally intrinsic to the "New Israel." One major effect of this gradual conversion of the Roman Empire was the transformation of the nature and uses of philosophic speculation. Despite its vast significance for the communication and defense of the Christian message, the openness of Greek speculation was lost. Post-Platonic forms of thought became the vehicle of Christian theology, which in turn became a dogmatic orthodoxy enforced by law and imperial power.

In the year 325 the emperor Constantine himself would be arbitrating subtle points of Christian orthodoxy. His successor, Julian, would discover that the old syncretistic past of Roman religion was gone forever—even though much of its form and spirit had passed into the piety and theology of the Catholic Church, both East and West.

Without going into details one can also observe in passing that Islam's expansion into many lands of the empire and of the church brought still another bearer of the Judaic tradition into the wider context of world history. And like Judaism itself it would also find the philosophic tradition of Greece invaluable for the reformulation of Mohammed's prophetic message. Due to the intellectual and social situation thus created, the dispersed "Sephardic" remnant of Israel would revive the old tradition of Philo and for similar reasons would also turn to Plato, Aristotle, and the Greek philosophic tradition. Most amazing, however, is the way in which Christian and Islamic expansion carried the Judaic tradition in some of its most essential features to the ends of the world, often enforcing orthodoxy by the sword, the scaffold, logical argument, and harsh denunciation. Since the mid-nineteenth century the Marxian movement has become as powerful a bearer of this tendency as any other.

Tolerance for deviation and for the idea of multiple solutions to perennial problems has come to acceptance in the West only slowly and very recently; and the gains made are often precarious. These gains, moreover, must be seen in large part as emerging from the West's Greco-Roman heritage. Before we discuss this aspect of our fate as Westerners, however, we must consider two other massive and more substantive legacies of Israel: first, its sense of time and history, and then that complex of attitudes and doctrines that conditions Western views of nature, or what I have elsewhere referred to as its exploitative mentality.[5]

Aside from the unequivocal Judeo-Christian commitment to a jealous God one can justly wonder whether any aspect of its life and faith has had a more powerful impact on the West than its unilinear sense of history, its conception of earthly reality as an inexorable and all-decisive movement from the creation to final consummation; its vision of mankind's destiny as a movement from the Garden of Eden to the messianic Kingdom, and its undeviating insistence that this movement through time, from the Alpha to Omega is *the* story and the *only* story, and that each human being has his one time and no other to play on that grand historical stage. There are no cycles, no returns, no transmigrations of souls, and no opportunities for second chances whether for persons, groups, kingdoms, or civilizations. Making the most of one's time, one's only time, is the burden and privilege that is laid not only on each person but on each age. Each deed, each institution, each government, each nation has its place in God's plan for the ages. Egypt and Babylon, as well as Israel itself, have a part to play in the redemption of the world which God is intending.

5. Sydney E. Ahlstrom, "Reflections on Religion, Nature, and the Exploitative Mentality," in Chester L. Cooper, ed., *Growth in America* (Westport, Conn.: Greenwood Press, 1976), pp. 13–25.

Fruitful grounds for controversy are indeed provided by this theology of history. The signs of the times have been read in different ways in succeeding periods and in different social and religious contexts. Our historical memory is crowded with conflicting apocalypses, with conflicting calls to duty, with opposing views of new heavens and new earths. Prophet is set against prophet, messiah against messiah: Daniel, John the Baptist, Jesus, Saint John the Divine, Augustine, Mohammed, Joachim of Flora, the Fifth Monarchy Men, Jonathan Edwards, Hegel, Saint-Simon, Thomas Jefferson, Edward Bellamy, and Joseph Smith. My list, of course, is purposefully a mélange of grossly divergent types, some of them being chiefly commentators on the Scriptures; but we recognize among them some of truly historic magnitude.[6]

Now, in the twentieth century, it would seem to be Karl Marx, rather than Moses, Jesus, or Mohammed who is the most decisive prophet of all. Certainly no other movement is gaining adherents so swiftly as that which is inspired by his vision of inevitable revolution, the withering of the state, and the ultimate victory of social justice. Historians would insist on Marx's indebtedness to greater prophets who preceded him, but the remarkable fact remains that in our own time we have beheld the incorporation of China and other parts of the ancient Orient into this Western form of world-historical passion, and anti-syncretist doctrinal orthodoxy, complete with Western-type accusations of heresy and deviation. In all of these Marxist lands, East and West, moreover, one also sees an almost rabbinic approach to the interpretation of authoritative "scriptures."

The culminating feature of our fate as Westerners has to do with the dramatic and dynamic expansiveness that has characterized the West and which for not very obscure reasons has come to its most extreme expression in the United States of America. What we see in the West is an increasingly obsessive concern for the exploitation of the earth's natural resources, a persistent search for the laws which govern the cosmos, the rationalization of the economic order, the harnessing of science to the needs of improved technologies, and a moral commitment to productive work. Part of this same syndrome was a growing emphasis on the doctrine of progress, and a strong conviction that the West had a mission to bring

6. Judaism, Christianity, and Islam have, of course, been the chief sources of eschatological interpretations, although Marxism has become a semisecular rival. The eminent Jewish philosopher, Salomon Formstecher, in his *Religion des Geistes* (Leipzig, 1842) saw Christianity and Islam as "missions" of Israel which brought distinctive witnesses to different peoples and cultures but which would ultimately lose themselves in a religion of the spirit represented by an evolving Judaism.

the rest of the world under its sway. From our own vantage point, moreover, we can see that its mission has in many respects been achieved, though not uniformly. Marxism in China, technological and industrial marvels in Japan, industrial pollution and decimated nature in Africa, enormous areas of metropolitan sprawl in Brazil, not to mention Western monopolies on the manufacture and sale of armaments—all of these signs point to the West's historic dynamism. The presence of such long-term characteristics, moreover, underlines the importance of Max Weber's efforts to show how Western belief and thought in the realms of religion, ethics, and values have been a vital factor in the generation of such activity, while the characteristic modes of Eastern thought and belief conduced to quite different attitudes and behavior.

To put the matter interrogatively we must ask, What was it that accounted for the emergence of the *modern* in the West—*and not elsewhere*? When one broaches this subject it is, of course, Weber's little classic, *The Protestant Ethic and the Spirit of Capitalism*, that first comes to mind. In actual fact, however, most of Weber's work, beginning with the study he wrote at the age of twenty-nine of the agrarian problem of eastern Germany, had as its aim the development of a theory broached by Wilhelm Dilthey and more remotely by Hegel as to the cultural significance of subjective experience—which is in large part to say religion and morals. This in turn led him to a massive study of the spiritual and moral "climates" which are characteristic of the religions of China and India as well as of Judaism, Islam, and Christianity, including those features that distinguish Protestantism from Catholicism.

In summing up the significance of Weber's work Talcott Parsons makes an evaluation to which I would gladly add my own small voice. "It is my view [that Weber's *The Sociology of Religion*] is the most crucial contribution of our century to the comparative and evolutionary understanding of the relations between religion and society, and even of society and culture generally.[7] The conclusions to which Weber came, though expressed in diverse contexts and from different angles, can be reduced to three major assertions: (1) that the Judeo-Christian traditions develop attitudes which more or less inadvertently and often unintentionally (indeed with effects sometimes counter to formal expectations) conduce to an activistic and production-conscious social order; (2) that the Jews due to their "pariah status" and Catholics due to the deep and

7. Max Weber, *The Sociology of Religion*, (Boston: Beacon, 1963), Introduction by Talcott Parsons, p. lxvii. Weber's *The Protestant Ethic and the Spirit of Capitalism* first appeared in 1904. The first English edition, translated by Parsons, appeared in 1930.

widespread effects of an otherworldly outlook are relatively far less important in this regard; and (3) that those forms of Protestantism which drew heavily from the Old Testament tended to reverse the characteristic attitudes of medieval Christendom. "The inner-worldly [this-worldly] asceticism of Protestantism first produced a capitalistic state. . . . [whereas] mystical religions had necessarily to take a diametrically opposite path with regard to the rationalization of economics."[8]

Weber by no means asserted that capitalism began with the Reformation or that any one factor such as religion explains this phenomenon by itself. He, like Marx, protested against simple-minded theories of economic determinism. What Weber did show with great care and sensitivity was that some religio-ethical systems encourage the formation of attitudes and practices that are conducive to the rise of a capitalistic social order.

When America is our chief consideration (as here and now) the important historical fact is that the Protestant Reformation was a full-scale assault on the Roman Catholic civilization that had been erected over the ruins of the Roman Empire. The reformers repudiated the religion of Rome, its syncretistic approach to old folk religions, its mystical propensities, and the vast philosophico-theological systems through which both Christian doctrine and a whole theory of natural reality were explained and defended. The positive side of this assault was a return to the Bible, and in the Reformed tradition especially, a return to the idea of Christians as covenant people. Accompanying this momentous shift was a strong reassertion of God's absolute sovereignty in all that pertained to the natural order and to the salvation of his people. In the English Reformation the effect of this double theological revolution would become especially strong. And it is the course of these developments that must become our next great concern, because their consequences for America would be enormous.

The radical movement for reshaping English religious life, which soon won the names of Precisionist and Puritan, was a product of that "Reformed" branch of Protestantism often associated with John Calvin. Desiring a total break from Roman error, deeply concerned about the implications of absolute divine sovereignty for the care of souls, and exceedingly fearful that England would not reorder its church life in accordance with the prescriptions of Holy Scripture, these earnest

8. Ibid., pp. 220–21, 250.

reformers began to advance their views of proper personal behavior, truly Reformed church government, and true piety. Under Elizabeth they became a powerful force in the land, although they also began to discover that their program of reform was creating irreconcilable conflict within the Established Church. Their search for assurance of election and their desire for a purified church membership gradually led them to the view that an inward (subjective) experience of God's grace was an essential mark of a Christian. What emerges therefore was a new and revolutionary conception of Christian piety which would in due course have profound but disruptive effects on religion, social behavior, and church order throughout the Protestant world.

The rise of a militant Puritan movement in England and not in other Reformed lands is perhaps best explained by Britain's unusually long and turbulent Reformation experience, which began with Henry VIII's largely political separation from Rome in 1530 and did not become stabilized until after the overthrow of James II in 1689. Since the actual course of events produced larger radical movements than elsewhere, a general collision was inescapable. Puritanism gathered force under Elizabeth and then began to encounter serious resistance under James I (1603–25), whose reign also saw the rise of a powerful parliamentary opposition. Under his less adept son (Charles I, 1625–49) adverse developments in almost every realm (finance, foreign policy, ecclesiastical affairs, and politics) lead to the formation of a coalition of dissenting elements which finally brought English government to an impasse. During what has been referred to as its menshevik stage Parliament simply asserted its authority. Then after the king declared war, its actions became more extreme. Plans were set in motion to reshape the official theology and structure of the church. Later, after the royal forces were routed by Cromwell's New Model army, a more radical "bolshevik" leadership took power; the king was beheaded and monarchy abolished. For almost a decade Cromwell carried out a large-scale revolution. Karl Marx would be quite right in seeing it as the first real social revolution in Western history.

In one sense, of course, the Puritan Revolution was a failure. Within two years of the lord protector's death, arrangements for a restoration of the Stuarts with Charles II as king had been completed; but as it turned out, neither he nor his brother James II was able to rule effectively. Far more important was the fact that the social revolution was transferred to America, where it struck root even in those colonies which were founded on aristocratic principles by the duke of York and various friends of the later Stuart court.

The first successful migration of Englishmen to the New World was carried out under moderate Puritan auspices in 1607, and every American schoolchild knows that Jamestown was the result. At the Virginia Company's behest Virginia had elective legislature functioning even before the more celebrated "Pilgrims" had signed the Mayflower Compact at Plymouth. In 1630 the well-planned Massachusetts Bay Company, with charter in hand, took up its lands in the Boston area, and then followed a long succession of others down to that last great venture in Puritan statecraft led by William Penn in 1681. By this time the Dutch and Swedish colonies had been brought under English rule and a diverse but overwhelmingly Protestant population was in a relatively flourishing state.

The Quakers, Baptists, Puritans, German Pietists, and others who occupied these colonies shaped their lives, organized churches, flouted laws and navigation acts, and developed political ways of subverting the aims of royal officials. Even the feudal leftovers in William Penn's benevolent realm were rendered impracticable. A new kind of society, never seen before in the world, was arising in America and it was inwardly steeled by a new set of attitudes that could turn into implacable resistance if confronted by external authoritarianism. In many places, moreover, these colonial efforts were informed by very precise theories of statecraft and led by strong-minded social architects who founded almost autonomous commonwealths on bold new principles.

This process of gradual social, economic, and political development was interrupted by the Glorious Revolution of 1688–89, when King James II was chased from his throne and replaced by act of Parliament, and an act of religious toleration was passed. In this way dissenters received some recompense for the humiliation and persecution that had followed the great St. Bartholomew's Day ejection of puritanical clergy from the Established Church. There followed a "moral revolution" designed to undo the profligacy of the Restoration court.

In America a whole series of disturbances ensued, some of them with revolutionary consequences. Proprietary rule was overthrown in Maryland as was James II's plan for an authoritarian reorganization of the Northeastern colonies. After a glimpse of greater liberties, the chief gains, however, were subjective: a growing awareness of the need for better guarantees of colonial rights. By 1730 nearly every major attitude to be expressed in 1776 was already being advocated by many colonial leaders. Then almost immediately came the onset of the French and Indian Wars, an imperial contest which continued for most of a century. This threat increased the national self-consciousness of Americans and deepened their anti-Catholicism. The military situation, to be sure, restrained their anti-British sentiments; but the practical and ideological significance of the wars has tended to be underestimated. After the fall of New France in 1759 and the Treaty of 1763 with its cession of New France and Florida to England, American attitudes quickly changed, and the revolutionary epoch promptly opened. ,

Between the Glorious Revolution and the War for Independence comes that great spiritual and institutional earthquake, the Evangelical Awakening, a vast and diversified religious revival—heralded by Solomon Stoddard's Northampton "harvests" at the century's turn, continued in the Middle colonies, given classic symbolization by the "Surprising Conversions" which Jonathan Edwards described in 1735, and gaining colony-wide force through the campaigns of George Whitfield during the 1740s, and then rumbling on in many places, but especially in the Southern back country down to and through the Revolutionary War. Everywhere the revivals challenged the standing order and disrupted churches; in retrospect it can be seen as a massive and enduring intensification of the Puritan impulse as well as a broad nationalization of the American self-consciousness. Among its most important effects were the solidarity it gave to the heretofore divided evangelical community and the sense of providential destiny, which in due time would infect rationalists and enthusiasts alike.

In 1743, in *Some Thoughts Concerning the Revival,* Jonathan Edwards propounded his conviction that the millennium would appear first in America. "And it shall come to pass," the prophet Hosea had said, "that in the place where it was said unto them, Ye are not my people, there it shall be said to them, Ye are the sons of the living God" (1:10). And Isaiah, too, had spoken: "I will give waters in the wilderness, and rivers in the desert, to give drink to my people" (43:20). There was moreover something just and reasonable about such a disposition of things for "God has made, as it were, two worlds here below, the old and the new. . . . God has already put his honor upon the other continent, that Christ was born there literally . . . so as providence observes a kind of equal distribution of things, 'tis not unlikely that the great spiritual birth of Christ, and the most glorious application of redemption is to begin in this."[9]

So runs the line of thought with which evangelicals from that time

9. Clarence C. Goen, ed., *The Great Awakening,* vol. 4, in *The Works of Jonathan Edwards* (New Haven: Yale University Press, 1972), pp. 353–58.

forward were to kindle their hopes for America's future. On Edwards's authority, though with an exegetical abandon that he could hardly have approved, they came to understand the coming of the Kingdom of God as something that would be accomplished within the ordinary processes of history. With the outbreak of war with England the state itself came to be the bearer of their millennial visions. And long before the war had been won, Edwards's grandson, Timothy Dwight, composed a national anthem in which "Columbia" was proclaimed as "queen of the world, and child of the skies . . . thy reign is the last and the noblest of time." Nor were these views restricted to evangelicals.

By 1776 Jonathan Edwards's notion that the Kingdom of God was commencing in America had been translated by the authors of the Declaration of Independence into an official dogma: that heaven smiled upon the new nation, making it a "new order of the ages" (E PLURIBUS UNUM . . . ANNUIT COEPTIS . . . NOVUS ORDO SECLORUM). Jefferson, Adams, and Franklin would agree that as Israel of old had been led through the wilderness to the Promised Land, so also had the United States become God's New Israel. Long before John L. O'Sullivan coined the phrase in 1845 Americans were convinced that their destiny was manifest, and that the old order of kings, aristocracies, irrational privilege, and institutionalized religious coercion was expiring. In his Second Inaugural Thomas Jefferson, despite his philosophical materialism, would describe the new nation (which now included his vast Louisiana Purchase) by invoking the classic Puritan vision: he spoke "of that Being in whose hands we are, who led our forefathers, as Israel of old, from their native land and planted them in a country flowing with all the necessaries and comforts of life, who had covered our infancy with his providence and our riper years with his wisdom and power." In 1811 John Quincy Adams, who in a few years would negotiate an international boundary with Spain that extended from the Atlantic to the Pacific, would voice this same confidence in a letter to his father, declaring that in the Providence of God this nation, speaking one language, would extend from sea to sea.

Giving still more force to this sense of destiny was the rekindling of the evangelical spirit that had been becoming ever more apparent since the turn of the century. The Second Great Awakening was gathering force, and with it came a new wave of millennial fervor which also carried within it a reformist impulse whose determination was to make the republic a Protestant beacon and model to the world. A new Evangelical United Front arose as a kind of Protestant quasi-establishment just when the last of the old state establishments of religion (in Massachusetts) was abolished. In the spiritual atmosphere thus created the enlightened rationalism of the Founding Fathers became a "lost world." Nationalistic enthusiasm filled the air and the republic became a "Redeemer Nation." Despite the nativist harassment of nonevangelical elements in society, the in-rolling tides of immigrants were amazingly receptive to the prevailing sense of America's providential mission to the world as well as the moral and economic attitudes which undergirded the social order. Not even the Civil War and the end of the old federal union broke the ideological cadence. Indeed, in the victorious North it became only more obvious that God's truth was marching on.

As for Southerners during the period between the rise of the antislavery movement and the War with Spain, they became the gentiles in God's New Israel.[10] Ever since the introduction of black slavery and the rise of the plantation system in the seventeenth century they had been becoming a region apart, convinced by and large that their social order was ordained by God and far more benevolent than the "wage slavery" in the North. In fact in the critical writings of George Fitzhugh and others one hears some of the most mordant and sophisticated criticism of *laissez-faire* principles and the acquisitive society before those of Marx.

Despite the rise of serious social criticism by Henry George and others during the Gilded Age, it was not until after the First World War, however, that any really fundamental changes in the national ideology became generally noticeable. And not until the 1960s or even the 1970s did the fact of ideological crisis become a fully manifested aspect of America's destiny.

During their Bicentennial era, therefore, Americans face a situation that is at once discouraging and challenging. A long and fervently celebrated patriotic tradition has lost its resonating power. The need for serious and thorough ideological reconstruction has become apparent. And nothing can be more relevant to that need than an examination first of the Revolution itself and then of the ways in which the revolutionary tradition has been implemented. As always such an examination to be significant must search out the values which have been expressed and objectified in our institutions, our policies, and our way of life. In this way we will come to know our fate. We may recognize the conditions that surround our exercise of freedom.

What then is the American Revolution which brought this new nation

10. Sacvan Bercovitch, *The Puritan Origins of the American Self* (New Haven: Yale University Press, 1975), p. 139. The passing reference to Southern "gentiles" is quite incidental to the book's larger and very important theme.

into existence? In answering this question it is clear to me at least that we can do no better than accept the position taken by John Adams as he evaluated the work of his generation: the Declaration of Independence simply articulated a loss of confidence and affection among colonial Americans that had been growing for many years before 1776. Their achievement was to have instituted a government that eliminated the evils which Adams attributed to the canon and the feudal law. In a modern way the Founding Fathers had institutionalized the principles of the Puritan Revolution.

Assaying the evidence in the perspective provided by the passage of two centuries, Bernard Bailyn nails down the same proposition:

> The primary goal of the American Revolution, which transformed American life and introduced a new era in human history, was not the overthrow or even the alteration of the existing social order but the preservation of political liberty threatened by the apparent corruption of the [English] Constitution, and the establishment in principle of the existing conditions of liberty. . . . What was essentially involved in the American Revolution was not the disruption of society, . . . but the realization, the comprehension and fulfillment of what was taken to be America's destiny in the context of world history.[11]

We do well to remember, moreover, that this was substantially the same interpretation which was wholeheartedly adopted by the Protestant establishment in the antebellum era. This indeed gave confidence to the likes of Lyman Beecher and led them to identify the state itself as the bearer of God's plan for America and to develop a form of nationalistic millennialism in which the Protestant churches of Puritan lineage were the special custodians.

It is important to observe with Bailyn that in America the War for Independence was not a revolutionary phenomenon; it ratified and guaranteed the continuation of the social order that had gradually taken shape. From an international point of view, on the other hand, it was a radical event. It was the first and fullest, and most thoroughly institutionalized example of the bourgeois revolution. By comparison the French Revolution was but a transient embodiment of democratic ideals which was soon overwhelmed by first Napoleonic and then Bourbon authoritarianism and reaction. Everywhere else in Europe the hold of

---

11. Bernard Bailyn, *The Ideological Origins of the American Revolution* (Cambridge: The Belknap Press of Harvard University Press, 1967), p. 19. To say that the Revolution was not revolutionary is to say that it did not result in social upheaval. All would agree that its effects on the American people were very great. In Europe it was apprehended as revolutionary.

"the canon and the feudal law" was still stronger—and remained so far into the twentieth century. Even today sharply defined forms of class consciousness remain—perhaps especially in England.

The clue to American values, including religious values insofar as they can be separated, must, therefore, be sought in the American revolutionary tradition. The fundamental elements in this libertarian social system were democratic government, the Bill of Rights, a free economic order, and the security of property. This was a body of thought whose most relevant origins can be traced to the leading Puritan theologians and social thinkers. In the economic realm its ultimate formulation was achieved in Adam Smith's *The Wealth of Nations* which was published almost simultaneously with the Declaration of Independence in 1776. According to Smith's golden chain of reasoning the free and unhindered pursuit of profit by all would lead ineluctably to the best of all possible societies. He thus provided a license for the economic anarchy which the new republic sponsored and on which course it stayed, almost without let or hindrance (except with regard to the whole matter of slavery) until the nation staggered into its first Centennial celebrations in 1876. At that gloomy time there was of course much talk of reform, but even the "best men" did little more than sack the Grand Old Party's reconstruction program and facilitate the industrial designs of the Robber Barons. The Supreme Court even converted the great civil rights amendment to the protection of private corporations. Despite the efforts of the Social Gospel, populists, progressives, and a few more radical social critics, there was very little structural reform and only very moderate regulatory legislation during the whole course of the "extended Gilded Age," which can be said to have lasted from the retirement of Grant to the retirement of Herbert Hoover.

Down to the Great Depression freedom of enterprise and the rights of property were the values which the American political system consistently enforced. Only with the coming of the New Deal in 1933, and its diverse and sometimes contradictory efforts to deal with depression, drought, hunger, oppression, and social insecurity does America's long era of economic anarchy come to an end. The Roosevelt program was moderate, however, and after the end of the Second World War a second industrial age opened in which the old forms of restraint, both moral and governmental, became outmoded. Powerful corporations, many of them multinational, came to dominate the formation of public policy, extending their influence into both the White House and the Congress. Tax reform languished and "benign neglect" defined the prevailing concern for social ills. As a result the world's most affluent nation staggered into its Bicentennial through the rubble of the Nixon administration and the aftermath of a tragic Thirty Years' War in Southeast Asia. With social inequality at an all-time high and public morale at an all-time low there were small grounds for optimism. The old forms of patriotic piety had lost their power to inspire. Except for a very small number of conservative chauvinists the proposition that the United States is God's New Israel was no longer credible.

When we move toward an explanation of the credibility chasm that separates us from the confidence and self-assurance that once pervaded our national experience, we naturally think first of malfeasance in high office, the disasters of our foreign policy, the energy crisis, and the malfunctioning of our economic system. Unemployment, inflation, violence, urban wastelands, and racial or ethnic unrest provide visual evidence of disequilibrium. In the economic realm the most easily apprehended sign of failure is the nationwide ubiquity of near insolvency—of states, cities, towns, educational systems, universities, social service agencies, and transportation systems of all types—except private automobiles which deepen the energy crisis and make a sizable contribution to the unhabitability and hence the insolvency of cities.

At another level entirely, Americans are experiencing rapidly changing views of religion, ethics, family structures, the role of women, the use of natural resources, and the ecological threats to the biosphere. Harder to apprehend are the high levels of alienation, frustration, and resentment among people of all ages and in almost every vocational realm. And so one could continue. But one must conclude more swiftly than litanies usually do. And this can be accomplished by a short summary diagnosis.

In the complicated root system that nourishes American social evils, two roots are of manifestly special significance. One of them is endemic in the human race—and we call it racism. It destroys our sense of community by keeping human beings and human groups irrationally and obsessively at odds with one another, and always to the greatest detriment of the weaker persons and groups. The other is endemic in the United States of America as in no other land (though a few rivals remain), and it may be called rampant anarchic economic individualism (RAEI) which destroys our sense of community by keeping human beings in a perpetual state of competition and instability from kindergarten to cemetery, and which also by the creation of corporate "persons" keeps cities, states, suburbs, regions, and neighborhoods in destructive contexts of unnecessarily rapid social change, which in turn conduces to immeasurable amounts of human woe and to the general institutional instability and insolvency.

These two vast forces, moreover, converge to produce and maintain a degree of inequality not found in any other industrially developed country. This is to say that these two forces tend to negate the egalitarian principle which is the major premise of the Declaration of Independence. As a result a large portion of the American population (estimates run from thirty to forty million people) are virtually excluded from the implicit social contract which provides the basis of their loyalty.

If, in accordance with the design of the present essay series, one asks how American religious values are related to these conditions, one must stress the fact that they have been powerfully supportive rather than critical. To a remarkable degree these ideological attitudes arose out of the Anglo-American Puritan movement; and during the whole course of American history the American Protestant quasi-establishment provided it with divine sanctions. Among the vast majority of America's fifty million immigrants the same views have been dominant. Religious movements for reform and social justice have by and large been small and relatively ineffective in marshaling strong support. Religious institutions have thus served a primarily legitimating function; and there are few grounds for thinking that they will change, except insofar as present-day trends weaken traditional forms of theology and ethics.

Yet there is another way of interpreting the relation of churches to social change, one that is suggested by Richard Niebuhr in his debate with his brother referred to at the outset of this essay. "The fact that men can do nothing constructive," he said, "is no indication of the fact that nothing is being done."[12] What in fact animates the seemingly impersonal processes of social change is often unobserved or even below the level of consciousness. The slow erosion of traditional attitudes toward work, leisure, sex, women, nature, resource exploitation, and even nationhood itself may slowly accomplish a revolution as profound as Puritanism's erosion of the grounds for popular acceptance of the old authoritarian structures of English government. An attack on magic and miracle in religion can undermine belief in the "royal touch" and the divine right of kings.

The real American Revolution, said John Adams in a reflective letter of 1818, was effected long before the actual war. "The Revolution was in the minds and hearts of the people; a change in their religious sentiments of their duties and obligations."[13]

12. Neibuhr, "The Grace of Doing Nothing," pp. 379, 380.

13. Adrienne Koch and William Peden, eds., *The Selected Writings of John and John Quincy Adams* (New York: Alfred A. Knopf, 1946), pp. 203–5; see also pp. 11–24.

A similar process is no doubt going on in our own time. Indeed, it is probably the leading factor in the "continuing revolution" of which so many people were speaking during the Bicentennial years. The real changes in mentality are constituted by gradual revisions in the values Americans are living by; and it seems to me that these quiet processes will in time confirm the obsolescence of our present commitments and restore the ideal of equality to its proper place in the dialectics of freedom.

Response

To Professor Ahlstrom has fallen the challenging task of presenting the introductory essay on our topic of American religious values and the future of America. Since his task has been general, that is, has not been limited to developing the topic from particular perspectives as other contributors have done, he has faced the problem of how to go about developing his presentation. What material from his vast competency as a scholar of religion in America should he employ? The answer is not easy. So, while I differ somewhat on the selection and emphasis of the material in his essay, I want to point out that I am sympathetic to the difficulties inherent in his task.

It seems to me that Professor Ahlstrom is so much under the dominance of assumptions relative to the formative role of the Reformed tradition in the religious history of the American people that he accords too little significance to the pluralism that is a statistical fact in this nation. His present discussion does not allow sufficient weight to the divergent cultural traditions and historical experiences that are part of the "soul" of the nation. Except for passing reference to blacks, who after all comprise about one-seventh of the nation's population, Ahlstrom draws a veritable straight line between the European derivation of some of the nation's founders and the present. To be sure, he mentions racism as one of two continuing "social evils," rampant anarchic economic imperialism being the other, but it would appear that he either underestimates the cancerous character of the former or is so convinced of the determinative character of "Western" cultures that he believes that all that is required are minor adjustments to the social organization rather than the radical surgery which is the prescription that others prescribe. He speaks of the "continuing revolution" as a basis for his conviction that these social evils are being brought under control.

Ahlstrom writes: "The real changes in mentality are constituted by gradual revisions in the values Americans are living by; and it seems to me that these quiet processes will in time confirm the obsolescence of our present commitments and restore the ideal of equality to its proper place in the dialectics of freedom." I would submit that a nation cannot restore what it has not established. The nation exempted blacks and, to a large degree, native Americans from the dialectics of freedom. It has not succeeded to this day in including them. Whether blacks and other minorities will wait for the "quiet processes" to "confirm the obsolescence of our present commitments'' is not yet assured. The multiplied consequences of white racism may have created a malignancy that will not wait for such gradual and self-interested therapy.

BENJAMIN E. MAYS

The Protestant
Experience
and Perspective

Introduction

Martin Marty is an impressive and wide-ranging scholar. Readers of his essay will profit from his capable presentation on American religious values and the future of America, as developed from the Protestant experience and perspective. Here I will comment only on Marty's remarks concerning blacks.

Dr. Marty's perceptive analysis of the place of blacks within the broad spectrum of American Protestantism is consistent with my own. My perceptions of blacks who are Protestants, however, emerges out of experiences which are widely divergent from those of Professor Marty. I shall speak of these experiences in the main body of my own text.

I wish first to address his thesis that the values of a given person or of a society can best be identified by taking note of what values are preferred operationally rather than through a philosophical analysis or through examination of formal creeds. If this be true, and I believe that it is, then one of the paradoxes of the black experience in America is that the values most vigorously "preferred" by blacks are precisely those which are stated in the founding documents of the nation. These values are those which whites enjoy as a matter of birthright but which they have not "proffered" to non-white minorities in the nation. The struggle of black Americans has been to actualize the rights and privileges which the Declaration of Independence and the Constitution were designed to guarantee to all Americans. Thus, black Protestants have had to be engaged on at least two fronts throughout the history of this nation, that is, to seek access to full citizenship rights in the civil community and to confront the apostasy of the dominant religious establishment with respect to the unity of the church. The very existence of segregated churches contradicts the prayer of Christ that believers "all may be one."

Marty speaks with some caution about the "refined tribalism" emergent among blacks and properly identifies the potentiality for both negative and positive effects produced by this development. He takes insufficient notice, however, of the rampant white tribalism which has rendered the "refined tribalism" of blacks necessary. The power and privilege which derive from membership in the "white tribe" inflict a myopia on some which makes it impossible for them to see a comparable sense of black tribal identity as, in part, their own creation.

Professor Marty rightly assesses the positive potential of this developing ethnic consciousness. It is a critical judgment upon and an impediment to the further deformation and exploitation of black humanity. It is an

28

"operation bootstraps" by persons no longer willing to be excluded from full participation in the society primarily because of the color of their skins. The national neurosis which feeds on assertions of racial superiority must be exorcised if the nation is to survive. The real danger is that the presence of large groups of minority persons who do not perceive themselves to be full citizens in the body politic and who respond in ways disruptive to public order may force the majority to engage in acts of repression which will make a mockery of both national and religious creeds.

BENJAMIN E. MAYS

The Protestant Experience and Perspective

MARTIN E. MARTY

To address futures, values, and *the* Protestant community in one essay is an almost impossible task. Futures are hidden from historians; historians have little special expertise for discussing them. They must "wait and see" before they have something to say. All that one can hope to do in the present context is to discuss what values from the past and present could be projected into some sort of future. But even that is most difficult. Some years ago, back in the sixties "when wise men hoped," there was a "Committee on the Year 2000." One of its subcommittees had to deal with "Values in the Year 2000." This subcommittee soon disbanded because its members recognized that they had not the faintest idea what values around 1960 were. No one knew what to project.

Just as "futures" give difficulties, so do "values" themselves. Because the philosopher Ludwig Wittgenstein wanted people to take care with words, he is said to have spit out a view of the problem: "Values. A terrible business. You can at best stammer when you talk about them." But stammer we must, because values, which involve "interests, pleasures, likes, preferences, duties, moral obligations, desires, wants, needs, aversions and attractions, and many other modalities of selective orientation," have become urgent in a pluralist society.[1]

Martin E. Marty is Professor of Modern Church History at The University of Chicago and associate editor of *The Christian Century*. At the university he teaches in the Divinity School, is an Associate Member of the History Department, and is on the Committee on the History of Culture. He has also served as Associate Dean of the Divinity School, where he received his Ph.D. in 1956 and whose faculty he joined in 1963. He is the author of many books including *Protestantism, Righteous Empire: The Protestant Experience in America*, and *A Nation of Behavers*. He is the author of the fortnightly newsletter *Context*, and a co-editor of *Church History*. His honors include the National Book Award (1971) and seven honorary degrees. Born in 1928 in West Point, Nebraska, he was for ten years a Lutheran parish minister.

1. Stephen C. Pepper, *The Sources of Value* (Berkeley: University of California, 1958), p. 7.

Suspicion can be well grounded: that value-talk in general is today designed to fill a vacuum left by religion itself in the discourse of our kind of society. Thus in Autumn 1975, the Society for Religion in Higher Education set in motion a process that has since led to a change of name. It is now the Society for Values in Higher Education. The society's leaders informed their publics that few members really were satisfied with the new choice of name. But it was felt that too many of these members were making their living studying cognate areas and that they thus could not be simply defined as scholars of religion. And, more important, the word "religion" was a handicap when they dealt with foundations and endowments they were approaching for possible scholarship support. Much talk about "values clarification" in elementary and secondary education is also a way of reintroducing categories that have to do with religious notions.

Many prophets have converged on the concept of "values" because they think it will be a preoccupying one in our troubled republic. Thus in 1965 Peter Drucker quite properly prophesied that in the decade(s) ahead "unfamiliar issues" of a new and different kind would come on the scene in America. "They will be concerned, not primarily with economic matters, but with basic values—moral, aesthetic, and philosophical."[2] Since then values have been advertised, as if in commercials. It is widely believed that they are good things. "Be the first kid on your block to have values."

What shall we mean by "values"? As a historian of religion in American culture I have found congenial some distinctions introduced by cultural historians, most notably by Philip Bagby in *Culture and History*.[3] "It is ideas and values . . . which provide the basis for differentiation between cultures. It is in this realm that we find the broadest uniformities in the cultures of groups of local communities and the sharpest differences between the cultures of groups." Popular Platonism thinks of these values "as floating somewhere over our heads or lying buried somewhere deep inside of us." Yet little can be said unless there is something to observe.

2. Peter Drucker, "American Directions: A Forecast," *Harper's Magazine* (February 1965), p. 39.

3. Philip Bagby, *Culture and History: Prolegomena to the Comparative Study of Civilizations* (Berkeley: University of California, 1963). The following quotations occur on pp. 109–12, 192.

Ideas and values are best thought of . . . as modes of discrimination, inter-relating and evaluating our experience, whether this takes place inside, as processes of thinking, feeling—or, to use a more general term, per-ception—or outside, in overt behaviour. If you accompany someone to buy a pair of shoes, you can actually see him distinguishing between different kinds of shoes, and choosing the pair he likes best. You assume in addition that he discriminates in his mind between the different kinds of shoes and his positive or negative feelings about them, but it is the whole complex process of thought, feeling and action which we call "choosing a pair of shoes" and on the basis of which you can say that he likes or "values," for instance, long, narrow, black shoes. Indeed, every human action can be thought of as involving some discrimination and evaluation of the world about us, and most actions will involve some inter-relation of the parts already discriminated.

This use, notes Bagby, differs considerably both from common usage and the usage of philosophical ethics. There a value is thought of

as some common element in the objects of experience towards which the observer has a consistent affective or emotional reaction, which he "evaluates" in some consistent fashion. For us, a value would be the common element in a series of acts of evaluation. Thus if someone prefers black shoes, the value in the common and philosophical sense would be "black shoes," in our sense it would be "preferring black shoes."

Such ideas and values would not always be conscious or formulated. Yet in the lives of people they become observable and they help us "analyze and describe the *ethos* of a culture."

Bagby concludes his discussion by noting that "the actual technique of describing cultural ideas and values is a fairly simple one. It consists of listing all or, at least, a number of the forms of cultural behaviour, the speech, and actions in which they are expressed, and the artifacts which result from this behaviour. It is left to the reader to perceive for himself how he would have thought and felt if he had engaged in the same behaviour." At this point we note, then, that our preoccupation is not "black shoes" but "preferring black shoes." In a typical instance, we would not talk about "money" as a Protestant value. But "preferring money" might be an element in "the Protestant ethic" if, indeed, there is any such thing.

So important is this distinction in the field of value-discussion that I would like to take a second run at it by reference to another historian, this time one who concentrates on social behavior in history. Robert F. Berkhofer, Jr., notes that "philosophers usually define values as ends, but sociologists follow John Dewey in stressing the evaluative side of values.''

> Thus to them a value implies a process of evaluation or valuation, and cultural values as opposed to individual values are the standards by which objects and objectives are judged according to an interpersonal process of ranking. . . . A cultural value, like any value, is not the object or objective itself; it is the standard by which those are judged.

For Berkhofer the act of valuation is an expression of belief that a specific mode of conduct or end-state of existence is personally or socially preferable to an opposite or converse mode of conduct or end-state of existence.[4]

The community that does the valuing becomes of prime importance in the cultural historian's approach. "Heaven" may be a value in common and philosophical usage, but it is not particularly interesting as the object of valuation by, say, the Protestant community, if for no other reason than that "heaven" is "out there" for *anyone* to dream about. What is important is the way in which the Protestant community has "preferred heaven" in the course of its history.

The Protestant community: to use that term as we have in the previous paragraph is to introduce another whole level of confusion. "Preferring heaven" ranks very differently in the Unitarian Protestant's scheme of things and in the conservative Baptist's or the Seventh-Day Adventist's. Instantly we are confronted with the issue of cultures and subcultures. The Protestant community in America is a subculture made up of subcultures. Another term awaits specific definition. Philip Bagby is again of help here. "Culture" represents "regularities in the behaviour, internal and external, of the members of a society, excluding those regularities which are clearly hereditary in origin." He quotes M. J. Herskovits: "a society is composed of people; the way they behave is their culture." A subculture is

> the aggregate of cultural regularities found in any society or class of human beings smaller than the group of local communities which serves to define a culture. . . . When we come to delimit the society or segment of a society which defines a sub-culture, the actual individuals to be included may often turn out to be defined by common elements in their behaviour, that is by the distinctive features of their sub-culture.[5]

4. Robert F. Berkhofer, Jr., *A Behavioral Approach to Historical Analysis* (New York: Macmillan, The Free Press, 1969), pp. 100–2, 104–7.

5. Bagby, *Culture and History*, pp. 84, 104–5; Berkhofer, *A Behavioral Approach*, pp. 87–88.

With this set of definitions as background, it can be seen at once to any informed observer that there is no set of acts of evaluation or preferring that belongs to the whole Protestant community or uniquely to the Protestant community. It is possible to trace the history of a putative "mainline" Protestant culture through all of American history, as Robert Handy and I among others have done, and then state some generalizations about regularities of behavior in this community's attempt to build a Christian civilization or righteous empire. But such authors have taken considerable pains to show that even they have been working with a culture among many. Both Handy and I, for example, have made it clear that our story had to do with the dominant white culture over against the inhibited black subculture.[6] And books such as the ones just alluded to are also quite emphatic about the fact that they are dealing with a community that has largely or at least partly disintegrated. Discussion of values for the future must presume the existence of these values in intact subcultures or subcommunities, and neither the "Christian civilization" nor "the righteous empire" advocates speak from sufficiently intact or representative communities today. They are part of the part, not the whole of the whole. The point deserves illustration.

One could begin a discussion such as this by referring to "America *as* a Protestant culture." On that basis whatever America does would be somehow connected with Protestants' acts of valuation. It is in this setting that one hears much about "*the* Protestant ethic." Yet such talk leads to enormous difficulties. Do all Protestants and all Americans, by secondary contact, hold to whatever is meant by *the* Protestant ethic? Books on the Japanese national character show that the Japanese cultures bear many manifestations of what is called the Protestant ethic, yet without having had much contact with any definable Protestantism. William McNeill's portrait of Venice before the Protestant Reformation is a description of a culture in which most of those Protestant-ethic features are vital. Were the Venetians crypto-Protestants? Hardly. Children of parents who inhabit "white ethic" subcultures will correct any speaker who presumes to locate the Protestant ethic in a Protestant America. "My parents are post-World War II immigrants, and they *brought* what you call 'the Protestant ethic' with them from Lithuanian Catholicism." And many who lived out what the generalizers call "the Protestant ethic"

---

6. Robert T. Handy, *A Christian America: Protestant Hopes and Historical Realities* (New York: Oxford University Press, 1971); Martin E. Marty, *Righteous Empire: The Protestant Experience in America* (New York: Dial, 1970).

took considerable pains to distance themselves from the clergy or anyone else who could bring specific Protestant values to bear, as George Smith has shown in a study of the Dutch in colonial New York.[7] It may well be that the behavioral and evaluational elements of "the Protestant ethic" are simply structural; they belong to "the human condition" and appear wherever certain possibilities for capital development and expansion elicit styles of aspiration.

America *as* a Protestant culture was a more plausible concept in the thirteen colonies, where not many practiced religion. But the elites who did were Protestant, and they were norm-givers and name-givers in that culture. In a society of from three and a half million to four and a half million, in which perhaps twenty to thirty thousand Roman Catholics and two to three thousand Jews (without rabbis) were at best tolerated, it would have been incredible to picture non-Protestants as having left a strong stamp on the acts of preferring or valuing that were characteristic of the dominant culture. Such a situation lasted until the 1830s and 1840s when substantial continental non-Protestant populations began to arrive. It was becoming a less credible picture by the end of the nineteenth century when the cities at least had seen the displacement of Protestant majorities by non-Protestants, who set many of the new terms in politics, labor, and the like. The immigration exclusion acts of 1920 and 1924 were last gasps of this Protestant culture. At that time André Siegfried's judgment, since given almost canonical status, that Protestantism is America's "only national religion and to ignore that fact is to view the country from a false angle," made some sense. But it made sense in the way that many summaries of a dying culture do. From within Protestantism, H. Richard Niebuhr in his classic *The Kingdom of God in America* traced that impact of Protestantism in a still plausible way.[8]

That was fifty years ago. After midcentury it was more accurate and credible to speak of America as a nation of fulfilling pluralism; some went further and stamped this pluralist congeries of subcultures "post-Protestant" for one clear and simple reason: Protestantism and Protestant churches had lost their near-monopoly in the culture and no longer

7. William H. McNeill, *Venice: The Hinge of Europe, 1081–1797* (Chicago: The University of Chicago Press, 1974); George L. Smith, *Religion and Trade in New Netherland: Dutch Origins and American Development* (Ithaca, N.Y.: Cornell University Press, 1973).

8. Siegfried is quoted by H. Richard Niebuhr, *The Kingdom of God in America* (New York: Harper & Row, 1935), p. 17.

were in position to dominate in the acts of preference and valuation.[9]

To speak of pluralism and post-Protestantism is not to deny the privilege given Protestantism by its priority (in the thirteen colonies but not in the rest of the North American continent) or predominance until the recent past. Protestantism does make up much of the moraine on the American landscape and is a familiar element in national cultural artifacts. But today we are seeing that in any discussion of the future of American values more attention must be paid to Iberian and Gallic Catholicism and the part they played from 1492 on. Similarly, the American version of the Enlightenment, of reasonable and natural religion in forms that were strong at the precise moment of the birth of the nation and the development of its prime institutions, has to be seen as a partner in the expression of regularities of behavior or acts of valuation. It is from this source that much talk of "the religion of the republic" or "civic religion" has issued.[10] Judaism, despite its minority status, tends to dominate today in many fields including entertainment, the arts, mass media, and publishing, and must be recognized in assessments of values. (Name any Protestant-culture novelists to match the dozen prime Jewish writers of fiction.) Non-white cultures are certainly engaged in acts of valuation or preference, and many of these have little to do with what most people associate with America *as* a (white) Protestant culture. Whatever pluralism is—and some have seen it as being host to simple secularity—it is a more accurate description of the whole culture than the idea of America as a Protestant culture could hope to be.

The disadvantages of seeing the whole culture or nation as Protestant are at least twofold. It is a perception that is unfair to the nation, which sets out to be, in the terms of the Supreme Court, "wholesomely neutral" in such matters. It is unfair to the Protestant churches as subcommunities, for they are not responsible for much that is called Protestant in the culture and they find the culture largely unresponsive to most of what they promulgate. So America is not Protestant in legal contests or so far as the whole ethos is concerned, at least not on any kind of scale comparable to the ways in which, say, a China is Maoist—by acts
– of the sword and altered consciousness.

Second, if America as a whole is not Protestant, then, according to

9. Sidney E. Mead, *The Nation with the Soul of a Church* (New York: Harper & Row, 1975) is a book-length argument in defense of the Enlightenment in America and an attack on "the post-Protestant concept."

10. See Mead, *The Nation with the Soul of a Church,* and Robert N. Bellah, *The Broken Covenant: American Civil Religion in Time of Trial* (New York: Seabury, 1975).

some, there must be a single Protestant subculture. The assignment given me as author of this essay was to speak from the viewpoint of *the* Protestant community. Troubles abound. Most values associated with any significant number of Protestants are not shared by significant numbers of other Protestants but are shared by many non-Protestants. The American Protestant community is not held together by anything so decisive as what Judaism experiences. Judaism is necessarily concerned with survival and secondarily with identity in urgent ways. Shaping events in the modern period, especially the Holocaust and the rise of Israel, have no counterpart among acts or agencies tht might pattern Protestantism.[11] There is no hierarchy or magisterium or central papal authority system to provide form for Protestantism as they do for Catholicism.

The Protestant community: do we speak of Carl McIntyre with his hatred of things ecumenical and liberal or of Eugene Carson Blake, who is both ecumenical and moderately liberal in outlook? Both have large Protestant clienteles. Members of each do not speak to those of the other. Protestant culture: is one of its largest subcommunities led by Jesse Jackson or Joseph Jackson? One heads Operation Push and is seen on the assertive and progressive side of the spectrum; the other probably commands the attention of far more followers as head of the five-million-member National Baptist Convention. The two value almost nothing in common. Is the Protestant community represented by Billy Graham, the second-most admired man in America, or by the Niebuhrs and Paul Tillich, the most celebrated theologians of Protestantism in the third fourth of this century? What have the Possibility Thinkers and Positive Thinkers in common with those who struggle to give voice to the Appalachian poor Protestants? Two-thirds of America's Protestants are in the South and the Midwest. No matter what their denominational names, do many of them have much in common with the tiny elites of an ecclesiastically unresponsive and irresponsible white Anglo-Saxon Protestant "establishment" in the Northeast? I have attended sessions where the moderate left of the Protestant moderate right meets in conjunction with the moderate right of the Protestant moderate left and have seen that even in this hair-split field of differences entirely different sets of heroes, celebrities, cultic goals, habits, and nuances prevailed. How does one speak of the Protestant subculture?

11. Nathan Glazer, *American Judaism* (Chicago: The University of Chicago Press, revised edition, 1972); chapter VII discusses this theme in detail.

Were one to restrict himself or herself to the cognitive deposits in the textbooks of Protestant dogma it is possible that a few ideas and values would survive as representing all that is in common. My own study of world Protestantism found only one splendidly isolatable item of this kind, however; it is applicable also, one presumes, to the American species of the world-Protestant genus: a refusal to accept the authority of the Roman pope.[12] Along with that may go a corollary teaching or two: I assume that few Protestants assent to the idea of the Immaculate Conception of Mary or of her Bodily Assumption. But if the negative part of this teaching does go far to define Protestantism within Western Christianity, the positive corollaries of it are few and not of much help.

Shall one move on in the textbooks and see how many of the more conventional of these see Protestantism shaped by a "material principle" that somehow accents the grace of God, justification by grace through faith, or whatever? Fine. Except that the historian of culture has to look for distinctive elements of behavior in the community that is doing the valuing. Of few things is the historian of American culture more sure than that the experience of such grace does not distinctively mark Protestant communal life. That is, it is no more a Protestant property or expression than it is a Roman Catholic or Orthodox one—and it may be rarely perceived by historians who look for external behavior in a culture. If anything, what is observable is the opposite of response to grace. Most admirers and critics of Protestant subcultures in America have noted how grimly productive and programmatic they have been, how Pelagian and synergistic, how sure that God is somehow dependent upon Protestant cultural artifact.

That should leave the formal principle of most Protestants, as expressed in their dogmatic texts: a fidelity to and awe for the authority of the Bible. It is true that when Protestants in ecumenical and pluralist America sit down to meet each other they have no basis other than the Bible for expressing themselves. Protestant renewals are characteristically biblically informed renewals. From the most conservative to the most liberal, Protestants in many senses have had nowhere to go but to the Bible as a source and norm. Here is one element in regularities of behavior and in acts of preferring and valuing—although, at least since the Second Vatican Council, it is increasingly difficult to see the biblical faithfulness as a unique and even distinct Protestant expression. And the spectrum of fidelities within Protestantism is vast. The Bible is used

12. Martin E. Marty, *Protestantism* (New York: Holt, Rinehart and Winston, 1972), finds rejection of papacy the chief distinguishing mark of Protestantism (pp. x–xi).

critically by some and as a talisman or icon by others; for some it has legal and juridical qualities while for others it witnesses to the gracious saving acts of God.

Protestants more than anyone else did bring to America the sense that the nation's history was somehow prescripted. Not even the most literalistic have done so literalistically, at least not with any consistency. Thus the pretribulationist premillennialists, probably several million strong, can find Russia (Gog and Magog issues) in the Bible. They can find the British, with the use of word-play—they can see Israel and Armageddon prophesied. But they cannot find America in the Eastern hemispheric plot of the Bible. The more imaginative, however, beginning with the Virginians and Pennsylvanians and perhaps most of all the New Englanders, symbolically read their peoples' story into the biblical stories of exodus and exile and mission. Providential views of history were deeply stamped into their habits and reflexes. These have been combined with a lively sense of experiment to provide, if not a Protestant distinctive, then at least a consistent accent.[13]

So far we have come up only with the biblical accent, though in at least more remote history that was decisive for many acts of valuation in America. It is hard to move much further. No doubt one could find that the cult of the preacher as an attracting agent is stronger in Protestant than in more sacramental systems (since most of American Protestantism does not overstress sacramental and priestly views of ministry). Protestantism as an evaluating agency brings to the whole society a debate over salvation versus social action, but so do almost all other religious forces. Class-consciousness is characteristic of Protestantism, but no more so than it is in Catholicism or Judaism or other faiths. Protestant behavior focuses on the gathering of money and the use of music, but are these culturally unique?

So we leave the discussion of *the* Protestant community concentrated on the important biblical and experimental motifs. They have served genetically to code the life of these valuers in America, have been a kind of exoskeleton into which the community grew, the eschatological pull that gives the community a sense of future, the matrix of most of the major symbols. Beyond this one must chart and map Protestant sub-communities and subcultures and from them draw a complex of valuating expressions. And on the assumption that the more intact a

13. See Jerald C. Brauer, *Protestantism in America* (Philadelphia: Westminster, 1953), p. 7, for accent on "constant free experimentation" and "a sustained effort to avoid going beyond the truth and light already known in the Bible . . . free experimentation and enduring Biblicism."

subculture is the more decisive will be the acts of valuing or the regularities of behavior, it is profitable to take these subcultures from the viewpoint of their relative intactnesses. A different pattern emerges, then, from the one that comes when people lightly generalize without reference to the Protestant community and with only a kind of Platonic sense that certain ideas and values are "in the air," floating.

A glance at the map which the reader will find in the back cover[14] shows one intact subculture that stands out above all others, that raises the greatest problems for the historian, and that should merit the exempt status I intend to give it. I refer to the fact that nowhere is there a Protestant subculture or subcommunity that is more clearly defined, imperial, and even theocratic than the Latter-Day Saint sector. Not a single county in the state finds more members of any church other than the Mormons—though no county outside Utah has a Mormon majority among church members. A map reflecting the situation twenty years earlier did show numbers of counties that were Mormon in southern Idaho and eastern Nevada, but even the rapidly expanding Mormons evidently cannot hold territory so exclusively in an ever more pluralistic America. The Latter-Day Saints, more than almost any other group, produce regularities of behavior and consistent norms for evaluation. But there are problems.

First, Mormons do not think of themselves as Protestants and Protestants do not think of Mormons as Protestants. The case here is somewhat different than that of, say, high-church Anglicans and Lutherans, who want to be Catholic and not Protestant. Sociology is against *their* ecclesiology and sociology. Whatever private definitions they wish to use, the namers in the culture around them will think of them as Protestant. Mormons definitely rose on Protestant soil, out of a sense of rejection of other Protestantisms yet taking up elements from them. But they also have a separate quasi-biblical canon in *The Book of Mormon,* are considered to be consistent polytheists, and depart too much from the codes of conventional Protestantism to be included even in its tolerant spectrum. (One could also list here other groups that are more than marginal, that are true outsiders. Among these would be the Jehovah's Witnesses, who repudiate any ties to Christianity and thus to

14. The map here referred to appears in Douglas W. Johnson, Paul R. Picard, and Bernard Quinn, *Churches and Church Membership in the United States 1971* (Washington, D.C.; Glenmary Research Center, 1974), insert; the earlier version was in Edwin Scott Gaustad, *A Historical Atlas of Religion in America* (New York: Harper & Row, 1962), insert.

Protestantism; but they do not show up on the map as the Mormons do.)

The second problem with the Mormons is that their cultural expression at most points of valuation, so far as public understanding is concerned, blends into middle-American culture as a whole. From having been repudiated as alien because of theocratic tendencies and the legitimation of polygamy, they have become the typical Americans. In as yet unpublished research, Professor Jan Shipps of Indiana University has come to speak of Mormonism as America's *Reader's Digest* religion. Beginning in the 1930s its members became known for "taking care of their own," not depending on welfare, making much of the family and domestic virtues, being clean and honest and all those other things that Americans like to think or wish of themselves as being. From the viewpoint of a Peter Schrag, who in *The Decline of the Wasp*[15] saw Protestant valuation being replaced by "plastic culture," the Latter-Day Saints would add nothing to cultural discussion that would not already be there if their subcommunity is overlooked. They are already behaviorally where straight post-Protestant America is heading. Aware that my United States is now down to forty-nine states, we can discuss other intactnesses in the subcultures of Protestantism.

The largest of these is black Protestantism.[16] The map shows white Baptists predominating in the South and Roman Catholics in Northern cities, but had the mapmakers taken pains to include black Protestantism, they would have only reinforced the Baptist-Methodist impressions of an imperium in the South and would have found a counterpart to Catholics in the cities, which are changing to black.[17] One illustration: four-fifths of the Protestants on Manhattan in America's largest city are non-whites. About one in every six American Protestants is black and the vast majority of church-going blacks are Protestant: here is an excellent place to foresee the future of American values from a Protestant viewpoint. Let it also be said that ideologically much of black Protestantism is truly Protestant; that is, it exercises the principle of prophetic protest against human artifact, including especially the churches and even the black churches—as one glance at the critical and

15. Peter Schrag, *The Decline of the Wasp* (New York: Simon and Schuster, 1973), chap. 4, "The Plastic American," pp. 185ff.

16. Benjamin Mays's chapter in this book details the black community at greater extent and from a different perspective, but there was no way for me to fulfill my assignment conscientiously without treading on his chapter's territory.

17. Regrettably, the maps mentioned in note 14 do not include data on the black churches, presumably because their statistics are not consistently reported.

even haranguing books issuing from black church circles will reveal.[18] No one can say that the black community is not in many cultural senses Protestant or that its Protestantism is *ersatz*. It has simply been overlooked by many mainline Protestants and by cultural analysts who cannot see any Protestantism beyond the mainline.

Within the black Protestant subculture there are many denominational subcultures; they add up to an impressive whole. More than ten years ago the statistics already had reached something of this proportion:[19]

DENOMINATION	MEMBERS	CHURCHES	PASTORS	SUNDAY SCHOOL MEMBERS
National Baptist Convention USA	5,000,000	26,000	27,500	2,407,000
National Baptist Convention of America	2,668,000	11,398	7,598	2,500,000
AME Church	1,166,000	5,878	5,878	363,432
AME Zion Church	770,000	4,093	2,400	199,250
CME Church	444,493	2,523	1,792	115,424

In 1973 there were only about as many black Roman Catholics as there were members of the fourth largest black Protestant denomination—and about as many as there were blacks dispersed in the largely white denominations. Add to this black Protestant nexus the countless storefront independents and the Pentecostals, and impressive figures emerge. Thus the largest Pentecostal group, the expanding Church of God in Christ, now claims three million members—about as many faithful as can be summoned in the whole Church of England in England by the archbishop of Canterbury and his counterparts, colleagues, and minions.

Whoever doubts the impact of the regularities of behavior and the acts of valuation consistently expressed in these churches simply reveals ignorance of black Protestantism and of the heritage of the "invisible institution," the *only* institution malleable to the purposes of blacks for a hundred and fifty years. It was the matrix and repository *par excellence* of

18. The concept of "the Protestant principle of prophetic protest" is a theme that runs through the writings of Paul Tillich.

19. John P. Davis, ed., *The American Negro Reference Book* (Englewood Cliffs, N.J.: Prentice-Hall, 1966), p. 402.

black values until at least the urban migration and concomitant secularization of much of that black community. Of course, denominational fragmentation means that the community is a *communitas communitatum*, a community of communities. It would be inaccurate and unfair to impose absent unities on it. But blacks, like Jews, have been shaped together by certain external pressures that have been consistently felt at least as strongly as today's Jews feel the issue of survival. Slavery, racism, discrimination, segregation, generalizing by outsiders, negative valuations, xenophobia, ethnocentrism have made life as *black* Protestants inescapable for black Protestants.

The roots of this community go back to Africa, which elicits a sense of what W. E. B. DuBois called "doubleness,"[20] comparable to that which Jews feel for their Israeli Zion and their American Zion—a doubleness without much sense of conflict. To this was added the growth of slave religion, which, as Eugene Genovese and others have shown, gave dignity and hope to an enslaved people.[21] The church in the age of Jim Crow then devised its own distinctive styles and patterns of behavior. The recent accent on black power, beauty, and identity has elicited new expressions from the black Protestant churches. In this complex are there values for the American future? Out of many possibilities I shall list three.

First, a sense of peoplehood, a refined tribalism. Most students of American social location and identity, whether they concentrate on religion, white ethnicity, or orientations to sex or age, credit (or blame) the newly assertive black religionists for having brought or brought back a sense that God saves a people or saves through a people, that a "chosen" people can be a "light to the nations." Positives and negatives go with this new tribalism, and the Protestant principle will need more assertion than it has received if blacks are to avoid what Harold Isaacs calls *Idols of the Tribe*.[22] But in the midst of the experience of identity-diffusion, the sense of peoplehood has again brought dignity and power to people and may be foreseen as an enduring element in the American future.

The second style of black valuation (though one need not say "preference") sees the inevitability of a tragic sense of life. Much of

20. J. Deotis Roberts, *A Black Political Theology* (Philadelphia: Westminster, 1974), p. 54; see the entire chapter II, "Ethnicity and Theology," pp. 47ff.

21. Eugene D. Genovese, *Roll, Jordan, Roll: The World the Slaves Made* (New York: Pantheon, 1974).

22. Harold R. Isaacs, *Idols of the Tribe: Group Identity and Political Change* (New York: Harper & Row, 1975).

white American Protestantism has been a success culture, rich in optimism; whatever was tried seemed to work. *Annuit coeptis:* God has blessed our beginnings so says the seal on the dollar bill. But the black was denied success and reasons for optimism—if not for hope—in most of American history. He knew of the evil in the heart of the human, by looking at the enslaving society and often at what it did to him. Many blacks could take the measure of the cramping boundaries of existence—and still affirm. This is a value that will be needed in the American future, since citizens have run out of space and their nation is increasingly cramped so far as assertiveness and success in world affairs are concerned. When the tragic sense shows up in American civic religion, as in Abraham Lincoln, the historians are impressed. If it ever shows up in mainline church religion, they are stunned.

Third, the liberation theme has been embodied in much of black Protestant religious life. Here one need not go along with either the tribal solipsisms one hears from many black theologians—one must *be* black not only to "do" black theology but to "do" theology at all—whatever that neologism of "doing" may mean.[23] Nor need one share all the romantic notions proposed as having been consistent in the black churches; not all that they did exemplified the liberationist motif. But if one takes the overall view, it is clear to see that the black churches have better kept it alive even if only because they were forced to respond to the evangelical reality that sees the gospel as preached first and chiefly to the poor and the oppressed. It gives people the experience of liberation, the freedom to be free. As rarely as this motif is heard or exemplified in other Protestant behavioral communities, the more the fairly consistent black assertions stand out. It is hard to picture an American future that will not need the liberational word and act or to picture a subcommunity with more credentials for asserting it than black Protestantism.[24]

The second most intact Protestant community is defined spatially as being Southern. Here the map is stunning: except for southern California—where Protestants are strong but Catholics dominate—in the more sparsely settled states of Arizona and New Mexico, and in the southern tips of Texas, Louisiana, and Florida, which are also predominantly Catholic, the South is solidly, massively Protestant. If one adds to this Baptist–Methodist–Church of Christ "nation" the mid-

---

23. James H. Cone, *A Black Theology of Liberation* (New York: Lippincott, 1970) argues for this monopoly.

24. See Albert B. Cleage, Jr., *The Black Messiah* (New York: Sheed and Ward, 1969) for more on liberation motifs; Cone has dealt with these consistently.

South with its Methodist dominance and the denominations made up of Southern in-migrants or of a Southern "feel" in the Northern cities, well over half of American Protestantism can be called culturally Southern. Thanks in part to Kirkpatrick Sale's *Power Shift*,[25] an overstated and crude book, the concept of a "Southern rim" in American politics and culture will have currency in the latter years of the 1970s. There, are the growth, the wealth or at least the new wealth, the new political power, and the location of most of Protestantism's "warm bodies." Generalizations about Protestantism that rely on superficial contact with semisecularized Northeastern white Protestantism or on the partly compromised Midwest and Western versions will be simply inaccurate and misleading.

Within this Southern Protestantism at least two large subcultures operate. The first of these may well be described as the most overlooked in America: that of the Appalachian white poor. An astonishing number of these are "secularized," dechurched, disaffected, far from being classifiable as fundamentalist hillbillies. But others of them do find the churches to be their organizing center. Much of the time organization is minimal and no one knows any one else in another valley or hollow; spokespersons are necessarily lacking. These people have no counterparts to the leaders of black, white Catholic ethnic, and other subcommunities. They share some of the valuings of the black community: a tragic sense of life has been punctuated by ecstatic Christian affirmations in their churches.[26]

When they urbanize they can be expressive of values that frighten the rest of America. The Kanawha County, West Virginia, controversy about school textbook values, which is ostensibly over evolution and "pornography" in the schoolbooks, is just as frequently to be seen as a reaction against the fact that the radicals—that is blacks, Jews, Catholics, Chicanos, women, and countercultures—all are represented positively in the literature. But the poorer white Protestant peoples' experience is slighted or negated. Behind the ugliness of some of this expression the poor Southern white serves to nag the rest of America's conscience and, with the blacks, to remind other Americans of the gospel's role among the poor and the wretched of the earth.

25. Kirkpatrick Sale, *Power Shift: The Rise of the Southern Rim and Its Challenge to the Eastern Establishment* (New York: Random House, 1975).

26. David Edwin Harrell, Jr., *White Sects and Black Men in the Recent South* (Nashville, Tenn.: Vanderbilt, 1971); Samuel S. Hill, Jr., ed., *Religion and the Solid South* (Nashville, Tenn.: Abingdon, 1972).

At the other extreme are the *nouveau riche* Southerners, many of whom remain faithful supporters of Protestantism. A very worldly evangelical subculture has here emerged. This is the land of *The Total Woman* with its combination of materialism-and-sex for Jesus, of beauty queens and "jocks" for Jesus, of "Texas Baptist millionaires," and the like—against which evangelicals themselves are beginning to rail.[27] This subculture is impressively intact. A Christian Booksellers Association has come to serve as an indexer of *Index Librorum Prohibitorum* and a guide to the safe books for evangelicals in Bible bookstores. White Christian academies are springing up to provide parochial education. The periodicals and radio-television programs that enter the homes in this culture are consistently conservative or Pentecostal in orientation. It is possible to speak of the Southern Baptist Convention as being "the Catholic church of the South," so pervasive is its influence in so many dimensions of the culture.

It is easy to find much to criticize in this culture, particularly because so many assumptions of culture criticism arise out of "Yankee" over against "Cowboy" academies and media or literary centers. Such polarities usually divert people from careful analysis. Whatever the negatives, it is also possible to point to some positive accents that might have something to do with the American future. Here we shall concentrate on one: this Southern Protestant culture more than any other large community has nurtured and renewed the combination of religious experience and the context of a churchly tradition. All of Protestantism was once warmly experiential—most religious movements are born in what Emile Durkheim calls "effervescence"[28] and the religion of the first two Great Awakenings (1730s, 1800s) were as much Northern as Southern in their experiential accents. But the effervescence was bottled, the ferment crystallized, and much of Northern Protestantism forgot that it had been nurtured in both personal and communal experience of God and grace.

When in the late 1960s many in the culture had grown weary of seeing religion only as a community of interpretation and action it was necessary for many, especially the young, to "go shopping" for values associated with experience outside the context of their tradition. The vogue for occult and Eastern religions filled the old vacuum, and even the early

27. For an example, see Donald G. Bloesch, *The Evangelical Renaissance* (Grand Rapids, Mich.: Eerdmans, 1973), p. 24.

28. For discussions of "effervescence," see Steven Lukes, *Emile Durkheim: His Life and Work* (New York: Harper & Row, 1972), pp. 422, 462, 476, 508.

Jesus movements were nontraditional and determinedly "freakish." Some of these impulses have institutionalized themselves and will exert some influence; others have become suffusive presences to color the larger communities' experiences. But many have been gossamer, ephemeral, evanescent; they have disappeared.

The Southern white Protestant churches have been as free as the black churches to give expression to the experiences of repentance, conversion, and the like. They may be accused of exploiting the *Zeitgeist,* married to the spirit of the times. They fail to carry their experience into the realms of theological interpretation and social or even personal action; the result may be a spiritual narcissism and hedonism. But this form of religion need not be measured by its worst expressions any more than need Catholicism, Judaism, black Protestantism, and other partly exempt-from-criticism groups. *If* Americans are to continue to value the primacy of experience in religion, they would do worse than to give some empathic interest to Southern white Protestants. The experience among them, because it is rooted in the tradition that was handed down to the new generation, stands more chance of surviving than do many rootless growths—although it will also be in more need of Protestant prophetic protest precisely because it is so rooted and autochthonic.

The next most intact community in the sense that it has a territory, a turf, a domain in which in many counties its members consistently outnumber those of all other churches, is in the upper Midwest. A band of counties from Michigan and Wisconsin centering in Minnesota, stringing out through the whole Northwest, and dipping down into Iowa and Nebraska, has a Lutheran predominance. The Lutheran groups here are largely of the American Lutheran Church and the troubled Lutheran Church—Missouri Synod. This means that they combine conservatism, confessionalism, piety, and the desire and ability to develop cultural artifact less for the larger culture than for their own churches. Forget for the moment, if it can be forgotten, the current traumas over dogma, world view, and politics or personalities in the Missouri Synod. Under them (or before the controversy broke into public view) was a set of churches that were becoming nationally known for their impressive contemporary architectural experiment. The musical tradition is strong across the Lutheran spectrum here. There is less fear of and more appreciation of the liturgical and visual arts than in much of the rest of Protestantism. Despite cultural dominance, these people were not particularly effective in politics, carrying over as they did into that realm something of what H. Richard Niebuhr called "Christ and Culture in Paradox," and seeing taint and even the demonic in its structures of existence. But within the churches there was cultural affirmation.

As close as I am to this subculture, I am most aware of its shortcomings. My assignment here is to concentrate on values that might be carried over into the larger culture. We might speak of this subcommunity as an intact *liturgical* presence as opposed to an evangelistic presence. Despite the lineages of pietisms and the occasional presences of pentecostalisms today, most members of the culture are embarrassed or horrified at the idea of regaling others with their own guilts and conversion experiences and are not particularly emotional in their expression of faith. With members of Episcopalianism, Presbyterianism, the Reformed Churches, and others who do not have a territory on today's map, they represent that part of Protestantism that sees the activity of God as a kind of "given" in the sacramental and ordered life of the church. In classic Troeltschian terms, here is more of the "church" type of theology over against the "sect" type of the South. The typology does not hold consistently, for the upper Midwesterners have often looked more like sects in their withdrawal from, say, politics, while the Southerners have looked catholic for their involvements in political culture.

If tomorrow's America is to keep alive the sense of a liturgical-sacramental-confessional presence as a counterpart to evangelicalism-fundamentalism, it is possible that not all these Lutherans and their kin will drift, as many of them have begun to do, particularly in the Missouri Synod, into the generalized evangelical-fundamentalist cultures.

Of vastly greater influence in American history has been the last and the least intact of the geographically integral communities, Methodist America. We have already observed that it can be seen as "the North of the South," but it is also "the South of the North." A troubled, declining community that is now being challenged by what we here have typed as "Southern experientialism"—and that may be thereby diverted from its larger task of recovering its own Methodist roots—this subcommunity has embodied much of the American sense of progress and success. What the Methodists tried worked, from 1784 or so until the 1950s. They did much of the converting; they provided care-structures, set a pace for reforming the world around them, sent out missionaries, "churched" America, pioneered in social action and the Social Gospel, and the like. Much of the effervescence was gone as these impulses were bureaucratized or their religious capital expended in the institutionalism of the 1950s and the social action of the 1960s. Such social action is out of vogue today, and Methodism is often exhausted, dispirited, or stale.

But it represents another value that belongs in the Protestant picture for the American future: the virus to change the world. However much Protestants of the 1970s take refuge in transcendentalisms and other-worldlinesses, in the new spiritualities and selfishnesses, this virus remains latent—and nowhere does it do so more consistently than in Methodist culture and its kin. Today a new effort must be made to find paradigms for its expression.

Not on the map, except with a trace here or there, are two more Protestant subcultures. The first of these is the cluster of "sects," particularly of the "peace churches," chiefly Mennonite, Church of the Brethren, and others of Anabaptist lineage or the Quakers. They have influence far beyond their numbers and will continue to do so as long as war-and-peace and ethics associated with hunger and poverty remain urgent—as they give evidence of doing. The values of the sect-principle at work for the world and of culture criticism are expressed here.

Also not on the map is the remnant of the old Protestant majority, usually called the white mainline churches and their culture. Almost nowhere do its churches dominate except in a few sparsely populated counties of Indian reservations. But the "colonial big three" of Episcopalianism, Congregationalism (the United Church of Christ), and Presbyterianism, to which might be added the American Baptist Convention which derived originally and in part from the second of these, are a "thin spread" nationally, particularly outside the South. They used to be called "the establishment" or the domain of white Anglo-Saxon Protestants. As bearers of the old cultural values, they have instinctively born brunts of criticism disproportionate to their size and, quite probably, to their influence. When the Black Manifesto was posted, it is significant that the black spokespersons did not confront First Baptist Church in Dallas—which might only have been done at expense to life and limb—even though today "the money is there" and at least as much guilt for what has gone wrong racially reposes at such a church door. No, Riverside Church as part of "the establishment" would be a better locale. Liberals give everyone a hearing, often enjoy expressing their guilt, and usually—though not in this rather exotic circumstance—really try to do something about things.

The churches in this great subculture are not prospering today as they did in the 1950s. In some senses they have been yielding space ever since the Second Great Awakening around 1800. Selectively their congregations may grow and be healthy. But as a skein, a nexus, a network, a bureaucracy, an establishment, they tend to be demoralized and characterized by apathy and *anomie*. Their boundaries blur off into the secular order, and they are often held responsible for the actions of their unresponsive "alumni associations." If one links these twelve million Protestants with the twelve million Methodists there remains a substantial community. It is the one concerning which so much of the generalization about *the* Protestant community in America has been made. Having devoted part of a career to writing about it and having set forth its assets and liabilities in at least one statement, *Righteous Empire*, a book located in an ample genre in which we have also placed the historical work of Robert Handy,[29] it is not necessary to detail all the values that issue from this subcommunity. Let me concentrate them all in one phrase: here has been the locus in which churches have taken on the chief burden of interpretation, of experiment, of action in the culture. Here is "Christ transforming culture," the center of much or most of the creative theology, the risk-taking, the *use* of Christian community and experience in the world. Their stance has always made these churches vulnerable. They have been ready to make more mistakes and they have made more visible mistakes than did the more segregated and sequestered Protestant and other Christian groups. But without their influence and with the risk of further loss among them, Protestantism and much of the rest of American religion could appear to be even more a set of self-serving and self-preoccupied communities than they are.

What have we retrieved, in sum, from this scale of Protestant sub-communities measured by their degrees of integrality and intactness? Far from being shared by all others and thus not making up a composite, there is here at least a repertoire of possibilities based not on floating Platonisms but on substantial extant communities:

1. Enduring attentiveness to biblical witness and resource.
2. Persistent devotion to experiment in religion.
3. The sense of the validity of peoplehood and, on occasion, tribe.
4. The Christian gospel of affirmation in the face of the tragic sense.
5. The gospel seen as liberating.
6. An awareness of the value of the primacy of experience.
7. A paradoxical relation to culture based on a liturgical sense.
8. Carrying the impulse or virus that leads to reform of the world.

29. Handy, *A Christian America*; Marty, *Righteous Empire*.

9. The use of the sect not for the sect but for the larger culture.

10. The value of culture criticism from a disciplined base.

11. Taking on the burden of interpretation, experiment, and action.

To the degree that people see these as positive, humane, and Christian valuations and to the degree that they are indeed embodied in the communities and subcommunities to which we have pointed, it would seem that they will find here at least some possibilities for expressing values on Protestant grounds in the American future.

Response

Martin Marty makes an important contribution here to our discussion of "American Religious Values and the Future of America." First, he clarifies the value question, redirecting the focus of attention to the process of valuing and to the regularities of behavior which that process generates within distinctive cultures or subcultures. Like Sydney Ahlstrom and Robert Handy, Marty believes that once there was a relatively coherent American culture whose characteristic forms of evaluation were shaped by a dominant evangelical Protestant community. Even if that relatively intact community found its basis in somewhat negative modes of thought—knowing what it was against—it still had sufficient coherence and strength to generate a broad national understanding of a "righteous empire" or a "Christian America." That culturally powerful Protestant community has now "largely, or at least partly, disintegrated," Marty argues, and America has become post-Protestant and pluralist. Like others who adopt this view, Marty sets the stage then for a discussion of the contemporary scene which places that unity over against the jumble of voices in contemporary value discussion.

Perhaps it is temperament, perhaps insight, which makes Marty's writings somewhat more upbeat in tone than his argument would seem to justify. He is not particularly attracted to the old Protestant culture, nor overly nervous about the clash of views of pluralism. In this essay, in particular, he is content to clarify our thought about "the Protestant community," to describe a variety of intact Protestant subcultures, and to leave us with a "repertoire of possibilities" based on extant communities which may or may not make substantive contributions to the national dialogue and the future of America. Perhaps, in the interaction of these and other extant religious subcultures, sufficient discussion of values and evaluation will take place to preserve an open society and promote national progress. Perhaps values and processes of evaluation generated by other cultures in American society, such as those of academia, the military, the corporate bureaucracies, will envelop and overwhelm the values generated by religious subcultures. Which of these will happen, or whether other alternatives are possible, are questions left unanswered. The paper, indeed, seems to presume with perhaps too much optimism, that an overarching structure of pluralism and dialogue will be sufficient for the American future. Yet, one suspects that Marty might share the doubts which some of his readers will have about the prospect.

Several points in Marty's paper are worthy of particular attention.

Catholics, Jews, and others will benefit from Marty's clarifications regarding American Protestantism. Like Catholics of the pre-Vatican II era, he takes great pains to demonstrate that there is no single Protestant community, but in fact many quite distinct denominations, communities, and subcultures within the broad grouping of Protestantism. A certain unity once grew out of rejection of the pope, but that ground of unity is no longer sufficient. When asked questions of a more positive character—what is it that you believe? what is it that you wish to do in the world?—Protestants answer with many voices, all shaped by diverse understandings and experiences. Perhaps more than either know, Catholics and Protestants need each other, for their ability to define themselves over against the other provided a basis for unity which could transcend diverse subcultures. Now that they have lost that basis for unity their diversity becomes more evident. It may be celebrated as a new ground for possible Christian unity or because it frees each to pursue its distinctive possibilities with freedom. Yet, Catholics as much as Protestants share the somewhat nostalgic yearning for coherence, unity, unspoken agreement, which still characterizes Jews and blacks. Marty's own references to these two groups show a similar affection for the sense of peoplehood which, he acknowledges, both groups have derived from oppression, from knowing that there is an enemy out there, and from knowing that, however we may differ over who we should be, we at least know who we are not.

The new tribalism of which Marty speaks needs to be critiqued, to be sure, for it often creates enemies against whom group identity can be defined and propagated. Yet, neither mainline Protestantism nor liberal Catholicism can offer a positive alternative, it seems, of a vision and a sense of possibility powerful enough to move hearts, create communities, generate new and powerful subcultures, with shared values, common processes of evaluation, regularities of behavior. The world-transforming dynamics of Methodism, the risk-taking openness of the older mainline churches, both seem worn out, exhausted; liberal, Americanized Catholicism shares those qualities. Perhaps, as Marty seems to hope, the best sides of the extant subcultures will be adequate to national and to human religious needs. But might one not also suggest that the liberal tradition in the churches must find sources of regeneration, both for the sake of their own authenticity and for the sake of a world and a people who need visions of human possibility which transcend tribes and regions and promise some hope of providing a basis for evaluation of those issues which humankind must deal with if it is to survive.

From this perspective, the peace churches of whom Marty speaks in passing may have something more to offer than an important, though peripheral, response to perennial issues of war and peace and hunger. If, indeed, these have become not issues among many, but *the* issues of cosmic import, then the churches which have always spoken to those issues may be the most important of all. Some years ago Daniel Boorstin described the history of colonial Quakers in terms of their failure to build a solid culture in Pennsylvania. By their refusal to compromise, according to Boorstin, they condemned themselves to a minor, irrelevant role in American life. Marty would no doubt modify that conclusion, indicating, as he does quite rightly, that their influence has far outstripped their numbers. But something more could be said, in the context of this discussion. Amid all the ambiguities of their own history, the Quakers did make some consistent choices for fidelity to principle over influence, effectiveness, and cultural power. They did so without becoming simply a sect or a tribe, without rejecting the world, or refusing to accept some responsibility for the crimes of slavery and injustice and war which marked the world, their world. Their extant subculture, manifested today in the American Friends Service Committee and the Friends Committee on National Legislation, is based not on tribe, or region, or external enemy, but on fidelity to certain fundamental beliefs and *values*. As such, they may offer as important, indeed a more important, model and witness for mainline Protestants and Catholics than that offered by Jews or blacks or native Americans, whose experience and sense of oppression can and should never again be our own, unless, perhaps, on the basis of belief and principle, we choose such an experience. To paraphrase a Norman Mailer exaggeration, perhaps, the Quakers and pacifists in prison in protest against the war in Vietnam redeemed the soul of America and by their action joined themselves to the redemptive work of God in the world, a work which also operates in the suffering of many Americans, black, brown, red, and white.

Perhaps, then, the enemy is not out there, but is us. And perhaps the problem for many of us is not the absence of the supportive subculture which can consistently reinforce authentic evaluation, but our own lack of courage and commitment on the basis of which we might again construct such supportive subcultures. History will not do it for us, as it once did for my Irish and Marty's Lutheran forebears. We will do it, or it won't be done. And if we don't do it, the future will not belong to the tribes and the subcultures left intact because they do not disturb the powers of history at work in the state and the corporation and the other centers of force. It will rather belong to those centers, to the fatalism and the violence for which they too often stand. Then we will have to make further refinements of our understanding of values and evaluation, for the values will be provided, and the evaluation will be done, for us by others, and we won't even know it.

DAVID J. O'BRIEN

The Catholic
Experience
and Perspective

Introduction

In the essay which follows David J. O'Brien wrestles productively and provocatively with two distinct but interrelated problems, both of them fundamental to the welfare of the American republic. The first of these has to do with the prevailing ideological tradition and its capacity to recognize and rectify the forms of injustice that cloud the country's future. On this subject his criticism is directed first of all to his own historical profession, due to its constant propensity to interpret the country's predicament as the inexorable result of social and technological forces. This leads him, however, to an assessment of the nation's civil religion; but here again his stance is critical. Even when propounded at its best, as in the writings of Sidney E. Mead and Robert Bellah, its functions, he fears, are largely celebratory, and he doubts its capacity to sustain a consistently prophetic role. One senses the author's preference for the social criticism of the early Reinhold Niebuhr, Philip Berrigan, and others whose sympathies do not lie with the "liberal consensus." Our civil religion too often has conduced to pride and idolatry while ignoring the chaos produced by the *laissez-faire* state of mind.

Professor O'Brien's chief concern in this essay, however, is with the possibilities for a Catholic contribution to the country's manifest social ills. And on this topic a double movement of thought becomes apparent: criticism of the older tradition and support for more recent developments. *Mirari vos,* the stinging encyclical of Gregory XVI which in 1832 shattered the Catholic movement for social reconstruction which Félicité de Lamennais had inspired, provides his point of departure. The pope's reactionary response to the exhilarating surge of social optimism spurred by the revolutions of 1830 is seen as marking an era in Catholic social teaching that extends "from Metternich to Hitler." Even the great social encyclicals of Leo XIII and Pius XI are seen as flawed by paternalism and an insistence on hierarchical supervision. As a result the promising initiatives of the Catholic "Americanists" in the United States were unheeded or silenced during the nineteenth century, while the twentieth century revealed a "scandalous" degree of support for fascistic movements. In this context the author cites the unanimous support that Hitler received from the Catholic Center party in 1933, as against the unanimous negative of the Social Democrats. The church "blamed the victims" and alienated those in the tradition of Lord Acton and Dostoevski.

O'Brien's positive counsel emerges in his extended discussion of the

58

CAMROSE LUTHERAN COLLEGE
LIBRARY

career-long efforts of John Courtney Murray to develop a rapprochement between Catholic social teaching and democratic modes of thought and practice. Even more pronounced is his turning to those thinkers who were liberated or inspired by Pope John's revolution and by the positions taken in the Second Vatican Council. He fully recognizes that the reconciliation of Catholicism and democratic ideals, as well as the affirmation of the rights of conscience, disturbs the traditional attitudes and ecclesiastical practices that have long prevailed, yet he seeks to overcome such inertia and resistance by recurring to the positions taken by popes, synods, and theologians who reflect the impact of that great event, Vatican II.

O'Brien repeats Pope Paul's demand that "modern forms of democracy be devised" so as to counterbalance increasing technocratic impediments. He also quotes the Synod's warning that the "concentration of wealth, power and decision making in the hands of a small or private controlling group" must be curbed. And he closes with a long quotation from the splendid statement published by the twenty-five bishops of the Appalachian region. What we have here, then, is a strong, richly textured statement of an immensely significant Catholic position. And one cannot but wonder about the consequences of this line of thought if it were to become a proportionately strong force in American public life.

One thing is certain however: such a development would surely alter the nature of the "triple melting pot" which Will Herberg described in his widely read *Protestant, Catholic, Jew* (1955). In that book Herberg was, among other things, explaining the "contemporary upswing in religion" against a background of immigration and acculturation. His thesis was that for very many people religious affiliation had become a way of affirming the "American Way of Life," a means of establishing one's place in an increasingly homogenized culture. He quite rightly ascribed no great social-ethical significance to the process, except insofar as it denoted full acceptance of the status quo.

Professor O'Brien, on the contrary, is trying to build a fire under the Catholic melting pot. And this is the kind of incendiarism for which I earnestly hope. Should the desired results occur, it would bring about a radical change in the nature of American pluralism.

If I try to relate this set of purposes with my own contribution to this series of essays, it would be seen as entirely complementary. The country's traditional form of civil religion has been so drastically limited by its overwhelming Protestant bias as to become a major rationalization for many kinds of discrimination and oppression. Due to its extravagant claims for America's providential destiny, moreover, it has tended to deafen the American conscience to charges of injustice and imperialism. Even its many reform campaigns were narrowly conceived and remote from the country's need for structural reorientation.

Yet one massive problem would remain even if Mr. O'Brien's manifesto were to instigate an awakening that transformed the social stance of every Catholic in America. Its appeal would not be universal. It would not transcend the profound religious diversity of this most pluralistic of major nations. Above all it would not reach that majority of Americans who have no active affiliation with churches and synagogues, and whose attitudes are one of the factors that explain the declining hold of America's civil religion during recent decades. O'Brien seems to recognize this problem, however, in that his concluding summons calls upon Catholicism to affirm A. J. Muste's dream of a free democratic society. Muste was a genuinely eclectic disturber of American complacency: sometime Dutch Reformed pastor, sometime Communist labor leader, sometime liberal Christian pacifist. His last major change of position even occurred in the Church of Saint Sulpice in Paris!

Yet when all is said, Muste's message is also rooted in a biblical—albeit liberal—outlook. Despite its great value in this realm, therefore, it only builds a fire under yet another melting pot, important though that may be. It thus approaches but does not claim those grounds of ethical witness which place a universalized appeal before the American people. This, however, is what the nation most urgently needs: an appeal to justice that will arouse long overdue concern for the *general welfare* to which the federal Constitution commits the country. We must, in other words, get beyond a libertarianism which rests on the assumption that if every American does his own thing without impediment, the general welfare will take care of itself.

The principles of distributive justice have been expounded from the times of Aristotle to John Rawls in our own day. And one wonders if Professor O'Brien should not now be exploiting these resources in the Catholic tradition. In any case we must remember that the United States is a "new nation" in which sharp and serious cleavages of race, ethnicity, and religion persist. Our reconciliation and sense of national purpose require an appeal that transcends this diversity and truly seeks to give meaningful content to our ongoing efforts in behalf of the general welfare.

SYDNEY E. AHLSTROM

The Catholic Experience and Perspective

DAVID J. O'BRIEN

Choice

Either support what is going on, in which case you count for nothing because you are swallowed in the mass and great incalculable forces bear you on; or remain aloof, passively resistant, in which case you count for nothing because you are outside the machinery of reality.

Randolph Bourne's words of World War I accurately present the choice that again and again confronts decent men and women in modern times.[1] During the first of this century's wars, America's historical optimism began to crack, the nation's faith in itself began a long slide toward fatalism and accommodation to insanity. "I am against war," Fiorello La Guardia told his fellow congressmen. "Because I am against war I am going to war to fight against war."[2] Thus took form the American doctrine of warring for peace, as Woodrow Wilson regretfully led his people into the "war to end war."

Some progressives had always known what took Wilson so long to learn, that, as Theodore Roosevelt put it, "Peace will prevail in international relations, just as order prevails within a nation, because of the

David J. O'Brien was trained in American social and political history at the University of Notre Dame and the University of Rochester. He has written *American Catholics and Social Reform: The New Deal Years* and *The Renewal of American Catholicism*, both published by Oxford University Press. With Thomas Shannon he has edited a collection of Catholic documents on justice and peace, *Building the Earth*, published by Doubleday Image Books. Dr. O'Brien has taught at Loyola College in Montreal and at Holy Cross College and presently serves as Director of the Institute of Justice and Peace at Stonehill College, North Easton, Massachusetts. He has lectured widely around the country and serves on the Board of the Catholic Committee on Urban Ministry. During the Bicentennial he served as a member of the Bishops' Committee on the Bicentennial and as research consultant to the United States Catholic Conference responsible for documentation for the Call to Action conference.

1. Randolph Bourne, *War and the Intellectuals*, ed. Carl Resek (New York: Harper & Row, 1956), p. 221.

2. Quoted in Eric Goldman, *Rendezvous with Destiny* (New York: Alfred A. Knopf, 1952), pp. 200–201.

righteous use of superior force."[3] If Wilson agonized over the price the nation must pay for making war, many found the pull of power far more attractive than the sentimentality of old-fashioned idealism. Herbert Croly put the matter clearly as early as 1910:

> The American nation, just in so far as it believes in its nationality and is ready to become more of a nation, must assume a more definite and a more responsible place in the international system. It will have an increasingly important and an increasingly specific part to play in the political affairs of the world; and, in spite of "old fashioned democratic" scruples and prejudices, the will to play the part for all it is worth will constitute a beneficial and a necessary stimulus to the better realization of the Promise of our domestic life.[4]

Despite Croly's enthusiasm, Americans really hadn't expected to enter the war, and once in it they could not be sure what, beyond slogans, they were fighting for. "We dared not ask ourselves questions," Harold Stearns remembered. "For when we began to ask questions, we began to doubt. And we could not afford to doubt; the decision had been made and it was irrevocable."[5] To such a temper, the dissenter was especially unwelcome; those who were inclined to question the war either went to jail or, abandoning their questioning, went to work for the government. When the skeptic pointed out "unpleasant realities" he met the retort that "the ideal was so great that sacrifices must temporarily be made for it. By his tendency "to follow the drift of events and then to idealize the decision," Wilson is seen by many, in retrospect, to have personified the liberal collapse. American liberalism abandoned its pragmatic analysis of events when the results became embarrassing, Stearns believed: "Faced with the reality of war, liberals had hoped to control events by abandoning themselves to them." For Stearns, this was "the technique of liberal failure," the lesson of the war for American liberalism.[6]

Some, like Bourne, stood aside and refused to accept the drift, and they were told, as he was, that they "counted for nothing." The nation paid for its idealized surrender to events in the postwar disillusionment, which is with us still. In many ways, today's mood parallels almost exactly that of a previous generation of Americans who tasted the bitterness of loss of faith in the American dream. Listen to H. L. Mencken telling why

---

3. Herbert Croly, *The Promise of American Life* (New York: Macmillan, 1909), p. 312.

4. Ibid., p. 289.

5. Harold Stearns, *Liberalism in America* (New York: Bonn and Liveright, 1919), p. 93.

6. Ibid., pp. 110, 135, 147.

he would vote for Warren Harding in 1920 and see if it does not sound familiar:

> Today no sane American believes in any official statement of national policy, foreign or domestic. He has been fooled too often and too callously and impudently. Every idea that has aroused him to sentimental enthusiasm and filled his breast with the holiest of passions has been dragged down into the mud by its propounders and made to seem evil and disgusting. He wants a change. He wants a renaissance of honesty even of ordinary, celluloid politicians honesty. Tired to death of intellectual charlatanry, he turns despairingly to honest imbecility.[7]

The high idealism of Wilsonian progressivism and "the war to end war" left as its legacy only Versailles and prohibition. Confusion and disappointment spread; that day's best and brightest could only offer the fruits of their profound alienation in the form of autobiographical reminiscence; preoccupation with personal consciousness replaced critical social thought, offering aesthetic daring in place of social responsibility. "A generation aware of its predicament is at hand," Joseph Wood Krutch wrote.

> It has awakened to the fact that both the ends which its fathers proposed to themselves and the emotions from which they drew their strength seem irrelevant and remote. With a smile, sad or mocking, according to individual temperament, it regards the works of the past in which was summed up the values of life. The romantic ideal of a world well lost for love and the classic ideal of austere dignity seem equally ridiculous, equally meaningless, when referred not to the temper of the past but to the temper of the present.[8]

The roots of this disillusionment lay not simply in the fact that liberals had surrendered to the drift of events and called their surrender patriotism. Equally important, they institutionalized modern critical scholarship in a professionalism which eventually led them to lose sight of the moral grounds on which that scholarship had been born, the commitment to reason and freedom. Over the next generation men like Charles Beard and Carl Becker would fashion out of the anguish of skeptical relativism a renewal of chastened faith in America and in democratic ideals, but their example remained lonely and uncharacteristic, and was often considered eccentric.

7. Malcolm Moos, ed., *H. L. Mencken on Politics* (New York: Vintage Books, 1960), pp. 33–34.

8. Joseph Wood Krutch, *The Modern Temper* (New York: Harcourt Brace and Co., 1929), p. 17.

In the wake of Watergate, Charles Reich argued that "we are responsible for what we call reality. It is not something that is inevitable, but something we choose." If we would only stop going along, Reich pleaded, we might "regain the sacred power that human consciousness gives us, the power to choose by what truths we shall live."[9] But the mass of Americans remain convinced, as Jonathan Kozol put it, that history is always made by someone else, in some other time and place.[10] Those who suggest otherwise threaten "the command mechanism of the established order," as John Kenneth Galbraith noted in commenting on Reich's *The Greening of America:* The established scholars' attack on such men demonstrates, to Galbraith's satisfaction, that "they are the most in the thrall of the convenient belief and hence [are] the least capable of envisaging any alternative."[11]

More characteristic by far than the demand for choice is the rationalization of existing definitions of the possible by scholars like Thomas C. Cochran, who argued in his presidential message to the American Historical Association in 1973 that the contemporary "cultural crisis" arises from the conflict between massive bureaucratic structures created by complex social forces and a renewed, romantic belief in human equality. "Is democracy or egalitarianism the kind of value or belief that can by itself cure antisocial behavior and the loss of social morale?" Cochran asked. His answer was unequivocal: complex, centralized, hierarchical structures are inevitable; equality is thus impossible:

> Since some hierarchy seems inevitable in the conduct of human affairs and since equality can never be complete, what is required is the justification of gradations, not the virtual elimination of them. . . . A cure of the cultural crisis must be some compelling doctrine which will lead Americans to *play their roles* with the *orderliness* necessary for the operation of a good society.[12]

Those who would "choose the truths by which they shall live" are, as Bourne foresaw, condemned to irrelevance, allowed a limited tolerance if harmless, made objects of hatred and contempt if they make a serious effort to translate their beliefs into effective action. One need only assess the mid-1970s public status of Hubert Humphrey, Henry Kissinger, and

9. Charles Reich, "The Greening of America," *New York Times,* 14 June 1973.

10. Jonathan Kozol, "History Returns to Boston," *New York Times,* 11 December 1974.

11. John Kenneth Galbraith, *Economics and the Public Purpose* (New York: Signet Books, 1973), pp. 222–23n.

12. Thomas C. Cochran, "History and Cultural Crisis," *American Historical Review* 81 (March 1973), pp. 1–10.

Arthur Schlesinger, Jr., as opposed to that of Eugene McCarthy, Noam Chomsky, and Philip Berrigan to appreciate the truth of this contention. The dominant cultural fatalism well serves the interest of academic and governmental elites; it also saps the people's self-confidence and erodes the popular will. Yet the democratic spirit does not die, but struggles for life. In this century we have witnessed successive people's movements, each affirming the dignity and worth of ordinary people: the middle class revolt of the progressive era, the dramatic rise of trade unionism in the 1930s, the civil rights movement of the postwar era, and the assertion of pride and determination on the part of black, brown, and red Americans, and of women, in our own times. Whatever the ambiguities of these movements, and however limited their results, each has indicated the strength of a historic vision of human possibility, alive in resistance to arbitrary power. Despite the cynicism of the powerful, the spirit is described by Bernard Bailyn:

> . . . faith ran high that a better world than any that had ever been known could be built where authority was distrusted and held in constant scrutiny . . . and where the use of power over the lives of men was jealously guarded and severely restricted. It was only where there was this defiance, this refusal to truckle, this distrust of all authority, political or social, that institutions would express human aspirations, not crush them.[13]

The question, then, is not whether American religious values will influence the future of America, but whether human beings themselves, and those hopes which many ordinary persons have invested in America, have a future. For Christian religious values include faith in God and his Son, fidelity to his word, and dedication to his will, but, today, we see those values quite properly in the context of freedom. If, as Vatican II taught, every person has the right and the duty to follow his conscience, then the opportunity to form a conscience and the power to choose are the truly fundamental issues. Those who would issue the Christian invitation and be faithful to the Christian gospel must, in the days to come, learn once again the reality of oppressive power and help one another become, with all people, truly free, both in external conditions and in the life of the Spirit.

---

13. Bernard Bailyn, *The Ideological Origins of the American Revolution* (Cambridge, Mass.: The Belknap Press of Harvard University Press, 1967), p. 319.

Civil Religion

Cochran's appeal for a new consensus to restore order and promote acceptance of present insanity includes a realization that "to be effective, new values must attain the force of religious belief." It is evidence of the self-serving character of the argument that he provides a major role for historians in supplying this new "religion," to use his word. As many critics have noticed, historical study, particularly in its modern institutional form, is a highly effective instrument for promoting public accommodation, adaptation, acceptance of the idea that the way things are is the way they have to be.

Some years ago, writing in *Playboy* magazine, Newton Minow, former head of the Federal Communications Commission, urged a more effective utilization of the limited resources available for public broadcasting. Fearful that experiments would dissipate available funds while leaving nothing of lasting benefit, Minow called for the concentration of energy, money, and talent on one major project at a time. The first project to be undertaken, he argued, should be a course on American history which would help bind up a divided nation, making all the people, old and young, rich and poor, black and white, aware of their common heritage, their common commitment to this country and its institutions.[14]

Rarely has anyone expressed so clearly the potential utility of American history as an instrument for defining and propagating a sense of common national purpose. Minow's article reflected the deep divisions of the late 1960s, to be sure, but it was by no means untypical or insignificant. "Attitudes toward the past frequently become facts of profound consequence for the culture itself," Warren Susman writes.[15] History as actuality—the past itself—is no neutral arena of cold hard facts to be discovered, recorded, and analyzed, but a battleground, where contending forces struggle for control of the people's soul and of the nation's future.

The search for a usable past is no new phenomenon. Crèvecoeur called the American a "new man." Jefferson believed that "this whole chapter of the history of man is new," and this theme was renewed by Frederick Jackson Turner. Newness and novelty suggested that the past had been left behind. Nevertheless, Americans needed a history, a story of the nation's origins and development which could serve as a point of focus for

14. Newton D. Minow, "Must the Tedium Be the Message?" *Playboy* 15 (July 1968), pp. 117, 197.

15. Warren I. Susman, "History and the American Intellectual: Uses of a Usable Past," *American Quarterly* 16 (Summer 1964), pp. 243–44.

a restlessly mobile and diverse people. "While the past itself has been almost wholly an old world possession and preoccupation," Henry Steele Commager has written, "Americans have resolutely studied themselves as if they were an isolated chapter in history and exempt from its processes."[16] American history must validate the nation's uniqueness and provide those common beliefs without which, Tocqueville tells us, "no society can prosper, say rather, no society can exist." Tocqueville further understood that the function of historical mythology was particularly crucial in a democracy. "It is required that all the minds of the citizens should be rallied and held together by certain predominant ideas," he wrote, "and this cannot be the case unless each of them draws his opinions from the common source and consents to accept matters of belief already formed."[17]

In recent years a number of scholars have noted the existence of just such "beliefs already formed," a consensus on values and goals which might be celebrated or deplored, but which in any case constitutes a major feature of national existence. As early as 1941, Ralph Gabriel described an "American democratic faith" centered on belief in the centrality of individual freedom, the existence of a higher law, and the special role or mission of America. Gabriel regarded the national creed favorably, but the postwar generation had its doubts. Louis Hartz saw America's monolithic liberal tradition as an impediment to national self-understanding which resulted in a provincial outlook and intolerance of dissent. Richard Hofstadter noted similar failures in the American consensus; indeed he turned it on its head, associating popular democracy in America with cupidity rather than freedom, and spelling out the dangerous emotionalism and naiveté of American reformers. At the same time, Will Herberg explained the postwar religious revival in terms of the desire for respectability on the part of newly mobile Americans, who found that, as ethnic identity faded, religious affiliation provided a stable location in America. The American democratic faith became for Herberg an "idolatrous new religion of Americanism" which could only deserve the scorn of people seriously committed to the truths of the Judeo-Christian tradition.[18]

16. Henry Steele Commager, *The Search for a Usable Past* (New York: Alfred A. Knopf, 1967).

17. Alexis de Tocqueville, *Democracy in America,* Mentor Books edition, ed. Richard D. Heffner (New York: New American Library, 1958), p. 141.

18. Ralph Gabriel, *The Course of American Democratic Thought* (New York: Ronald Press, 1940); Richard Hofstadter, *The American Political Tradition* (New York: Alfred A. Knopf, 1948); Louis Hartz, *The Liberal Tradition in America* (New York: Alfred A. Knopf, 1957); Will Herberg, *Protestant, Catholic, Jew* (New York: Doubleday, 1955).

John Courtney Murray was one of the few Catholics who discerned the importance of the national consensus, and his life was dedicated to the task of bringing to a conscious level the long-held intuition that the American civil creed corresponded with the "principles and doctrines . . . of western constitutionalism, classic and Christian." While Murray was the very model of the critical intellectual, he knew well the dangers of an undisciplined and irresponsible intelligentsia. He joined his more conservative Catholic colleagues in vigorous assault on those referred to as the "new barbarians" who undermine standards of judgment and corrupt the "inherited intuitive wisdom by which the people have always lived" not by spreading new beliefs "but by creating a climate of doubt and bewilderment in which clarity about the larger aims of life is dimmed and the self-confidence of the people is destroyed." In 1960 he wrote:

> Today the barbarian is the man who makes open and explicit rejection of the traditional role of logic and reason in human affairs. He is the man who reduces all spiritual and moral questions to the test of practical results or to analysis of language or to decision in terms of individual subjective feeling.

If intellectual discourse required, indeed presupposed, a framework of agreement on principles of logic and reason, so civil discourse required a constitutional consensus by means of which the people acquire an identity and society is endowed with vital form and given a sense of purpose. The principles of the Declaration and the philosophical framework of the Constitution provided that consensus for Americans, a consensus which, Murray argued, Catholics endorsed because it was their patrimony as Americans, because it corresponded with the principles of their own tradition and, most important, because it was true. The civil consensus "is not simply a set of working hypotheses whose value is pragmatic," Murray wrote. "It is an ensemble of substantive truths, a structure of basic knowledge, an order of elementary affirmations that reflect realities inherent in the order of existence."[19]

The most significant work on civil religion went largely unnoticed. Sydney Mead's many fine explorations of the "religion of the Republic" were well known to scholars, but rarely were drawn upon to illuminate present problems or to provide a framework for judging alternative actions. Yet Mead's was in many ways the most profound treatment of the

19. John Courtney Murray, *We Hold These Truths* (New York: Doubleday, 1960), pp. 27–45.

question. Informed by the Turner vision of American religious history, reinforced by Whitehead's process philosophy, Mead's analysis of the experience of the churches and of the American people was open ended, tracing patterns in the past which opened new vistas to the future. Writing in a spirit of faith in America reminiscent of the progressive scholars, Mead insisted that the heritage of religious beliefs shared by all Americans contained abundant resources for understanding our present predicament and pointing toward a future alive with promise. Where others had noted the manner in which the American creed was used to justify present realities, Mead argued that "the religion of the Republic is essentially prophetic, which is to say that its ideals and aspirations stand in constant judgment on the passing shenanigans of the people, reminding them of the standards by which their current practices are ever being judged and found wanting."[20] Robert Bellah's famous essay, which inaugurated the current wave of interest in civil religion, offers a similarly complex understanding, combining a realization of the manner in which the national religion, like others, both comforts and challenges, finds its healers and disturbers, its crusading knights and its peaceful mystics and seers.[21]

Mead and Bellah were unique in arguing that the civil creed is a genuine religion, offering some real truths of universal validity, providing people and a nation with a framework of ultimate meaning and significance by which they can guide their actions and judge their accomplishments. "I would argue that the civil religion at its best is a genuine apprehension of universal and transcendent reality as seen in, or one could almost say, as revealed through, the experience of the American people," Bellah wrote. It is this insight into the complexity of the national mythology, its potential for both unifying the nation and challenging it, that makes its exploration so vitally important in an era marked by the collapse of long-accepted institutions and the decline of confidence in traditional values. Perhaps Norman Mailer best captured this in a characteristic moment of illumination during the 1972 Democratic convention:

> As he stood near McGovern now, there came to him the first strains of that simple epiphany which had eluded him through these days, and he

20. Sidney Mead, "The Nation with the Soul of a Church," *Church History* 36 (September 1967), pp. 262-83; see also Mead's *The Lively Experiment* (New York: Harper & Row, 1967).

21. Robert Bellah, "Civil Religion in America," *Daedalus* 96 (Winter 1967), pp. 1-21; and *The Broken Covenant* (New York: Seabury, 1975).

realized it, and it was simple, but he thought it true. In America, the country was the religion. And all the religions of the land were fed from that first religion, which was the country itself, and if the other religions were now full of mutation and staggering across deserts of faith, it was because the country had been false and ill and corrupt for years, corrupt not in the age old human proportions of failure and evil, but corrupt to the point of terminal disease, like a great religion foundering.

So the political parties of America might be the true churches of America, and our political leaders the Popes and prelates, the bishops and ministers and warring clergymen of ideologies which were founded upon the spiritual rock of America as much as on any dogmas, and so there was a way now to comprehend McGovern and enter the loneliness which lives in his mood, for he inhabited that religious space where men dwell when they are part of the power of a church and wish to alter that church to its roots. For yea, the American faith might even say that God was in the people. And if this new religion, not 200 years old, was either the best or the worst idea ever to shake the mansions of eschatology in the world beyond, one knew at least how to think of McGovern; if he had started as a minister in the faith of his fathers, he had left that ministry to look for a larger one.[22]

The existence of the civil religion has been aptly demonstrated. Its manipulation by the state and the dangers involved in its identification with political and economic self-interest have also been clearly defined by scholars from Reinhold Niebuhr to the recent critics of national policy like Senator Fulbright. What is less clear is whether the civil religion necessarily leads to pride and idolatry, or whether, rooted in a universal dream of equality and brotherhood, it contains resources for transcending its own particularistic national origins. Mead believes that it does, and Bellah argues that in its "third time of trial," the national faith must provide a corridor to a higher, more universal reality.

It is important to note that Tocqueville saw the national consensus, the pool of beliefs and values held beyond doubt and questioning, as especially important to enable society to engage in common action. The rise of a preoccupation with the civil religion parallels almost precisely the rise of the power of the state. Tocqueville and Murray both saw the indispensable role that the consensus played for civil discourse and all forms of public life, but for many others, the hidden agenda was war and rumors of war. That tough-minded realist George Kennan concluded his antimoralistic, realistic treatment of the Russian threat with the statement that "the thoughtful observer of Russian-American relations

22. Norman Mailer, *St. George and the Godfather* (New York: New American Library, 1972), p. 112.

will welcome the Kremlin's challenge to American democracy for it will enable Americans to pull themselves together as a people and accept the responsibilities which history plainly intended they should bear."[23] Even as thoughtful and consistent a critic of national righteousness as Reinhold Niebuhr could on occasion decry both McCarthyism and parochial schools because both divided a nation that badly needed unity in the face of the Communist danger.

Murray himself walked a Catholic tightrope characteristic of the 1950s, attempting to define a national consensus in terms which allowed, even encouraged, Catholic support without at the same time allowing it to become "religious," for it was just that escalation which inhibited Catholic accommodation to liberalism abroad, rationalized Protestant righteousness at home, and opened Catholics to the charge of separatism. By restricting discussion of civil religion to the constitutional and juridical spheres, and by relying on the peculiar historical perspective of "end of ideology" social scientists like historian Daniel Boorstin, Murray was able to reshape Catholic understanding of religious liberty and church-state relations. But he seriously underestimated the extent to which the national symbols both shaped and expressed personal and group life; he misjudged national self-confidence in history and reason, and failed to grasp fully the emotional and cultural dimensions of national life. Murray himself offhandedly dismissed the slavery controversy of the nineteenth century and argued that the Civil War was primarily a fight over constitutional interpretation. Those raised in the Murray tradition understandably had difficulty dealing with the passionate issues of race and war in the 1960s.

Murray's approach, with its emphasis on reason and civility, left little for moralism and could easily become simply a Catholic counterpart of the broader, secular drift toward historical fatalism. Neither did it leave much room for the people. If Murray feared that secular liberalism might undermine the intuitive wisdom of the people, he clearly understood that the people could never reach a level of intelligence to appropriate for themselves the truths of the civil creed. No more than his Vatican adversaries did Murray abandon the fundamentally antidemocratic heritage which had been the legacy of Catholicism's hostility to liberalism. "Man lives both his personal and his social life always more or less close to the brink of barbarism," Murray wrote. "Society is rescued from chaos only

23. Kennan's words conclude the famous "Mr. X" article; see Norman Graebner, ed., *The Cold War* (Boston: Little, Brown and Company, 1963), p. 38.

by a few men, not by the many. It is only the few who understand the disciplines of civility . . . [who] hold and check the forces of barbarism that are always threatening to force the gates of the city."[24] Murray's genius remained Jesuit, Catholic, classical, a gift to his community of faith of enormous value, but flawed by an aloofness which failed to recognize that the forces of barbarism operate in the hearts of the civil and the urbane—and of the powerful—as well as in the hearts of the masses. Murray helped Catholics to live more authentically in a liberal society, but they still were left to choose whether they would be of it. The full implications of accepting the "self-evident" truths as true are still to make themselves felt.

Catholicism and Democracy

In early 1933, Adolph Hitler was seizing absolute power in the German streets. The Reichstag, or German Parliament, was faced with a demand to give legality and legitimacy to the new Nazi regime by approving an Enabling Act granting the new leader dictatorial powers. The Center party, the largest party in the assembly, was also the Catholic party; acting under Roman direction, the party voted to a man for the new law. The Social Democrats, Germany's major socialist party, knew full well the law would be passed; they knew too that the costs of dissent and resistance would be frightening. Nevertheless, they voted to a man against the Enabling Act. Such events, multiplied far too many times, provided the real seedbed for the contemporary renewal of the Catholic community around the world.

Democracy has not been Catholicism's long suit. Modern historians agree with such nineteenth century figures as Lamennais and Acton that in general the Catholic Church set its face with equal firmness against political democracy, social equality, and religious liberty. Its conservative stance enabled the church to level scathing criticism at the liberal era. Perceiving liberalism's tendencies to produce alienation, rootlessness, and the tyranny of private capital and the military state, Catholics developed a negative position of almost prophetic power. Yet the church was unable to offer a positive option which could capture the imagination of the working class against the chaos of *laissez-faire* capitalism and the drifting helplessness of mass unchanging faith and the far from alluring vision of a restored medieval order. Against the socialists' idealistic vision of the worker Christ, Catholicism offered Christ the King, an image of power and authority linked inextricably to a church which saw itself in

24. Murray, *We Hold These Truths*, p. 13.

monarchical terms, and too often subordinated the human values of freedom and self-determination to its own interests.

From Metternich to Hitler, governments have found in the Catholic Church a willingness to deal if and when its freedom could be guaranteed and its work supported, and this for the best of reasons, the welfare of the people themselves. "Let it become more and more evident," Leo XIII argued, "that the tranquillity of order and true prosperity flourish especially among those people whom the church controls and influences."[25] This being true, it followed that the modern world, beset, as Pius XI put it, by "the greatest of evils," could never find order, harmony, and prosperity unless it returned to the church. Quoting Leo that "if human society is to be healed, only a return to Christian life and institutions will heal it," Pius completed the argument: "For these alone can provide effective remedy for that excessive care of passing things that is the origin of all vices; and this alone can draw away men's eyes, fascinated by and wholly fixed on the changing things of the world, and raise them toward heaven."[26] As these words indicate, the Catholic Church and its leaders, more than they realized, "blamed the victims," and in doing so insured that they not only would never contact the hopes of ordinary people, but would eventually face the issue of integrity which sensitive observers, like Acton and Dostoevski, perceived a century ago.

At the beginning of the nineteenth century Félicité de Lamennais led a multifaceted drive for reform of the pastoral life of the French Church, a movement for renewal of seminaries, clerical life style, and church practices. The movement enlisted the dedication and enthusiasm of hundreds of young French Catholics. Lamennais and his friends knew as well as any others the dangers of liberalism; they had indeed fostered the birth of an ultramontane papacy precisely because they had learned from Napoleon the totalitarian potential of change unchecked by religious and moral restraint. As Montalembert put it in 1863, "The more one is a democrat, the more it is necessary to be a Christian, because the fervent and practical cult of God-made-man is the indispensable counterweight to that perpetual tendency of democracy to establish the cult of man believing himself God."[27] Yet they knew, too, that the modern

25. Pope Leo XIII, "On Christian Democracy" in Etienne Gilson, ed., *The Church Speaks to the Modern World* (New York: Doubleday Image Books, 1957), p. 328.

26. Pope Pius XI, "*Quadragesima Anno*" in Terence P. McLaughlin, ed., *The Church and the Reconstruction of the Modern World* (New York: Doubleday Image Books, 1957), p. 264.

27. Montalembert in E. E. Y. Hales, *Pio Nono* (London: Eyre & Spottiswoode, 1954), p. 267.

movements were powerful precisely because they appealed to the hopes and aspirations of people. A revitalized church, they believed, must similarly rest upon confidence and fellowship among priests and people, united around a papacy and episcopacy dedicated to liberty and justice. But such a position, to be authentic, required commitment to liberty in political and cultural as well as religious life. This was more than their superiors could bear.

The "pilgrims for God and liberty" appealed to the pope, and they received the stinging rebuke of *Mirari Vos*. "From the evil-smelling spring of indifferentism flows the erroneous and absurd opinion—or, rather, derangement—that freedom of conscience must be asserted and vindicated for everyone." Pope Gregory XVI went on to condemn "the vile attack on clerical celibacy," "the deleterious liberty, which can never be execrated and detested sufficiently, of printing and publishing writings of every kind," and, finally, "the detestable insolence and impudence of those who, burning with an unbridled desire of baneful liberty, dedicate themselves entirely to the weakening and the destruction of all rights of government." Instead, the pope commended the example of the early Christians who, in the midst of violent persecutions, "worked to the best of their ability for the emperors and the welfare of the empire, not only by faithfulness in carrying out accurately and promptly those things which were not contrary to their religion, but also by their courage and by shedding their blood in battle." Rejecting Lamennais's love for the people, Gregory spoke of "this perverseness of men" and appealed to "our beloved sons in Christ, the rulers," who should consider that their authority has "been granted to them for the government of the world, but more especially for the defense of the church."[28]

The condemnation of Lamennais established a consistent stance for modern Catholicism. The combination of internal authoritarianism and external opportunism both rested on a profound distrust of human nature, particularly as that supposed nature expressed itself among the "lower order." It accounted for the increasingly undemocratic "social movement" which aimed to alleviate mass suffering by means of private paternalism and the power of a state subject to Catholic influence. Leo XIII's ecclesiastical diplomacy was complemented by his determination to maintain hierarchical authority in the church. Although he called for action for justice, Leo insisted that "whatever projects in-

28. *Readings in Church History*, vol. 3, ed. Colman J. Barry (Westminster, Md.: Newman, 1965), p. 41.

dividuals or associations undertake . . . should be formed under
episcopal authority," while he warned the bishops to be solicitous "in
controlling, compelling, and also in preventing" such efforts, "lest any,
under the pretext of good, should cause the vigor of sacred discipline to
be relaxed or the order which Christ has established in his church to be
disturbed."[29] The repression of lay political action, the condemnation of
modernism, and the engines of intellectual control it spawned, the
manipulation of Catholic Action and the scandalous flirtation with
fascism, all expressed the dominance of a political ecclesiology which
rested upon a profoundly prideful self-righteousness and an equally
regrettable suspicion of ordinary people.

However skillful Catholic apologetics were yesterday or are today, it is
very important that contemporary Catholics recognize the truth of
Lamennais's bitter judgment.

> Catholicism is languishing and tending to die out in Europe. The peoples
> are becoming detached from it. Kings either openly attack it or secretly
> undermine it. How can it be revived? How can the vigour which day by day
> it seems to be losing be restored to it? Such was the problem to be solved,
> and there were two possible solutions.
>
> Full of faith in the truths which fundamentally constitute Christianity
> . . . one could have broken the bonds that bind the church to the state,
> and have liberated it from the dependence that impedes its action. One
> could have associated the church with the social movement which is pre-
> paring new destinies for the world—with liberty so as to unite it with
> order and to correct its errors with science so as to reconcile it, by way of
> unfettered discussion with . . . dogma; with the people so as to pour
> upon their immense miseries the inexhaustible streams of the divine
> charity. In a word, one could have risen above all earthly interests and have
> embraced the naked cross, the cross of the carpenter who was born poor
> and who died poor; the cross of him who lived only for the love of his
> brethren and taught them to give themselves for one another. The cross of
> Jesus son of God and son of man might have been set up at the entrance to
> the ways along which the human race is now advancing. This could have
> been done; at least that is what we believed.
>
> But it was also possible to tighten the ancient alliance with the absolute
> powers, to support them against the peoples and against liberty, in order
> to obtain from them a tolerance of sorts; to weld the altar to the throne, to
> rely upon force, to turn the cross toward the past, to entrust it to the
> protection of diplomatic protocols, to entrust it to the care of soldiers who
> have been ordered with fixed bayonets to keep back the trembling nations.
> Rome has chosen the latter course; she had a right to do so.[30]

29. Pope Leo XIII, "On Christian Democracy," p. 327.

30. Quoted in Alec Vidler, *Prophecy and Papacy* (New York: Scribner's, 1954), pp.
260–61.

This is a harsh judgment to be sure, but it had enough truth to generate a profound suspicion of Catholicism everywhere the democratic spirit flourished, including in more than a few Catholic hearts.

American Catholics long prided themselves on their patriotism and love of country, their love of democracy and respect for the American Constitution. Indeed, in at least two celebrated episodes, they sought to instruct the universal church in the theological and political lessons to be learned from the American experience. In the second half of the nineteenth century, Isaac Hecker, John Ireland, John Keane, and Dennis O'Connell offered an American perspective on a range of outstanding issues. Not only did they describe the practical benefits derived from church-state separation, they even argued that both within and without the limits of the church, much could be gained by trusting the people.

As Hecker argued:

> A political society based on the maxims of man's capability of self-government, and which carries it out practically by the exercise of universal suffrage, presupposes man's possession of reason and free-will and the existence of natural rights, laws and justice.[31]

This is something Hecker believed quite in line with Catholic teaching. On this basis the Americanists argued that modern society was in fact superior to medieval society, that in fact the Holy Spirit did operate in enlightening and activating the lives of ordinary people and the world they lived in. These Americanists were condemned and silenced; while the language was more measured than that addressed to Lamennais, the message was the same.

Six decades later, John Courtney Murray enjoyed greater success. Initially suppressed on the quite legitimate grounds that he sought drastic revisions of accepted teaching, he was eventually to enjoy vindication at the Second Vatican Council. A tougher minded person than his Americanist predecessors, he avoided their uncritical assertion of the superiority of modern progress and the American way of life. Murray argued that the American First Amendment embodied a political and juridical arrangement which met the criteria of Catholic teaching and his argument helped shape the Vatican Council's Declaration on Religious Liberty. Official acceptance of church-state separation and strong affirmation of freedom of conscience seemed to many to mark a real turning point in Catholic history and a final accommodation with democracy.

31. Margaret Reher, "Americanism: A Theological Issue," unpublished paper presented to conference on American Catholic history, University of Notre Dame, October 1974, p. 4.

Yet, the nature of this turning point has not yet become fully defined. At the passage of the Declaration on Religious Liberty, historian H. Stuart Hughes asked if the principle that "each man has the right, and indeed the duty, to follow his conscience" was to be applied to Catholics in their relationship to their church.[32] A less sympathetic observer, Paul Blanshard, continued to be puzzled by the effort of an authoritarian church to enlist on the side of liberty. Father Edward Duff put the problem with almost prophetic clarity in 1957. "What does the advocacy of ordered freedom mean for life *within* the Catholic Church?" Duff asked. "The theme is not even alluded to directly in the Declaration, though it certainly preoccupied the adversaries, nervous that their religiously undereducated and spiritually underprepared people would be confused by the notion of freedom." Even its proponents had not calculated the impact which the "notion of freedom" would have on the life of the church. "The dignity of the human person—the basis of the Declaration of Religious Freedom—is a theme calculated to release new energies in American Catholicism," Duff predicted, "and, perhaps, introduce changes in the interpersonal relations within the church in the United States."[33] Less than a decade later it is clear that Duff's was at best an understatement.

In this context it becomes increasingly clear that the reconciliation of Catholicism and democracy is a far more complicated matter than Murray and his Americanist predecessors believed. There is more involved here than the question of due process or the issue of authority. What is at stake is the degree to which the church, having affirmed the rights of conscience and the dignity of the human person, is prepared to translate these values into pastoral policies based on trust and confidence in its own people. Bishops jealous of their prerogatives, priests fearful of lay initiative and control, educational experts dedicated to "raising the consciousness" of their ignorant students, children and adults, and lay people anxious for security and repose, all have failed to take seriously either the principle of human freedom or the vision of Christian community so eloquently set forth by Vatican II or in the best writings of the postconciliar church.

Lacking confidence in themselves and trust in other people, liberal and conservative Catholics alike too often manipulate, harass, or generally treat with contempt their brothers and sisters in the faith. Only personal

32. H. Stuart Hughes, "Pope John's Revolution: Secular or Religious?" *Commonweal* 83 (December 1965), pp. 301–4.

33. Edward Duff, S. J., "Anniversary as Anachronism," *American Ecclesiastical Review* 164 (May 1971), p. 308.

conversion to trust the people and a pastoral policy based on a commitment to self-determination in the faith can begin the authentic Catholic reconciliation with the truths of the democratic heritage. For the power to choose, which is fundamental, cannot be awakened by elites or by what is called education, but only by honest, sincere love for and faith in ordinary, sinful, ambiguous, flesh and blood men and women.

John Courtney Murray argued that the question of Catholicism's compatibility with American democracy in the Catholic hierarchy of values would have to be reversed, to ask rather whether America was compatible with Catholicism. Yet, if the American experience, and the symbols with which Americans endowed their experience with meaning, embodies values and beliefs which Catholics have ignored or violated, then the original question may have theological and religious significance. Part of the responsibility of the American Catholic intellectual today is to assess the truly religious values of America and, if they are found worthy, assess Catholic life and practice in light of those values. The task takes on special urgency if those values are endangered today, as many sensitive citizens believe they are.

Persons, Peace, and Justice

While the full commitment to popular liberties and self-government has still to be made, the Catholic Church today has begun to articulate democratic values more forcefully than in the past and perhaps more forcefully today than any other institution in the world.

Pope Paul has emphasized both human rights and democratic structures:

> In the design of God, every man is called upon to develop and fulfill himself, for every life is a vocation. Endowed with intelligence and freedom, he is responsible for his fulfillment as he is for his salvation. He is aided, or sometimes impeded, by those who educate him and those with whom he lives, but each one remains, whatever be these influences affecting him, the principal agent of his own success or failure. By the unaided effort of his own intelligence and will, each person can grow in humanity, can enhance his personal worth, can become more a person.[34]

The 1971 Synod of Bishops defines this "Right to Development" as "a dynamic interpenetration of all those fundamental human rights upon which the aspirations of individuals and nations are based."[35] Implicit in

---

34. Pope Paul VI, *Populorum Progressio*, par. 15, in Joseph Gremillion, ed., *The Gospel of Peace and Justice* (Maryknoll: Orbis Books, 1976), pp. 391–92.

35. Synod of Bishops, "Justice in the World," par. 15, in Gremillion, *The Gospel of Peace and Justice*, p. 516.

all this is a powerful commitment to democratic forms in social and economic, as well as political, life. Pope Paul states that "in order to counterbalance increasing technocracy modern forms of democracy must be devised, not only making it possible for each man to become informed and to express himself, but also to involve himself in a shared responsibility."[36] Amidst all this there is a note of high urgency, a sense that only powerful and determined action can prevent disaster. "Unless combatted and overcome by social and political action," the Synod warns, "the influence of the new industrial and technological order favors the concentration of wealth, power and decision making in the hands of a small or private controlling group. Economic injustice and lack of social participation keep a man from attaining his basic human and civil rights." While neither pope nor bishop any longer speaks with assurance as to the exact form that action should take, they powerfully denounce "the network of domination, oppression and abuses which stifle freedom and which keep the greater part of humanity from sharing in the building up and enjoyment of a more just and a more fraternal world."[37]

In perhaps the most remarkable document ever to issue from the American hierarchy, the twenty-five bishops of the Appalachian region, gave testimony to a new democratic spirit entering into the life of the church. They acknowledged, "Our words are not perfect, for that reason this letter is but one part of an unfinished conversation." After eloquently testifying to the beauty and strength of the mountain people and the outrage of injustice under which they live, the bishops called for deliberate, decisive action by all the people of the region, together. Remarkably, for bishops, they concluded with thanks, to people "who all along have been struggling in hidden or dramatic ways for justice and unity among people." They thank "youth who have not given up hope and who continue to believe in freshness in human experience"; they thank "parents whose lives have been such that our youth have reason to hope"; the elderly "who despite great hardships continue to survive with spirit and grace and whose quiet wisdom inspires us all"; they even thank "women in the region, for we cannot but note the great role women have played here in the struggle for justice." If we think the times are bad in church, listen to their final words:

36. Pope Paul VI, *Octogesima Adveniens*, par. 47, in Gremillion, *The Gospel of Peace and Justice*, pp. 508–9.

37. Synod of Bishops, "Justice in the World," par. 9, in Gremillion, *The Gospel of Peace and Justice*, p. 515.

> Dear sisters and brothers,
> we urge all of you
> not to stop living
> to be a part of the rebirth of utopias,
> to recover and defend the struggling dream
> of Appalachia itself.
> For it is the weak things of this world,
> which seem like folly,
> that the Spirit takes up
> and makes its own.
> The dream of the mountain's struggle,
> the dream of simplicity
> and of justice,
> like so many other repressed visions,
> is, we believe,
> the voice of the Lord among us.[38]

"With us therefore worldly standards have ceased to count in our estimate of any man," St. Paul tells us. "When anyone is united to Christ, there is a new world; the old order has gone, and a new order has already begun" (2 Cor. 5:17 NEB). If this be so, then we have at least one ground for reconciliation among peoples. The old order is relativized, and can claim our unlimited allegiance no longer. The claims of no state, or party, or institution, can rise above the claims on us made by Christ; his Kingdom becomes the Christian goal, alive as a real possibility even within the midst of life itself. And it is the gift of God to every person, available to him or her, not in some end time only, but as an experience of human possibility and meaning today, living wherever people struggle for a fuller life, embodied explicitly and self-consciously in that fragile and earthly community called the church. "In our natural condition we, like the rest, lay under the dreadful judgement of God," St. Paul told the Ephesians. "But now in union with Christ Jesus you who were once far off have been brought near. . . . Gentiles and Jews, he has made the two one, and in his own body of flesh and blood has broken down the enmity which stood like a dividing wall between them. . . . This was his purpose, to reconcile the two in a single body to God through the cross, on which he killed the enmity" (Eph. 2:3–4, 13–16 NEB). The Christian, then, becomes a person who has a new way of seeing, seeing life, seeing history, seeing society, seeing people. The life of each and every man and woman who comes into the world is rich with possibility; the dignity and worth of each person are infinite.

---

38. "This Land Is Home to Me: A Pastoral Letter on Powerlessness in Appalachia by the Bishops of the Region," Prestonsburg, Ky., Catholic Committee on Appalachia, 1974.

In an age which has witnessed the atrocity of Vietnam and speaks with relative ease of the starvation deaths of the millions of innocent people, we should know with increasing force that even the simplest affirmations of these Christian truths are difficult to maintain with integrity. The Lordship of Jesus, over people and over history, the presence of his Spirit, God's fidelity to his promises, the dignity and worth of every human life that comes from the hand of the Creator, these are not "self-evident truths." Set against the awesome realities of contemporary life, they seem increasingly remote, less and less active principles in shaping the decisions which determine the fate of the people of the world. However comforting such beliefs may be in our personal world, they are mocked and scorned in the broader world whose life we must shape. To once again pledge belief in these doctrines is to take a stand against the history-making powers of our times, to form in those simple statements of faith a community of resistance, which in saying "yes!" to life says "no!" to death. Reconciliation of Christians, breaking down the "walls of enmity" of which St. Paul speaks, means both a renewal of awareness of those common, fundamental truths, about life, about people, about God, but it must also mean a renewed understanding of the responsibilities and demands which that common faith places on all its adherents. Among those demands is the requirement that we live the equality, justice, and love of the reconciled community in the life Christians share together, and the equally serious requirement to speak those simple truths to a world whose rulers today, as in Christ's day, regard them as foolish at best, subversive at worst. In their words and their lives, many people have tried to do that. In his own way, so has Pope Paul. In his speech to the World Food Conference in 1974, he spoke truth to power, irritating among others the American secretary of agriculture:

> The present crisis appears in fact to be above all a crisis of civilization . . . which shows itself . . . when only the model of society that leads to an industrialized civilization is considered . . . when too much confidence is placed in the automatic nature of purely technical solutions, while fundamental human values are forgotten . . . when the accent is placed on the quest for mere economic success deriving from the large profits of industry. . . . It is inadmissable that those who have control of the wealth and resources of mankind should try to resolve the problem of hunger by forbidding the poor to be born, or by leaving to die of hunger children whose parents do not fit into the framework of theoretical plans based on pure hypothesis about the future of mankind.[39]

39. Pope Paul VI, Address to World Food Conference, reprinted in *Origins* 4 (November 21, 1974), pp. 349–51.

Pope Paul's words clarify the fact so hard for modern scholars to understand, namely, that the reconciling affirmation of human life and the worth and dignity of human personality rest on a faith which must always set its adherents in a stance of resistance to the powerful. As A. J. Muste put it in 1940:

> The problem of democracy which concerns so many in this country today is . . . in the last analysis a problem of the nature of the human being, the quality of the individual. If human beings are essentially animals, even if they be very complicated and very clever animals, then every society . . . will be essentially a wolf pack . . . and then the distant as well as the immediate future will be with the dictators, since they are in that case building on the realities of human nature. Only if the human being is a creation of spirit, a being capable of making moral decisions and therefore of governing himself, is the dream of a free, democratic society capable of fulfillment.[40]

Insofar as Catholicism is able to begin to enter into this kind of affirmation, it may be able to make its finest contribution to American society. It seems much longer, but it was only sixteen years ago that John Courtney Murray told Catholics that they might be the last custodians of the American consensus. In our day, the time may well have come. Catholics have the theological resources to argue convincingly that those truths which often do not seem self-evident are, after all, truths for which people should be prepared to sacrifice fortunes, honor, even life. Equally important, Catholics share a worldwide community of faith with people who are living those truths in daily struggles against tyranny and oppression. To strengthen those bonds, at home and abroad, to share those struggles while renewing our own commitment, may be the finest contribution Catholics can make to national life today and in the days to come.

40. A. J. Muste, *Non-Violence in an Aggressive World* (New York: Harper & Bros., 1940), pp. 4–5.

Response

The work of David J. O'Brien is distinguished by several strong virtues: by his voracious reading and research; by his concern for ordinary people and his watchfulness over potential abuses among elites; by a profound Christian spirit—contemplative, activist, idealistic: and by a concern for forces, movements, and events in the cultural and political life of our time. All these qualities are exhibited in the present essay .

There are two points on which I find myself in some disagreement with Professor O'Brien, and yet it may be that through further discussions we should find ourselves not far apart at all. Some of his sentences, some of his paragraphs, are shaded in a way that makes me uneasy; whether I actually disagree is sometimes not quite plain. Let me try to formulate, then, the two sources of uneasiness. The first concerns an interpretation of where power actually lies in American society; the second involves a difference concerning optimism about human beings and institutions. Professor O'Brien seems to me a little too one-sided on both points. Not that I am sorry he takes the positions he does; if he did not, someone else would have to, for they represent a permanent part of the Catholic dialectic. (If no one else voiced them, I myself might feel obliged to argue for them.) Yet his positions, it seems, do require a corrective from the other side of the Catholic dialectic, and it is precisely that other side that appears to be more in need of articulation and defense today.

O'Brien opens his essay with a reflection on the intellectuals and World War I, but he neglects one of the main points in the discussion by Randolph Bourne and his critics. That point is that the intellectuals not only erred in becoming more supportive of the war, and more patriotic, than an appropriate critical distance would have allowed. The point is that this was their *second* error. Their first error was made in the period *preceding* the war when too many intellectuals failed to grasp the seriousness of the time, the need for preparedness, and the role of military power in international affairs. Reinhold Niebuhr went from pacifism to support for the war; and then a decade later went through the same journey once again: became again a pacifist and again a supporter of war. O'Brien stresses the "surrender" to the warring spirit, but does not mention the earlier surrender to a wish that the world would be nicer and more rational than it is.

Indeed, there is a larger lesson here, one with which O'Brien is probably sympathetic. It is necessary always to be somewhat skeptical about the conventional wisdom of intellectuals. In order to do intellectual work, intellectuals are liberated from many of the responsibilities and constraints that weigh upon other elites. This liberation does not mean that they are always right, or always wrong; it does mean that ideas and sentiments sweep through them very quickly. The financial and institutional responsibilities of other elites often make the latter discount the trend of ideas and sentiments; intellectuals, slowed by fewer inertial realities, feel the full weight of such trends—indeed, articulate and champion them. Conventional wisdom among intellectuals blows with the strong winds of social "change." Schemes of plausibility shift swiftly. Those who go with the current hardly have to argue at all; those who do not accept the prevailing plausibilities seem faintly immoral, irrational, and out of touch.

In the last thirty years, the numbers of persons in the intellectual class have multiplied by a factor of ten. Perhaps as many as 35 percent of all workers today are involved in "the knowledge industries"—in teaching, the media, the professions, consultants, social workers, and other managers of ideas and programs. Social change is the lifeblood of such professions. The more the government invests in social programs, the more jobs become available for intellectual workers. In this context, the "intellectuals" are no longer a small, powerless minority; they are a massive social force.

O'Brien, however, tends to think of intellectuals as a relatively small and powerless minority, whose underlying fidelity is to ideals, utopian visions, moved by "the sacred power that human consciousness gives us, the power to choose by what truths we shall live" (Charles Reich). This image of the intellectual is, I think, old-fashioned and romantic. O'Brien cites John Kenneth Galbraith's attack upon the "established scholars" who criticized Reich. Charles Reich teaches at Yale, Galbraith at Harvard, and Reich's much heralded book appeared first in *The New Yorker*, swept the campuses, and was anything but ignored. John Kenneth Galbraith himself is, one would think, the epitome of an "established scholar." To write of Reich and Galbraith as outsiders to the conventional wisdom, when in fact they are two of the rather more successful architects of the conventional wisdom of the time, is to miss an important turn in the tide of social power.

O'Brien picks up this theme in another sentence: "One need only assess the mid-1970s public status of Hubert Humphrey, Henry Kissinger, and Arthur Schlesinger, Jr., as opposed to that of Eugene McCarthy, Noam Chomsky, and Philip Berrigan. . . ." To defend Hubert Humphrey in intellectual contexts in 1968, or 1972, or even 1976 was not the most fashionable, inspiring, noble, and admired course of action. It made one's moral and intellectual credentials faintly—not even faintly—suspect. One has only to read the pages of *Rolling Stone, The New York Review of Books, The New Republic*—or to note the candidates preferred by intellectual workers during that period—to see how shabbily Hubert Humphrey was treated. (Compare the treatment of supporters of Humphrey and of McGovern in 1972). Concerning Henry Kissinger, one should note that *The Wall Street Journal* has been among his harshest and most penetrating critics over the last few years, and that the Right as well as the Left has had ample reason to criticize him. Arthur Schlesinger, Jr., has done all he can in recent years to rehabilitate himself among radicals, supporting candidates like George McGovern and Bella Abzug over candidates like Hubert Humphrey or Daniel Patrick Moynihan.

Eugene McCarthy, Noam Chomsky, and Philip Berrigan, on the other side, have had ample status as celebrities and heroes, and have been quite potent in setting the agenda, style, and even substance of "the new politics"—probably the politics presented most favorably by the media. O'Brien suggests that Humphrey, Kissinger, and Schlesinger have been more potent in the universities and in the media than McCarthy, Chomsky, and Berrigan. The situation is more complicated, and less unequal, than that.

There is now a conventional wisdom that pictures the war in Vietnam as (in O'Brien's word) an "atrocity"; that suggests that the leaders, people, and institutions in the United States are responsible for starvation in other lands; and that recites litanies about Watergate, corruption, profits, and the like as if what were wrong with the world is America. The power of dissenting and critical intellectuals to establish the parameters of public opinion in the television networks, in the cinema, and in the major publications is far greater—and far more questionable—than O'Brien suggests. From his point of view, his favorites may seem too weak; from other points of view, they seem to have been dominant for most of a decade. Power is not exactly where O'Brien pictures it.

The second point on which I disagree with O'Brien is even more difficult to articulate. O'Brien does write of "faith in ordinary, sinful, ambiguous, flesh and blood men and women," and he does note that "the power to choose . . . cannot be awakened by elites or by what is called education." He does note that "liberal and conservative Catholics alike too often manipulate, harass, or treat with contempt their brothers and sisters in the faith." And yet there is an undertow in his essay (and in other writings) that seems to me unguarded and far too optimistic about individuals, their consciousness, and their will.

O'Brien does not, I think, take with sufficient seriousness two profound limitations to the freedom of the person: (a) the individual's inalienable needs for institutional supports, for a state, a party, and a host of other institutions, within which to live embodied; and (b) the individual's own propensities for evil, irresponsibility, laziness, and self-seeking. O'Brien sometimes suggests that the individual with the grace of God rises above these limitations and that, in some utopian age, all individuals *will* do so. "The claims of no state, or party, or institution, can rise above the claims on us made by Christ; his Kingdom becomes the Christian goal, alive as a real possibility even within the midst of life itself." Unexceptionable words, but necessary to modify in context. "The old order is relativized," he writes, "and can claim our unlimited allegiance no longer."

"Unlimited" is the weasel word. Of course not. But the old order—and by that I mean the Bill of Rights, the Constitution, democratic capitalism modified by many socialist components, a free trade union movement, free elections, military power, an effective and disciplined secret service (in that silent war that in fact goes on day by day, in lieu of open war)—does not require our "unlimited" allegiance. It suffices that it receive our full, provisional allegiance until a better order—probably only incrementally better—comes along. For we are creatures of flesh and blood. We cannot live outside a social order. Order is required if life is to go on in even partial justice, partial equality. Such gains in justice and equality as the United States has painfully achieved in a short two hundred years may be lost in a single generation. (India recently lost many such in a single year).

O'Brien's eyes are fixed upon ideals. In addition, his ideals are not sufficiently concrete. The political and economic shape they would have is not easy to discern. Does he wish greater socialism, with the still vaster bureaucracy necessary to embody it? Many do. But it is not yet plain to many of us, studying existing forms of socialism around the world (most nations being both socialist and totalitarian), that socialism in practice multiplies either liberties or bread. O'Brien presses us toward ideals which he himself calls "difficult to maintain," "increasingly remote, less and less active principles in shaping the decisions which determine the fate of the people of the world." He wishes us to say "yes!" to life and "no!" to death. These words, of course, are metaphors. Their content in social policy is far from clear. Ideals are not enough.

It is the genius of capitalism that it has grasped the depth of human selfishness and, modified by other institutions, figured out a way of making this selfishness enhance the possibilities of life—through the freedoms of science, the arts, speech, demand and supply, and self-government. (In many nations, capitalism is, in fact, a form of state capitalism, a form of fascism, and results neither in broader democratic liberties nor in advancing the basic standard of living of its workers). It is the genius of American democracy that it affirms belief in self-government by denying belief in the goodness of human beings. The American Constitution is built upon distrust of the executive, the Congress, the courts, and the people. It establishes checks and balances upon each. It arises out of a most profound sense of human sinfulness. Watergate was not a revelation of the Constitution's inadequacies, but a fulfillment of its basic assumptions and realistic fears. Liberty is by no means easy to achieve or maintain. It is never pure. It is hemmed in by checks and countervailing forces.

Indeed, American democracy, unlike the French, is based upon pessimism with respect to human beings. Montalembert could write in 1863 of "the perpetual tendency of democracy to establish the cult of man believing himself God." In the same decade, Abraham Lincoln made in behalf of American democracy no such usurpation of the wisdom or designs of the Almighty. Not in man does our democracy trust. It says upon our humblest coins: "In God we trust."

In its lack of emphasis on the power of human evil, on the modest possibilities open to human institutions, and on the fact that our redemption does not occur in the world of history, Professor O'Brien's essay falls short of expressing the full Catholic dialectic. The vision is too individualistic, too voluntarist, too trusting in the goodness of human beings and the miraculous grace of God—too little expectant of the time upon the cross that is the lot of every social order in human history.

MICHAEL NOVAK

Values, Events,
and Features
in the American
Religious Experience

Introduction

Rabbi Tanenbaum sounds a very important note in his paper on American religious values and the future of America. He recalls us to the moral basis of government that was an intrinsic part of both the classical and the Puritan heritage. Civic virtue or moral public spiritedness was understood to be the essential foundation of a government of a free people. What has caused this sense of public virtue to decay? Certainly a widespread opinion of most Americans today is that politics is, by nature, "dirty." Politicians are expected to act in corrupt and selfish ways. It became hard for Americans to be scandalized even by such an event as Watergate, because the ingrained judgment that "all politicians act like that" had become widespread. Such attitudes encourage a populace to withdraw from active vigilance in public affairs into an attitude of privatism. Opinion polls show a great increase in cynicism toward public affairs in recent years. These attitudes spell the decay of that public spiritedness which earlier Americans saw as fundamental to the moral basis of government.

One cause of this decay of public spirit is rooted in a partial failure of the American "melting pot" fully to integrate successive groups of people into a sense of being one political community with an equal stake in participating in the maintenance of public order. Ironically enough, the very groups that were responsible for much of the original vision of American society as a moral order also helped initiate this failure. As successive groups of immigrants came to these shores after the Civil War, and the Negroes of the South were released from bondage, a paranoia developed among the peoples of the original Anglo-Saxon and Northern European Protestant stock. More and more Americans seemed to their eyes to be "aliens." There were Catholic Irish, Catholic Italians and Poles, Eastern European Jews, Slavs, Greeks, not to mention the black ex-slaves and the Orientals who began to enter from the West. Anglo-Saxon Protestants began to see themselves as the embattled "natives" no longer sure of holding their own.

It was in this atmosphere of paranoia that there developed a peculiar theory which we might call "the Anglo-Saxon Israel" complex. This theory drew on the Puritan roots that identified the English dissenter with the elect people of Hebrew Scripture. Only this idea of America as Zion now took on an ethnic note. It was not simply that this people, like Israel of old, had been called to faithfulness and must see its peoplehood under God's judgment. This idea, understood contextually, might be applied to many peoples. Rather, America as Israel came to be seen more particularisticly. If the Anglo-Saxon was God's new elect people, it followed that peoples of earlier religious eras: Catholics, Jews, "pagans" were marked down for obsolescence. The negative side of the doctrine of Progress is that other people were seen as "superseded." Brown, black, red, and yellow peoples could be regarded as negated by the triumphant march of divine choice and historical destiny. The Anglo-Saxon Protestant was the favored people of history, destined to annihilate, assimilate, or supersede all other peoples. The chauvinism of Anglo-Saxon Manifest Destiny found typical expression in publications such as *Our Country* (1885) by the Social Gospel clergyman Josiah Strong:

> By 1980 the world Anglo-Saxon race should number at least 713,000,000. Since North America is much bigger than the little English isle, it will be the seat of Anglo-Saxondom. If human progress follows the law of development, if "Time's noblest offspring is the last," our civilization should be the noblest, for we are the "heirs of all the ages in the foremost files of time". . . . Then will the world enter upon a new stage of history—the final competition of the races for which the Anglo-Saxon is being schooled. If I do not read amiss, this powerful race will move down upon Mexico, down upon Central and South America, out upon the Islands of the sea, over upon Africa and beyond. And can anyone doubt that the result of this competition will be the "survival of the fittest"?[1]

Along with this sweeping vision of the Anglo-Saxon superseding all the world's races went a great doubt as to the ability of this race to assimilate peoples of other races and cultures here in America and still maintain its "democratic institutions." Cries of alarm were sounded that broadly suggested that democracy and the characteristic representative institutions of American government were not a universal possibility, as is suggested in the language of the Declaration of Independence, but rather belong to a specific "race genius." These governmental institutions are the peculiar product of the racial history and genius of Anglo-Saxon and perhaps Germanic Protestant peoples. Those of other backgrounds, who did not share this history and race genius, not only do not share the same capacity for virtue required for these institutions, but their admixture in the American body politic will gradually "pollute" the native capacity for sound government. General Francis Walker, professor of political economy at Yale in the late nineteenth century, expresses this widespread "racial" view of aptitude for American government:

---

1. Thomas Gossett, *Race: The History of an Idea in America* (New York: Schocken, 1965), p. 188.

The entrance into our political, social and industrial life of such vast masses of peasantry, degraded below our utmost conceptions, is a matter which no intelligent patriot can look upon without the gravest apprehension and alarm. These people have no history behind them which is of a nature to give encouragement. They have none of the inherited instincts and tendencies which made it comparatively easy to deal with the immigration of the olden time. They are beaten men from beaten races, representing the worst failures in the struggle for existence. . . . They have none of the ideas and aptitudes which fit them to take up readily and easily the problem of self-care and self-government, such as belong to those who are descended from the tribes that met under the oak-trees of old Germany to make laws and choose chieftains.[2]

This racial theory of aptitude for democratic government justified some very undemocratic responses to ex-slaves and immigrant Americans which prevented them from becoming voting citizens. The franchise was treated as a privilege of the Aryan and the "Aryanized" for which others need not apply.

Yet, despite this frank effort to apply racial-ethnic limits to full American citizens, immigrant and black Americans to a remarkable extent have taken the universalism of the American democratic promise at its word. Against the racism of the founding groups, they have used the language of the Constitution and Declaration of Independence to insist on their own full inclusion. Thus the original American political language has proven capable of expanding to cover peoples not originally included. It has proven its capacity to critique those who would use it in a particularistic way. But the questions raised by the racial misuse of the American democratic heritage have yet to be fully answered. We are not yet sure on what basis we all: black, white, brown, red, and yellow, Catholic, Protestant, Jew, and perhaps Muslim and Buddhist, come together as one political community with a common sense of identity.

Are there limits to becoming "Aryanized in spirit"? Can a German do it, but not a Pole, an Irishman, or an Italian? Can Jews become Ayran in spirit? Are there some groups—blacks, Orientals, Indians—excluded by their very race from assimilation? More fundamentally, does American identity depend on losing one's own group biography into one which flows from classical Greece and Puritan England? Can the American social covenant be "renegotiated," so that cultural groups that were not a party to the original contract contribute more than their minds and bodies to be melted into the WASP mold? How might these groups

2. Ibid., p. 303.

preserve their own distinct cultures and histories in order to add them to the mix?

Becoming an American would then mean, not just learning Puritan history of Massachusetts, but black history and Indian histories, as the other side of this Anglo-Saxon history. It might mean that the heroic tale of Scandinavian settlement in Minnesota, Jewish flight from the pogroms of Russia to New York City, the Chicano struggle in the Southwest, and many more might become memories and heritages that all Americans could learn as a part of their national identity? The story of *Hester Street*, of the *Immigrants*, the book and televised version of *Roots*, the story told in *Bury My Heart at Wounded Knee* represent recent attempts to communicate to many Americans these suppressed histories. We have only begun to experiment with this enlarged understanding of the base of American identity. The Jewish community particularly lives and defines itself in the constant tension between public "Aryanization" and private group particularity in an effort to discover what it means to be American and Jewish. One would have liked Rabbi Tanenbaum particularly to have said a few words in his paper about this issue.

ROSEMARY RADFORD RUETHER

Values, Events, and Features in the American Religious Experience

MARC H. TANENBAUM

The observance of the Bicentennial commemorating the American Revolution was in many ways a moral tragedy. Given the magnitude and frightening seriousness of the problems of human survival that our nation and the world community face, the Bicentennial could well have been a singular opportunity for raising the consciousness and mobilizing the moral will of the American people and of world society about the central critical issues of our age, which, at their deepest levels, are moral, spiritual, and universally human issues.

With all the national publicity and consequent expectation that something "meaningful" would emerge from the Bicentennial year, many had hoped that this observance would become an occasion for reflecting seriously and systematically on the values and ideals for which the American Revolution was ostensibly fought, and what relevancy those ideals and values might have to help guide and sustain us in this complex and difficult time—a time of potential nuclear annihilation; of an insane arms race; of vast human suffering through poverty, hunger, and malnutrition; of decline of human liberties and human rights in many parts of the world; of the rape of the environment and the shrinking of nature's resources; of economic inequalities that border on the criminal; of pervasive crime, terrorism, and violence; of moral corruption in

Rabbi Marc H. Tanenbaum, National Interreligious Affairs Director of the American Jewish Committee, has been a pioneering leader and thinker in interreligious relations for nearly twenty-five years. A religious historian and authority on Judaism and Jewish-Christian relations, he has written and lectured extensively on the history, theology, and sociology of Judaism and Christianity. He is a founder and co-secretary of the joint Vatican-International Jewish Consultative Committee and of a similar liaison body with the World Council of Churches. A graduate of Yeshiva University and the Jewish Theological Seminary, Rabbi Tanenbaum has received many honorary degrees, awards, and honors. He has edited and authored numerous books including *Speaking of God Today in the Age of Auschwitz and Technology*, *A Guide to Jewish Traditions and Holy Days*, and *Jewish Christian Dialogue*.

governments, multinational corporations, business, law, medicine, labor, religious and educational institutions themselves.

Despite the multivolume report prepared by the national American Revolutionary Bicentennial Commission that purported to document "the achievements" of that year-long fiasco, the dominant images left by the Bicentennial observances were those of "Op-Sail," of graceful preindustrial ships sailing languidly and pointlessly up the Hudson River, and of tons of red-white-and-blue junk, that made advertisers and commercial hucksters rich, but neither enriched the spirit nor nourished the understanding of the American people. If one judges by the opinion polls and subsequent political events, the American people (and other peoples elsewhere) are looking for bread, and by and large they were fed circuses. The rare exceptions to these generalizations were some of the programs, seminars, studies, and publications conducted mainly and independently by Christian and Jewish institutions and by some universities, such as Villanova. But these reflective activities reached modest numbers of Americans, and their constructive influences may yet take years before they percolate down into the general culture, which is far more decisively influenced by advertisers and the mass media than by moral philosophers and historians of ideas.

These critical comments are not an effort to achieve any kind of notoriety as a sensationalist Jeremiad. They are based on a reading of polls and studies of the present state of "the American mood," as well as on personal experiences through travel in every part of the United States during 1976, and before and after then.

Thus, a Louis Harris Poll issued on November 18, 1976, reports: "An 88 percent majority of the American people feel the top priority for the next Congress is to 'clean up corruption in government.' " Close behind are the following mandates for Congress and the White House that "sum up the prevailing mood" today:

Listen to the people more	83%
Show trust in the people more	79%
Help the poor, the elderly, and others hard hit by inflation	78%
Begin to represent the consumer more, and big business and big labor less	78%
Make sure no more Watergate affairs can take place	78%
Make government less secret and more open to what is really going on	76%
Have courage to ask people to make sacrifices when necessary	66%

Pass much stricter legislation to protect the environment and to curb air and water pollution	59%
Curb the power excesses of the White House	57%
Pass legislation for a national health program	53%
Reduce imports of oil from foreign sources in the short run	50%[1]

In a later poll issued by Harris on December 24, 1976,[2] Americans were questioned on areas of life including violence, war, unemployment, tension, religion, and discrimination against minorities. The survey showed that 100 percent of the American people wanted to see a decline in violence, but a 67–22 percent of the majority did not believe they will see such a decline in their lifetime. While 98–1 percent majority of Americans want to see an "end to war," 82–8 percent said they did not believe this will happen. In 1968, the "pessimistic majority" was 55–32 percent.

By 97–2 percent, Americans said they would like to see "an end to unemployment," but an 81–11 percent majority was pessimistic that unemployment would be ended. In 1968, 42–39 percent majority did not believe unemployment would end.

"Life without constant tension" was hoped for by a 96–2 percent majority, but expected by only 11 percent. The only area of reform in which the American people are prepared to express much optimism is that of eliminating discrimination against minorities; 90–4 percent majority said they would like to see "equality for blacks," and a 44–42 percent majority indicated they believed it would be achieved.

Such polls as these reflect episodically what many social commentators have been aware of for some time, namely, that America, and postindustrial societies generally, face a "malaise of civilization"—a deep, pervasive crisis in values. Robert Heilbroner, author of *An Inquiry into the Human Prospect,* describes this condition in these words:

> There is a feeling that great troubles and changes loom for the future of civilization as we know it. Our age is one of profound turmoil, a time of deep change, and there is a widespread feeling that the world is coming apart at the seams.
>
> We have gone through "a drubbing of history," and a barrage of confidence-shaking events have filled us with a sense of unease and foreboding during the past decade or so. No doubt foremost among these has

1. Louis Harris poll, November 18, 1976, Religious News Service, New York, N.Y.

2. Louis Harris poll, December 24, 1976, Religious News Service, New York, N.Y.

been the experience of the Vietnam War, an experience 'that has un-
dermined every aspect of American life—our belief in our own invincible
power, our trust in government, our estimate of our private level of
morality.

But the Vietnam War was only one among many such confidence-
shaking events. The explosion of violence in street crime, race riots,
bombings, bizarre airplane hijackings, shocking assassinations have made
a mockery of the TV image of middle class American gentility and brought
home with terrible impact the recognition of a barbarism hidden behind
the superficial amenities of life.

We switch on the evening TV and learn what's going to hit us next on
the head—a hijacking, a murder, a rape, or some other daily terror. These
things profoundly affect our outlook.[3]

If the Bicentennial itself did not succeed in clarifying the nature and
extent of the "malaise" the majority of the American people continue to
feel about the future prospects of American democracy and the American
way of life, certainly candidate Jimmy Carter demonstrated that he had
nearly "perfect pitch" for the signals of that condition. Two years before
the election he was a virtual unknown nationally. On the basis of his
constant refrain, "Trust me, I will tell you no lies," he was catapulted
into the most powerful office of the greatest superpower on earth. Carter
had an unerring insight into the malaise of the American people, and
responded to their yearning for a vision of "what is right about
America." His advocacy of the cause of human rights in the world, and
the broad-based support of that advocacy, is a demonstration of the
degree to which Americans wish to recapture some of the ideals and
values of the past, and seek to live them in reality today.

But it will take more than a few idealistic slogans haphazardly selected
from the American revolutionary quiver to sustain American moral and
political will in the face of the foreign and domestic challenges that
confront us, both short-term and long-term. In an effort to provide some
clarity and depth to an understanding of the distinctive nature of
American ideals and values, I will review the sources of American value
concepts and will seek to make some connections between those perceived
ideals of the "American Experiment" and the contemporary problems
we face together.

What are those "distinctive values and ideals" symbolized by the
American Revolution; what have been their sources?

3. Robert Heilbroner, *An Inquiry into the Human Prospect* (New York: Norton, 1974),
p. 13.

In his brilliant study *The Ideological Origins of the American Revolution*,[4] Prof. Bernard Bailyn of Harvard University writes:

> In the intense political heat of the decade after 1763, the long popular, though hitherto inconclusive ideas about the world and America's place in it were fused into a comprehensive world view, unique in its moral and intellectual appeal. It is the development of this view, to the point of overwhelming persuasiveness to the majority of the American leaders, and the meaning this view gave to the events of the time, and not simply an accumulation of grievances, that explains the origins of the American Revolution. . . .
>
> Study of the sources of the colonists' thought . . . reveals, at first glance, a massive, seemingly random eclecticism. . . . But ultimately this profusion of authorities is reducible to a few, distinct groups of sources and intellectual traditions dominated and harmonized into a single whole by the influence of one peculiar strain of thought, one distinctive tradition.[5]

Professor Bailyn identifies the following five "distinct groups of sources and intellectual traditions" from which we derive our nation's values, ideals, and practices: classical antiquity, Enlightenment rationalism, English common law, New England Puritanism, and opposition radical thought.

References to the classical authors abound in the writings of the American colonists. They saw parallels between their situation and the history of early republican Rome and the tyranny which followed. Nevertheless, Bailyn says, this classical learning illustrated but did not determine their beliefs about politics and society.

The same can be said of the European Enlightenment writers whom the colonists frequently cited. While they were more influential than the classical authors, they were "neither clearly dominant nor wholly determinative," according to Bailyn.

Nor did English common law finally determine their political beliefs. The colonists were well aware of its tradition as they were of Enlightenment rationalism, but they looked to the common law primarily as a source of history and experience.

Another "major source" was New England Puritanism, particularly covenant theology. Bailyn observes that the ideas developed in the course

---

4. Bernard Bailyn, *The Ideological Origins of the American Revolution* (Cambridge, Mass: The Belknap Press of Harvard University Press, 1967). The "five distinct groups of sources and intellectual traditions" are a summary of material presented by Professor Bailyn in his chapter "Sources and Traditions," pp. 22–54.

5. Ibid., pp. 22–23.

of colonial history by writers and preachers contributed to America's sense of destiny.

Other historians have stressed the importance of the covenant.

> For the covenant, the congregations claimed direct authority from the Bible and direct precedent in the history of Israel. "The Covenant of Grace is the very same now that it was under the Mosaical dispensation," stated William Brattle [MS, Sermons, Harvard College Library]. . . . Uriah Oakes in his election sermon of 1673 [*New England Pleaded With*] emphasized God's covenant with the Children of Israel and how they were led into the land of promise. When this question was considered at a general convention of ministers at Boston, on May 26, 1698, all save one agreed that "under the Old Testament the Church was constituted by a Covenant" [Increase Mather, *The Order of the Gospel*, p. 39].[6]

Mediated by the Puritans in New England, the Hebrew Scriptures became in many ways the "intellectual arsenal" of the American Revolution. The patriots "found precedent and inspiration" in the Hebrew Scriptures, "and the pulpits of the land, where public opinion was molded, resounded with their revolutionary summonses," as Rufus Learsi asserts in his volume on *The Jews in America* (1954).

> The exodus from Egypt was the classic model of liberation from tyranny; the colonies of America should also make their exodus. The ten tribes of Israel defied the arrogant son of Solomon and established their own government: the thirteen colonies should do likewise. The Hebrew prophets denounced kings and potentates, and God-fearing Americans may do the same. Even the call [selected from the Book of Leviticus] engraved on the Liberty Bell: "Proclaim liberty throughout the land unto all the inhabitants thereof" [was symbolic of the attachment of the Founding Fathers to the Hebrew Scriptures]. Revolutionary doctrine became crystallized in the slogan "Rebellion to tyrants is obedience to God." Indeed, those were the words which Franklin, Jefferson and John Adams proposed for the seal of the United States: they were to be inscribed around a picture of the children of Israel crossing the Red Sea. . . .
>
> Not less potent was the influence of the Hebrew Scriptures in determining the basic political system of the new society that emerged from the War of Independence. To discredit the monarchy, preachers like the bold and brilliant Jonathan Mayhew of Boston held up the warning of the prophet Samuel against royalty. Samuel Langdon, the president of Harvard, considered the Jewish government "a perfect republic," and Ezra Stiles, the president of Yale, found in the American government the fulfillment of Biblical prophecy. In his classic work, *History of the Rise*

---

6. Thomas Jefferson Wertenbaker, *The Puritan Oligarchy: The Founding of American Civilization* (New York: Scribner's, 1947), pp. 57–58.

and Influence of the Spirit of Rationalism in Europe, the eminent nineteenth century historian, William Edward Lecky, declared that "the
Hebraic mortar cemented the foundations of American democracy."[7]

Professor Clinton Rossiter emphasizes the role of the clergy in developing colonial thought.

> Had ministers been the only spokesmen of the rebellion, had Jefferson,
> the Adamses, and Otis never appeared in print, the political thought of
> the Revolution would have followed almost exactly the same line—with
> perhaps a little more mention of God, but certainly no less of John Locke.
> In the sermons of the patriot ministers, who were responsible for one fifth
> to one fourth of the total output of political thought in this decade, we
> find expressed every possible refinement of the reigning political faith.[8]

But, most significant of all, was the mobilization of the ideas germi-
nating in the fertile soil of the new land.

> Not to find out new principles, or new arguments, never before thought
> of, not merely to say things which had never been said before, but to place
> before mankind the common sense of the subject, in terms so plain and
> firm as to command their assent, and to justify ourselves in the in-
> dependent stand we are compelled to take. Neither aiming at originality of
> principle or sentiment, nor yet copies from any particular or previous
> writing, it [the Declaration] was intended to be an expression of the
> American mind, and to give to that expression the proper tone and spirit
> called for by the occasion. All its authority rests then on the harmonizing
> sentiments of the day, whether expressed in conversation, in letters,
> printed essays, or in the elementary books of public right, as Aristotle,
> Cicero, Locke, Sidney, etc.[9]

Professor Bailyn credits the opposition writers with bringing together
the most important thoughts of New England Puritanism, English
common law, Enlightenment rationalism, and the classical authors—
ideas of social contract, English liberty, natural rights. In summary, the
opposition radicals:

> provided also a harmonizing force for the other, discordant elements in
> the political and social thought of the revolutionary generation. Within

7. Rufus Learsi, *The Jews in America: A History* (New York: World, 1954), pp. 40–41.

8. Clinton Rossiter, *Seedtime of the Republic* (New York: Harcourt, Brace & World,
1953), p. 328.

9. J. Bronowski and Bruce Mazlish, *The Western Intellectual Tradition* (New York:
Harper Torchbooks, Harper & Row, 1962), p. 378; cf. Letter of May 8, 1825, to Henry Lee,
Writings of Thomas Jefferson, ed. P. L. Ford, 10 vols. (New York, 1892–99), vol. 10, p.
343.

the framework of these ideas, Enlightenment abstractions and common law precedents, covenant theology and classical analogy—Locke and Abraham, Brutus and Coke—could be brought together into a comprehensive theory of politics. It was in terms of this pattern of ideas and attitudes—originating in the English Civil War and carried forward with additions and modifications not on the surface of English political life but in its undercurrents stirred by doctrinaire libertarians, disaffected politicians, and religious dissenters—that the colonists responded to the new regulations imposed by England on her American colonies after 1763.[10]

The American revolutionary spokesmen realized that they needed a moral principle to underpin their political ideas. Professor Rossiter in his discussion of "the Moral Basis of Government"[11] develops the role of virtue that was rooted in colonial America and became increasingly important in the years of crisis preceding the Revolution.

In addition to approving all recognized Christian [and Jewish], Roman, and English virtues, colonial theorists singled out several attitudes or traits of special consequence for a free republic: first, the willingness to act morally without compulsion, to obey the laws of nature as interpreted by reason and the laws of man as established in consent; second, the love of liberty, the desire for the adventure and sacrifices of free government rather than the false security of tyranny; third, public spirit and patriotism, . . . fourth, official incorruptibility, a state of virtue saluted by Jefferson in the *Summary View* when he reminded George III that "the whole act of government consists in the art of being honest"; and fifth, industry and frugality, hard work and plain living, the only path to personal liberty and national independence. Special attention was devoted to the fifth of these qualities, for industry and frugality were essential to the success of America's program of economic resistance.[12]

To promote virtue the colonial thinkers prescribed "hortatory religion, sound education, honest government, and a simple economy," Professor Rossiter observes. In sum, "just as religion, education, government, and agriculture could raise the level of public and private morality, so morality could strengthen each of these great human undertakings. . . . The business of political philosophers is to discover the virtues that lead to free government, and the form of government that leads men to virtue."[13]

10. See Bailyn, *Ideological Origins*, pp. 53–54.
11. See Rossiter, *Seedtime of the Republic*, pp. 429–37.
12. Ibid., p. 431.
13. Ibid., p. 435.

The writer of this brief summary is not unmindful of the vulnerability of such an idealized presentation to the criticism of the "scientific historians" of the Johns Hopkins school and of the earlier "new historians" once led by James Henry Robinson, Charles Beard, Frederick Jackson Turner, and Carl Becker. Around the turn of the present century, this small group of seminal historians disowned their traditional function as "preservers and adapters of myths," and audaciously proclaimed that they would thenceforth seek and report only "the truth."

They unearthed long-forgotten facts demonstrating that the Founding Fathers had been a cantankerous lot, who fought one another in unseemly fashion for power and wealth. They revealed that intrigue and factional strife in Congress were common, and men of all factions embezzled funds, profiteered in securing army supplies, and that even George Washington and Robert Morris, "the great man" and the treasurer who financed the Revolution, were greedy and ruthless land speculators who made fortunes at one time or another on the basis of secret information.

Forrest McDonald, in his book *The Formation of the American Republic, 1776-1790,*[14] cut close to the bone when he wrote, "Where patriots stood in the spring of 'seventy-six, depended upon whether they believed in Original Sin." The hard-shelled republicans, Eastern and Southern, he observes,

> shared a reverence for the classical republican virtues and a tendency to carry them to vices. The rectitude of their intentions was rarely questionable, but it sometimes veered to petty self-righteousness; they believed in and practiced simplicity, but ofttimes demanded impossible austerity of others; they were dedicated sometimes to the point of bigotry, and militant, sometimes to the point of paranoia. In public life, they heartily embraced the rationalist tradition, which meant that their thinking was systematic and encumbered by a minimum of superstition and sentimentality and that they believed in the natural rights of man and the possibility of a clean, rational break with the past. It also meant that when considering human affairs they tended to reason in straight logical lines from generalities to particulars, even when observation told them that the path to truth is variously curved. In private life, from aristocratic cultivation in Virginia and from Calvinistic indoctrination in Massachusetts stemmed a seriousness and sense of propriety that precluded enjoying humor or play or the pleasures of the flesh, save with a long hangover of guilt.

> The nationalists [McDonald notes] were more flexible and somewhat more charitable in their views, of others as of themselves. All men were

14. Forrest McDonald, *The Formation of the American Republic, 1776–1790* (Baltimore: Penguin Books, 1965). The following quotations occur on pp. 1–4.

ruled by avarice and ambition, and so must they be; but some men were less so than others. Indeed, some men were even worthy of trust; those who recognized that their motives were a compound of good and evil. In war, one served one's country out of patriotism, but also in pursuit of personal glory; in government, one filled public office out of esteem for a public trust, but all the while pursued personal gain. Those who pretended otherwise could never be trusted, for they were either knaves who masked their evil behind virtuous utterances or fools, who, believing their own purity, would also believe themselves damned to total corruption upon committing their (inevitable) final corrupt act.

In face of such diversity of motives and experiences, it is clear that a study of the American historic past will not contribute to any generalized knowledge of human behavior—once proclaimed as the primary purpose of American historians who studied "history as identity." Dr. Thomas Kuhn of Princeton University seems closer to realism when he declared:

> Where one has got from history some sense of how to act in a particular pressing contemporary situation, one has got it not through generalizations produced from history, but from exposure to concrete historical narratives which increase one's experience of concrete events, very much in the absence of generalization that one could apply directly to the situation.[15]

Such cautions are a necessary antidote to messianic pretensions as well as to an apocalyptic eschatology which have bedeviled American history at its worst moments. At the same time, such caveats should not be allowed to obscure the formidable dynamic power of "the American dream" in which, as Jürgen Moltmann[16] has written, "the biblical, particularly the Old Testament symbology, dominates."

Asserting that " 'the American dream' was dreamed in Europe," Professor Moltmann declares:

> It was and is the dream of freedom for every human being; the land of unlimited possibilities and of justice without privileges. This was the dream of the politically oppressed, the religiously persecuted, the socially humiliated and the racially defamed. . . .
> The *American dream* is basically nothing other than the transferral of the European dream of America to American soil. It is the fulfillment and the disappointment, the continuation and the reshaping of the European dream of America. Consequently, the American dream did not represent a

15. Thomas Kuhn, "Dialogues in History," *Daedalus* (Spring 1961), p. 247.

16. Jürgen Moltmann, "The American Dream," *Commonweal* 104:16 (August 5, 1977), pp. 490–96.

hope limited to America but had universal significance for all people who sought America as the fulfillment of the hope for freedom and justice.

. . . .

The dream of freedom, equality and happiness for all human beings— "We hold these truths to be self-evident that all men are created equal, that they are endowed by their Creator with certain inalienable Rights, that among these are Life, Liberty, and the pursuit of happiness"—is a *human dream.* It can only be fulfilled by humanity as a whole. As long as human beings are alienated from each other . . . this dream cannot be fulfilled. It also cannot be fulfilled as an *American dream;* for as a nation, a world power and a culture, America must take part in the alienation, separation and oppression of human beings. The human dream cannot be Americanized without being falsified through the ideological self-justification of the American empire and the free enterprise of the multinational corporations. As a human dream, the American dream is a true and necessary one. As an American dream, however, it makes the human dream impossible.

This contradiction, Moltmann adds,

is similar to that of Soviet ideology: the "establishment of socialism in one country" destroys through race identification the socialism of humanity. "Socialism" is falsified through the self-justifying terms of Russian hegemony. If the United States understands itself as "this nation under God" (Abraham Lincoln) or as the "champion of democracy" then ambiguities inevitably arise. Was the Vietnam war really executed for the freedom of the Vietnamese people or for the United States' own interests? At the time, one could hear both claims. The humanization of the American dream would make the United States a blessing for other peoples. But the Americanization of the human dream also makes the United States a burden for other peoples. Thus, the test question for United States foreign policy will be: will the "moral conscience" (Jimmy Carter) be realized in the demand for liberation and the respect for human rights in Latin America, Asia and Africa, or will the interests of American big business be further served through the ideology of "national security" (through the National Security Council) at the cost of other peoples?

The "humanization of the American dream"—that could well serve as the beacon light for our nation and for the world community through the dark decades ahead. Leaders from every field who speak to the human conscience need to help people, humankind, break out of the obsessional preoccupations with personal, materialist satisfactions, petty intergroup and interreligious rivalries, and concentrate on understanding and coping with central priority issues of our time, on whose resolution the very survival of mankind itself depends. And, above all, people need hope, a reinvigoration of morale, that can come from a recommitment to the fundamental moral and ethical values that, despite ambiguities and detours, are the foundation stones of the American experiment.

The challenges and opportunities have been well stated by Isaac Asimov in his essay "Is There a Hope for the Future?"[17]

> It is particularly easy to be pessimistic about the future right now. We need merely assume that population will continue going up; that national rivalries will continue to place the well-being of Group X ahead of the welfare of the world; that racist and sexist prejudice will continue to generate hatred and alienation; that personal and economic greed will continue to ruin the earth for short-term private profit—in short we need merely assume that things will go on, exactly as they have been, for another thirty years, and we can confidently predict the destruction of our technological civilization.

And Asimov adds, "I suspect, that the chances are better than 50 percent that this will happen; how much better, I am not certain."

But his conclusion is no less important than his fatalistic analysis.

> If, however, we can shift quickly enough in the direction of population control and world government [implying, I take that to mean, an effective means of stemming the deadly nuclear proliferation, containing the absurd arms race, meeting the needs of the starving and the impoverished, finding jobs and decent shelter of the underclass here and abroad, putting the lid on political-ideological warfare as in Ireland, Lebanon, Cyprus, Uganda, and elsewhere, promoting human rights and civil liberties as in the Soviet Union and East European countries as well as in Latin America] and can hang on for thirty years, the long-range future—within the later lifetime of the young people alive today—can be made incredibly bright.
>
> We will then have a twenty-first century that will be the dream of an older generation of science-fiction writers (writing prior to the current fashion of darkness and doom) come true. Imagine a world in which the scourge of war is eliminated and the horrors of sexism and racism are wiped out, in which lives are expanded and enriched, and in which all of space is opened to us.
>
> If we can only get through *this* crisis.[18]

---

17. Isaac Asimov, "Is There a Hope for the Future?" *Science Past, Science Future* (New York: Ace Books, 1975), pp. 413ff.

18. Ibid., p. 430.

Response

Responding to our theme, Marc Tanenbaum has made an eloquent and provocative presentation. I hope he will be heard in all the centers of power in America, whether governmental or multinationally corporate, but especially by the sovereign people of this republic which desperately needs an awakening to the cause of justice.

He evaluated the nation's observance of the Bicentennial, in some detail described the major influences affecting the deeds of the Revolutionary generation, and finally dealt with the various ways in which the actualities of American development have fallen far short of the ideals so hopefully announced two centuries ago. He expressed some reluctance to classify his essay as a Jeremiad, but he nevertheless undertook that prophetic function with regard to several problems. He concluded with judgments that could hardly be considered optimistic. Since his words are before the reader, a more detailed review is hardly needed here.

The prophetic (rather than analytic) stance which is assumed in this discourse has been so thoroughly appropriated by Western thinkers, from Augustine to Karl Marx, that it can no longer be described as characteristically Judaic. Given the shaping power of the biblical tradition this is, of course, not surprising. Only from the non-Communist East could we expect a distinctly different mode of critical discourse, and even that probability is rendered increasingly unlikely due to the Westernization of the non-West by either capitalistic or Marxian influences.

In the light of these circumstances, I would have appreciated a more specific and critical exposition of Tanenbaum's views of the Judaic component in the prevailing ideologies of the West, and particularly those which have figured so strongly not only in the formative colonial period, or in the Revolutionary era, but also throughout the country's development. We are, after all, a nation which has with singular unanimity and over long periods of time seriously identified itself as God's New Israel as Elect Nation with a Manifest Destiny (as I have suggested in my own contribution). In many other ways, moreover, America—by way of Calvin and the Puritans—has been more significantly shaped by the Hebrew Scriptures than any other country I can think of except for the republic of Israel itself. With regard to the presentation he gave (as against one I might have hoped for) my own satisfaction is so pronounced that I have only a few relatively modest qualifications or questions that seem worthy of further consideration.

The first of these has to do with our perceptions of the nature of the Bicentennial observance which he refers to as a "fiasco" and a "moral tragedy." Many social scientists, to be sure, would say that none of us know what happened and that nothing less than a million-dollar research project could deliver a judgment on so sprawling an event. But I still must say that my own fairly extensive participation in those activities, as well as my professional attention to what was going on, left me with a very different view.

It happens that I was lecturing nearby at Brandeis University on the eve of President Ford's inauguration of the Bicentennial era at Lexington. What makes those days so vividly memorable, however, is surely not the president's words nor even the counter-demonstrations for economic democracy which dogged the presidential trail. What makes those days in April 1975 unforgettable for every conscient American was the simultaneous news that our entire thirty years' political and military involvement in Southeast Asia was collapsing into nearly total disarray. With this addition to the patriotic shock and ideological confusion created by Watergate and the collapse of the Nixon administration, the American people were in no mood for capricious celebration of the nation's glory. As a result the primary elections and then the national election were carried out in a very subdued and somber manner. The fact that Americans did not spend the year in irresponsible self-congratulation or patriotic nonsense almost qualified them to enjoy the better than usual fireworks that marked this not-so-glorious Fourth of July. They could legitimately celebrate at least the *principles* of the Revolution. To my mind the Bicentennial comportment was remarkably serious and constructive. The visit of the Queen was for many a pleasurable reminder of an old and significant political and cultural relationship. As for the presence of the tall ships along the Atlantic seaboard, it was an inspired way of evoking our temporal distance from the Revolutionary era.

Far more important than any or all of these considerations, moreover, were the very particular observances that were planned and carried out in almost every locality and institutional context. Americans were examining themselves and their values in the light of the national heritage as well as their separate heritages. Never before in American history, I suspect, have so many historians, ethicists, and other serious observers been summoned to so many conferences. And by no means were these gatherings limited to a few universities and large religious organizations. Newspapers, church papers, churches, clubs, patriotic organizations, and literary societies pursued these problems. It has seemed to me and to many others that much of this concern stemmed from the increasingly depersonalized social order in which Americans are living. They were thus trying to rediscover their own relationships to the past—whether the accent be familial, institutional, religious or—as was too frequently the case—ethnic. In my small home town in Minnesota a stunningly well-designed historical museum was carried to completion, and a full-scale historical study of the area was arranged for. I am sure that similar projects were initiated in countless other places.

My final observations on Marc Tanenbaum's essay pertain to his thoughtful account and discussion of the American Revolutionary heritage. They take the form of three very brief comments on issues that deserve more extended consideration. They can be tagged with three simple terms.

1. *Slavery.* Any account of influences and dominant points of view that does not make explicit those sentiments, phobias, and well-considered views that rationalized and constitutionalized the institution of chattel slavery in the federal Union ignores the single most calamitous fact in American history.

2. *The Unseen Hand.* Of all the many influences that shaped the founding of the republic none had greater or longer lasting significance than that which is so marvelously symbolized by the publication of Adam Smith's *The Wealth of Nations* in the year 1776. This magisterial presentation of *laissez-faire* principles was, of course, based on ideas and practical experiences that had been accumulating for centuries, with various Puritan influences becoming especially strong during and after the reign of Elizabeth. Of the several principles that constitute the Libertarian Revolution (democratic government, equality before the law, intellectual and religious freedom, etc.) the most crucial by far was that pertaining to the economic order. In this realm it was believed that things were so ordained by Nature and Nature's God that full security of property and diligent profit-seeking by all would, if free from governmental restraints, lead to maximum social felicity. What they could not foresee were the ways in which this system would lead directly and swiftly to enormous disparities of social and political power and almost catastrophic forms of social and economic stratification. This tendency was already apparent in 1776, and by 1976, it was leading the country toward institutional and social disaster.

3. *Ideology.* The usage of this term has varied widely during the last two centuries, and there is ample warrant for relating it to publicly accepted positions on social and political issues, as Bailyn does in *The*

Ideological Origins of the American Revolution, on which Tanenbaum to a degree relies. When the Marxian usage of this term is ignored, however, a very important dimension of the country's political life is lost, most notably those religious beliefs, historical myths, patriotic attitudes, rites, and symbols that in vague or semiconscious ways inspire loyalty and legitimate public authority. It would seem, furthermore, that the American Ideology, far more clearly than the "German Ideology" of Marx's day, is a phenomenon of great national significance. If we are to think of the future it is very important that we consider the degree to which the traditional forms of legitimation have been eroded during recent decades. Could this possibly be a sign of promise?

SYDNEY E. AHLSTROM

The Black
Experience
and Perspective

Introduction

A special feeling of kinship and unique solidarity engages a Jewish reader of Dr. Benjamin Mays's moving essay. His calm, even magisterial, depiction of the tragic victimization of the black people in America reverberates in the Jewish soul which has experienced analogous suffering in the Christian West, but only of longer duration and in some ways—climaxed in the Nazi Holocaust—more devastating.

That comment is not meant to minimize or to detract from the magnitude of the pain that our black brothers and sisters have been forced to endure. It would be macabre and pathological for victims to contest with one another over whose suffering has been greater! Rather, it is to suggest that Jews who are cognizant of their history during the past 1,900 years approach black Americans with an empathy that is existential, not learned abstractly from textbooks.

The parallel experiences of persecution and exile, of being reduced to pariahs, have cast both blacks and Jews in a prophetic circumstance. Both their histories and their biblical theologies require of blacks and Jews—indeed, their very identities as particular kinds of human beings compel them—to cast critical questions before every American ideologue, or any other ideologue, who wishes to proclaim his or her system of values or ideals as ultimates that demand total obedience or apotheosis. Neither an "imperial president" of the right nor a messianic liberator of the left whose totalist ideologies would demand idolatry—giving ultimate loyalty to that which can claim only partial loyalty—should ever be able to deceive especially blacks or Jews who have had engraved the Psalmist's warning in their scarred bodies: "Trust not in princes or in the son of man for in them there is no salvation."

As a son of Russian-Polish immigrants to the United States, I have a very deep appreciation, more than that, profound love for this democratic republic. To my impoverished parents, and to millions like them who came to these shores escaping from indentured poverty, vicious prejudice, and denial of basic human liberties, America has been the "promised land." And in our present world in which democratic liberties and human rights are increasingly restricted and are in retreat, the United States with all its failings stands out as still the freest of nations and the greatest hope of economic justice and social equality.

Precisely because the burden of defending human liberty and justice now weighs most heavily on the shoulders of the American republic can it least afford illusions and vanities. And the foremost vanity which Dr. Mays's essay (and the Jewish experience) would seek to submit to critical judgment is that of the continued traces in our nation of Anglo-Saxon Christian *hubris.* "Hubris" is defined by Ernest Becker in his *Escape from Evil* (New York: Free Press, 1975) as "forgetting where the real source of power lies and imagining that it is in oneself."

After careful reflection, I am forced to conclude that the Bicentennial observances, worthy as a national objective, failed miserably. It was in the main an exercise in manipulated nostalgia, boosterism, hucksterism, cheap and frequently vulgar commercialism. And its main failing derived from this national addiction to *hubris,* self-worship whose central liturgical affirmation after two hundred years was still that the proper way to be considered a true American is in the Anglo-Saxon Christian model.

With the rarest exceptions, the Bicentennial programs that proliferated in virtually every hamlet of America taught the vast majority of two hundred million Americans practically nothing about the actual, agonizing history of the black people of this nation. It took eight one-hour television programs called "Roots" to begin finally to tell that decisive chapter of American history to the entire American people. It took a brilliant black author, Alex Haley, and interestingly, the cooperation of a Jewish producer, David Wolper (who had earlier produced a much-less acclaimed documentary of the Jewish historic experience) to inform America—after two centuries—that there is no such thing as a single, monochromatic, "official" American history, but that America makes no historic sense unless the nation knows the histories of all its constituent parts.

Thus, Dr. Mays summons us all to a primary task on the eve of our third century—to confront our vast ignorance of our own peoples—blacks, but also Hispanics, Catholics, Protestants, Jews, Evangelicals, Greeks, the whole ethnic and religious depth of our nation which is the keystone of understanding our pluralism. Each of the religious, racial, and ethnic groups conducted education and information programs during the Bicentennial year—witness the especially ambitious program of the Catholic bishops. In the main, they were talking to themselves, not informing the nation and those who needed it most.

In the absence of that understanding, caricatures and distortions will continue to prevail. President Jimmy Carter had to suffer the latent and widespread stereotypes and hidden bigotries against Evangelical

Christians. Secretary of Agriculture Earl Butz could confidently, even arrogantly, discharge himself of dirty little jokes about Pope Paul and blacks. Chairman of the Joint Chiefs of Staff General George Brown felt free to repeat the most vicious canards against the alleged "Jewish conspiracy." FTC Commissioner Paul Dixon felt comfortable in a cruel attack on "that dirty Arab," Ralph Nader. When will the Anglo-Saxon "elites" of America—many of them good "churchgoing" people as were the slavemasters—learn that the vast majority of the American people are sick and tired of their vile abuses, their verbal violence against the dignity and honor of millions of our citizens?

The first Anglo-Saxons who settled this nation saw themselves as God's "chosen people." But blacks and Jews, who apparently have taken the Bible seriously as a lamp unto their feet and not as a weapon for suppression, will need to provide still the necessary hermeneutic—blacks and Jews both have understood "chosenness" to mean especial responsibility to live God's way of justice, compassion, and equality, and not an invitation to privilege and dominance.

If the nation at large will educate itself about the actual histories and religious lives of both blacks and Jews, not the caricatures and mythologies that continue to prevail, it will learn that in few places in America and elsewhere (in Africa and in Israel, for example) are the events of Exodus and Sinai as alive as they are among these saving remnants. Both blacks and Jews experienced the Divine Presence as a Liberator from oppression and slavery. Both blacks and Jews carry in their hearts and bones the experience and instruction of Sinai where a former slave people experienced the revelation as God's moral will which transformed them into "a kingdom of priests and a holy people." Both among blacks and Jews, with whom the Old Testament prophets live as almost nowhere else, is there a consciousness that "justice and righteousness" are the diadems engraved on the throne of the Holy One.

As often happens, the particular bursts with the universal. If we learn as a nation to know and to appreciate not only the agonies but the spiritual and human richness and accomplishment that inheres in each of these minority communities, and if we learn that they live and thrive in America's pluralism not by sufferance but by right, natural right and divine right, we may yet learn that this talent of valuing difference not as a threat but as a source of enrichment may yet become the most important legacy of our Bicentennial. And if we genuinely learn that monumental truth, we may still—if God gives us the time before a nuclear Armageddon—be able to learn to appreciate and live amicably with all the other nations of the world, who have the same claims as do we to be God's human family.

Marc H. Tanenbaum

The Black Experience
and Perspective

BENJAMIN E. MAYS

Movements of nonviolence as a way of perfecting social change began in the black church almost two centuries ago. All along, the black church has contributed to the religious experience of black people. It has served uniquely, and one can indeed speak of the genius of the Negro church or genius of the black church.

In the remarks which follow, I will briefly describe the founding of the black church, and discuss its life, meaning, and service. I will comment on slavery. I will discuss the special role of black colleges, pointing out their past and present importance. Religion and education cannot be separated in the history of Negro life in America. Finally, I will offer some comments on the future we must meet, both blacks and whites.

The Founding of the Black Church

Interesting insights into Negro church origins can be derived by reviewing some excerpts from early local church histories and other documents. Let us begin with the story behind the founding of the first of these churches.

The revolution to establish the black church started with a black man, Richard Allen. In his autobiography Allen writes: "I was born in the year 1760, February 14, a slave to Benjamin Chew of Philadelphia."

Dr. Benjamin E. Mays has had a long and distinguished career as a scholar, educator, and religious leader. Born in Epworth, South Carolina, he graduated with honors from Bates College in 1920. He received his M.A. and Ph.D. from the University of Chicago. He is the author of seven books including *The Negro's Church, The Negro's God,* and *Born to Rebel,* a social autobiography of the author. He has written chapters or sections in fifteen books and has contributed to more than fifty magazines and journals. He has served as Dean of the School of Religion at Howard University, and was the President of Morehouse College for twenty-seven years. He was a representative of the United States at the funeral of Pope John XXIII. He has been President of the United Negro College Fund. He holds honorary degrees from thirty-eight colleges and universities. He delivered the eulogy at the funeral of his former student, Martin Luther King, Jr. He has been a member of the Atlanta Board of Education since 1969 and has served as its president.

After spending some time away from Philadelphia, Richard Allen
returned and purchased his freedom.

> February 1786, I came to Philadelphia. Preaching was given out for me at
> five o'clock in the morning at St. George church. . . . I preached at
> different places in the city. . . . I soon saw a large field open in seeking
> and instructing my African brethren, who had been a long-forgotten
> people and few of them attended public worship. . . . We all belonged to
> St. George's church. . . . We felt ourselves much cramped; . . . We
> established prayer meetings and meetings of exhortation, and the Lord
> blessed our endeavors, and many souls were awakened; but the elder soon
> forbid us holding any such meetings; but we viewed the forlorn state of our
> colored brethren, and that they were destitute of a place of worship. They
> were considered a nuisance.
>
> A number of us usually attended St. George's church on Fourth Street;
> and when the colored people began to get numerous in attending the
> church, they moved us from the seats we usually sat on, and placed us
> around the wall, and on Sabbath morning we went to church and the sex-
> ton stood at the door and told us to go in the gallery. He told us to go, and
> we would see where to sit. We expected to take the seats over the ones we
> formerly occupied below, not knowing any better. We took those seats.
> Meeting had begun, and they were nearly done singing, and just as we got
> to the seats, the elder said, "Let us pray." We had not been long upon our
> knees before I heard a considerable scuffling and low talking. I raised my
> head up and saw one of the trustees, H—— M——, having hold of the
> Rev. Absalom Jones, pulling him up off his knees, and saying, "You must
> get up—you must not kneel here." Mr. Jones replied, "Wait until prayer
> is over." Mr. H—— M—— said, "No, you must get up now or I will call
> for aid and force you away." Mr. Jones said, "Wait until prayer is over,
> and I will get up and trouble you no more." With that he beckoned to one
> of the other trustees, Mr. L—— S——, to come to his assistance. He came
> to William White, to pull him up. By this time prayer was over, and we all
> went out of the church in a body, and they were no more plagued with us
> in the church . . . we had subscribed largely towards finishing St.
> George's church, in building the gallery and laying the new floors, and
> just as the house was made comfortable, we were turned out from enjoying
> the comforts of worshipping therein.
>
> We then hired a store-room and held worship ourselves. Here we were
> pursued by threats of being disowned, and read publicly out of meeting if
> we did continue to worship in the place we had hired; but we believed the
> Lord would be our friend. . . . Here was the beginning and rise of the first
> church of the denomination later known as the African Methodist
> Episcopal. Many of the colored people in other places were in a situation
> nearly like those of Philadelphia and Baltimore, which induced us, in
> April, 1816, to call a general meeting, by way of conference. Delegates
> from Baltimore and other places which met those of Philadelphia, and
> taking into consideration their grievances, and in order to secure the
> privileges, promote union and harmony among themselves, it was

resolved: "That the people of Philadelphia, Baltimore, etc., etc., should become one body, under the name of African Methodist Episcopal Church."[1]

The "Christian" people in St. George's could not stand for those colored people to worship God on a basis of Christian brotherhood. In heaven, yes, but not on this earth.

Here is another story, that of the first Negro Baptist church, established in 1841, in Richmond, Virginia. "Until that year, the congregation was mixed. The 387 white members then retired to Broad and Twelfth Streets, and 1,708 colored members remained in the old church of worship."[2]

> Many are under the impression that the old church was given to the colored members but they paid $6,500 for the building. . . . The Attorney General of the State, Hon. Sidney S. Baxter, gave his written opinion: "That it would be inexpedient to make any portion of the trustees people of color and that it might endanger the title to the property." This opinion and the refusal of the First Baptist Church (white) to transfer the property made the colored brethren warm. . . . It was transferred in 1849 to their trustees: David R. Crane, Robert H. Bosher (white), John S. Kinney, Jas. C. Ellis, and Wm. Lightfoot (colored).[3]

Out of experiences somewhat similar to this and to the AME Church, we got the AME Zion Church, the Colored Methodist Episcopal Church, now the Christian Methodist Church, and scores of black Baptist churches. The black church is mainly a child of rejection by white Christians.

The Black Church Serving

The black church is a part of the American religious experience that has not been adequately considered by white American religion. The black church is a product of the refusal of some white Christians to accept the black man as an equal before God and a brother here on earth. The black church is also a product of the desire of the black Christian to control his own destiny and to do his own thing. The black church is sensitive to the needs of black people. We have black preachers who can speak to the

1. Richard Allen, *The Life, Experience, and Gospel Labors* (Philadelphia: A.M.E. Book Concern), pp. 1, 19, 20, 21, 22, 32.

2. Souvenir Program of the 50th Anniversary of Dedication of the Building (Richmond, Va., First African Baptist Church, 1928), pp. 1, 5.

3. W. T. Johnson, *Historical Reminiscences of the First Baptist Church* (Richmond, Va., Hastings Deeds No. 82A, Richmond Chancellor), pp. 9, 11, also 328ff.

needs of black people, economically, socially, and spiritually. The black church has always ministered to the needs of black people, and has never been divorced from those needs. Let me concretize this statement.

I was born and reared on a farm in Greenwood County, South Carolina, ten miles from the nearest town. Life was tough for black people. Negro ministers preached from the Old and New Testaments. They were afraid to deal with the economic injustices of white people toward Negroes. But they could preach the literal interpretation of the Bible. Each church had what was called burial aid societies. When someone died every member of the church gave twenty-five cents to the family of the bereaved. If there were 600 members the bereaved family received $150—equal to about $1,500 today.

The church was and still is the social center. It was the center of all activities of the black people. They met and sang in their local churches and in singing conventions across the county lines. It was the spiritual life for the people. The minister interpreted the Bible in terms of the spiritual needs of the time. If he stuck to the Bible, quoting it, he could preach about Jesus, and the prophets of Israel, pointing out how God punished the wicked and came to the rescue of the faithful. Did not God deliver Daniel, destroy the Egyptians, and deliver the Hebrews from bondage? Did not God create of one blood all nations of men to dwell on all the face of the earth? Did not he send his own son into the world to save all mankind? The life of each person is sacred unto God; so much so that the strands of hair on his head are all numbered. Not even one sparrow falls to the ground without God's taking notice and caring. The Negro's faith sustained him in the darkest hour. The Negro saw his emancipation as an act of God—not of Lincoln and the Civil War.

Long before science discovered the commonality of man, religion had apprehended it by faith. Long before science discovered four kinds of blood, the Bible had proclaimed it. These encouraging words could have never come from white ministers.

Black people were segregated in the white churches; so they built their own churches. The black church made it possible for the Negro to walk the earth with dignity and pride. Negroes on the whole will never sacrifice their church for a one-way entrance into the white church. The black church will keep its doors open to all people for worship and membership, and many blacks will continue to join and worship in white churches but it will be a long time before we have a thoroughly integrated church with justice and equality for all.

Without apology I admit I am biased in favor of the black church. The black church, with all of its shortcomings, and they are many, has been the salvation of the Negro people here in the United States. The black church has kept the Negro from violent revolution. During slavery and after emancipation, it has kept the Negro from the extermination which would have followed a violent revolution. During 246 years of slavery and another one hundred years of segregation and denigration, the black church preserved the Negro people. Without the black church extermination would have been very probable.

The Negro slave was property, not a human being, not a citizen. He was chattel to be sold as cows, horses, mules, hogs, wagons, and plows. His body belonged to his owner, to be sold or kept for his personal advantage. The American Indians fought back and were mainly liquidated and set off on reservations. There is no reason to believe that the slaves would have fared any better. I am not saying that all slave masters were cruel to their slaves. Many were not and only a small percentage of whites owned slaves. But after all the slave was property and he could be protected and loved as one loves his faithful dog, but the dog is not human. Some owners used their slaves for breeding purposes, permitting slaves to mate in order to bear children so they could sell them. I never knew my grandfather but my grandmother on my father's side told us that she and her husband were sold into South Carolina as slaves. I never knew my grandparents on my mother's side. Bad or unruly slaves were more than likely to be sold. Religion enabled the slaves to endure slavery and survive.

Religion and song have always gone together. The slaves sang as they worked in the field, picking cotton, plowing with a mule, pulling fodder, knocking cotton stalks, scattering guano, and chopping cotton. The singing of slaves led some writers to misinterpret the religious behavior of the slaves. They were accused of being happy in their state of slavery. But it was a technique of survival, singing and working rather than crying and pulling off a revolution.

White sons of slave owners were often kind to the black slaves. My father could read printing but not handwriting. My oldest sister, Susie, related to me what our father told her about how he learned to read a bit. A son of one of the more kindly masters took a liking to my father and, against the law, and against his father's will, taught him how to read. He would take my father away from the house, and in some shady spot he taught father to read and count.

The poor whites were envious of the blacks because they saw the slave as one who kept them from getting jobs that they felt belonged to them.

The seeds were being sown for the race problem which developed full blown after emancipation. The antipathy between black and white stems from conditions that developed in slavery. The poor whites and blacks were set over against each other but the whites, poor and wealthy, white farmers, owners, renters, sharecroppers, white politicians, and white law enforcement officers all got together. The poor and wealthy whites all came together against the newly emancipated black man, for the poorest, most illiterate white man was better than a Negro. Negroes had their places in society, and any white man felt he had the right to define the black man's place. He not only had that right but he exercised it with the support of all the whites in the community. The segregated Negro after emancipation was treated as an inferior person.

The Negro church altered this situation, and only the Negro church could have altered it. The white church was the church of the privileged and reflected in the main the values of the privileged, and the main function of the privileged is to protect the mores of its class. The ethics and values set forth in the Bible had little place. But the black preacher said to Negro people stand tall, stand up straight, throw your shoulders back, for you too are sons of the living God. "God has created of one blood all races of men for to dwell on all the face of the earth." "In Christ there is neither male nor female, neither slave nor free, neither Greek nor Gentile for we are all one in Christ Jesus." "Then Peter opened his mouth, and said, 'Of a truth I perceive that God is no respecter of persons.' But in every nation he that feareth him, and worketh righteousness, is accepted with him." "God cares for the sparrow—not one sparrow falls to the earth without God's concern, and we are more than sparrows." "His eye is on the sparrow and I know he watches me." "God so loved the world that he gave his only begotten son that whosoever believeth in him shall not perish but shall have everlasting life."

Black peoplehood and black pride have been served by the black church and its preservation of the gospel.

American Ideals and Black Experience

The black preacher has always given body and meaning to those great historical documents which were never meant for black people. Jefferson, author of the Declaration of Independence, gave the following beautiful words: "We hold these truths to be self-evident, that all men are created equal, that they are endowed by their creator with certain unalienable rights, that among these are life, liberty, and the pursuit of happiness."

Negroes know that these words were meant for white people. How strange! Despite the words attributed to Thomas Jefferson, "I tremble for my country when I remember that God is just," Jefferson never freed his slaves before he died. Words of the Declaration of Independence meant freedom for white men, not Negroes. But we are glad that Jefferson gave the Declaration of Independence a solid religious foundation. God gave us life, liberty, and the right to pursue happiness. The prophetic voice of the black preacher is needed to prick the conscience of America in hopes that the ideals expressed in the document will become a reality in our time.

Lincoln's Gettysburg speech has been quoted and will be quoted forever. It has given hope to all men and has been translated into many languages. "Four score and seven years ago our fathers brought forth, upon this continent, a new nation, conceived in liberty and dedicated to the proposition that all men are created equal." He ends the speech with a prayer that this nation under God will not perish from the earth. But this Kentuckian born in a log cabin didn't have me and my people in mind. In his debate with Stephen Douglas, Lincoln did not argue for real equality for blacks. He long supported a movement to send Negroes back to Africa.

The Revolutionary War was fought to free not black men but white. The Civil War was not fought to free black people. I think Lincoln was against slavery, but it was not to free black people, but to save the Union with or without slaves that the war was fought. The Emancipation Proclamation, January 1, 1863, was aimed at breaking the back of those in rebellion against the federal government. In that document those not in rebellion against the United States could keep their slaves. The Proclamation maintained that "all persons held as slaves within any State, or designated part of the State, the people whereof shall be in rebellion against the United States, shall be then, thenceforward and forever free." There were 800,000 slaves in the border states who were untouched by the Emancipation Proclamation. Furthermore, the basic rationale offered in the Proclamation for freeing those slaves who were freed by it was that it was a "fit and necessary war measure." The last paragraph of the Proclamation stated that it was "sincerely believed to be an act of justice, warranted by the Constitution upon military necessity."

After the war was over Congress had to pass the Thirteenth Amendment freeing the slaves, the Fourteenth Amendment protecting his rights to equality before the law, and the Fifteenth Amendment giving the newly emancipated people the ballot. These rights were guaranteed as long as federal soldiers occupied the South. Right after the Hayes-Tilden Compromise in 1877, when the election between Hayes and Tilden was so close that the decision as to who was president had to be decided by Congress, Hayes was given the presidency with the understanding that federal soldiers would be withdrawn from the South, thus turning over the destiny of blacks to Southern whites. With the withdrawal of federal troops from the South, the South had its own way with Negroes.

Between 1877 and 1910 the black man was enslaved again. Segregation, mob rule, and lynching covered "Dixie like the Dew," sanctioned by the United States Supreme Court which overruled what Congress did in 1875 guaranteeing equal protection of the law. Segregation became God in the South. So by 1910 segregation was found in every crack and in every crevice of this nation.

The 1896 decision (*Plessy* v. *Ferguson*) of the United States Supreme Court made segregation constitutional provided that the two separates were equal—one for white and one for black, both equal. The nation had no intention of making the separate equal by virtue of the fact that neither the Congress nor the state legislature ever passed laws to equalize segregation, to abolish mob rule, and to make lynching a federal crime. The NAACP tried for decades to get Congress to make lynching a federal crime. But Congress just would not do it. So it was left to the black people and the black church to take up the cudgel of leadership to get Congress to restore what the nation had taken away. The first fight against the 1896 doctrine of separate but equal came in 1935 exactly thirty-nine years after 1896.

Black Colleges:
Their Past and Present Importance

From 1935 through 1954 black lawyers were attacking in court the inequality condoned by the national government, sanctioned by the white church, and accepted by white ministers. The work of attacking this situation was carried forward largely by the products of black higher education which, like the black church, has made a vital and in-dispensable contribution to black people and to all the people of the United States. Both the black church and black higher education have done for blacks what the white church and white colleges could not have done.

It must be said, however, that higher education for blacks took its beginnings from the white church. When the Christian people of the North came into the South more than a hundred years ago, they came to build institutions for blacks that would last forever. No one was wise enough to see that by today the doors of segregation, locked with cords of steel a century ago, would be broken down forever. Whether the missionaries came believing that when Negroes were born, if given a fair shake, they would develop their intellectual powers as well as other persons in the society did, I cannot say. But I do know they acted as if they believed it. An examination of the black schools which were founded shows that curricula were modeled after those of the North. Though the institutions initially were little more than grade or high schools, they were called colleges and universities, designations that were prophetic of the intentions of their founders. Thus were born Howard University, Lincoln University, Fisk University, Shaw University, Virginia Union University, Morehouse College, Talladega College, Dillard University, Bishop College, and others.

The founders of these institutions came with a sense of mission. They came to equip the slaves and their offspring with the skills needed to compete with white men in a highly competitive society. It was in great measure a prejudiced society, which believed that the Negro problem would soon be solved because the black man would soon die out, because, it was thought, he could never survive in a competitive society designed for white men. It must never be forgotten that the black man was never welcomed in the United States as a free man but only as a slave. When freedom came, several movements were at work to send blacks away from the United States. But God moves in mysterious ways, and instead of dying out, the four million slaves have multiplied to a black population of some twenty-five million today.

Black colleges have given many benefits to us all. If by fiat we somehow blotted out all the contributions that black colleges have made to Negroes, to the South, and the nation, the Negro would indeed be in a pitiful plight and the South and the nation would be equally in a terrible condition. Consider the city of Atlanta. If we somehow eliminated all the contributions that the black colleges of the area have made to it, Atlanta would not be the model that it is for economic growth and intelligent educated leadership. Ask any Negro or white man in Atlanta why it is that Atlanta leads the nation in good human relations, and they will say that one reason is that we have had six Atlanta black colleges developing leadership for Atlanta and the nation for more than a hundred years. Black and white leaders do more things together in Atlanta than perhaps in any other city in the nation.

The distinctive service of black higher education has not only benefited all by what it has done in the past and is doing in the present. These black schools are important for the future too. The black man's image in education will be preserved in those things that are uniquely his own. His image in education will not be perpetuated by a few eminent scholars at Chicago, Columbia, Harvard, and Yale. His image will be preserved at Howard, Lincoln, Fisk, the Atlanta University Center Colleges, Hampton, Tuskegee, Dillard, and other black colleges, integrated institutions but under the control and management of presidents, staff, and student bodies that know that these institutions are uniquely their own. If America says now abolish black colleges because they are black and we do not want to support them, it would be a calamity indeed. It would be a repudiation of the American Constitution, the Bill of Rights, the Declaration of Independence, the Thirteenth, Fourteenth and Fifteenth amendments, and the American Dream. It would be the grossest kind of discrimination based on race—a sin against black people everywhere. If we fail to support black colleges on the ground that Negroes are poor and that white colleges are now opened to Negroes, this would be worse. We do not close Brandeis and Yeshiva Universities because they are Jewish. We do not say that Catholic and Notre Dame Universities should be closed because they are Catholic. Institutions with an identity and roots enrich higher education, preserve diversity within it, and ultimately enrich us all.

From Desegregation to the Present and Future

A sense of identity and peoplehood can help make us aware of needs that might otherwise be forgotten. How long might America have drifted on in its officially sanctioned educational inequality if it were not for a group of black lawyers, trained in black colleges, schooled in the law in a black university? James M. Nabrit, Jr., professor of law at Howard University, who spent his undergraduate days at Morehouse, and Thurgood Marshall, a graduate of Lincoln and Howard, played key roles in bringing the fight against segregation through the courts to the famous *Brown* v. *Board of Education* Supreme Court decision of 1954.

This effort paved the way for the Southern Christian Leadership Conference under the leadership of a Baptist minister, Martin Luther King, Jr. The Montgomery bus boycott, the Birmingham and Selma marches, the battle against segregation in Albany, Georgia, the non-violent march on Washington in 1963, were mainly the results of black people led by black preachers. How simple! If the city fathers in Montgomery had been wise and even if they had been good men, the Montgomery bus boycott would hardly have begun. If Rosa Parks had not been arrested, or even if they had granted the three requests of the Montgomery Improvement League—provide bus drivers in Negro sections, instruct white streetcar drivers to be civil to black riders, and let whites stand if blacks filled the bus first and let blacks stand if whites filled it first—we would have had no Montgomery bus boycott. But when they refused to grant these requests, the boycott was on for a solid year. This was the black church and a black minister leading a peaceful revolution. The people came from across the world to see this black preacher turn the world upside down.

Only a black leader could have challenged this country as Martin Luther King did. White people would not have listened to a white preacher. I say further that King had to come out of Morehouse, not Chicago, not Harvard, not Emory, not Boston University. But out of Morehouse where men had been schooled in believing that a man could be bodily segregated but free in his mind.

I look back over my life to many experiences. I can recall when a minister in South Carolina dismissed church at eleven o'clock on Sunday morning to participate in a lynching. On one occasion women and children were there to get souvenirs from the victim's body. One would say give me a hand, give me a finger, give me a toe. Nobody will ever know the damage such incidents as these did to the minds not only of the black people, but also to the minds of the white people in the white church.

Much has changed, and one can speak today of a new nation and a brand new South, though things are far from perfect. Not long ago, I was going to Calloway Gardens, Pine Mountain, Georgia, and was looking for the Holiday Inn. I stopped at a "two by four" filling station to inquire how to get to the Holiday Inn. The attendant told me, and wanted to know where I lived. I replied, in Atlanta. In the brief conversation I said "yes." This did not set well with this white man dressed in overalls and chewing tobacco. He looked at me and said, "You say 'yes, sir,' to me!"

Whether racism in both its obvious and hidden forms can ever be abolished in the United States, I am not omniscient enough to say. When I consider the Jew, I find no comfort in history for the Negro's plight. No other group in the annals of time has contributed so much, with so few in number, to the well-being of mankind. And yet anti-Semitism is centuries' old and still shows its ugly face with alarming frequency.

Throughout history, on the other hand, there has also been a minority imbued with a sense of justice and faith in God who has worked to change the face of the earth. It may be that such a white remnant and blacks can lead the world to God. I cannot trust the moral, ethical, and spiritual leadership of the white man alone. If one judges from the past, the white man believes in war and power to keep peace in the world, not nonviolence. I am not saying that the black man is perfect, but God may have called the black man to provide the leadership which we need at this critical moment in time.

Blacks have not conceived of themselves as a chosen people, but they have looked to history as the arena in which the will and purpose of God would achieve its actualization. With infinite patience they have waited for, believed in, and contested for the coming "Kingdom of his reign." That the Kingdom would come has not been disputed. Sometimes the appropriate strategy that persons should employ has been debated, but the belief in God's ultimate victory has been held with a depth that actual events were seldom able to shake. God might be long in his coming, they reasoned, but his delay was not an occasion for despair or doubt. "Didn't my Lord deliver Daniel, then why not every man?"

Throughout this essay I have emphasized the importance of the black church. Black people and the black religious institutions are not co-terminus but they have been joined in a common struggle to enhance the quality of life available in their communities. In the churches there has been a healthy concern for salvation and attention to matters of human survival. At various times the black churches have emphasized one or the other of these concerns, but even when an "otherworldly" emphasis has seemed to dominate, the perennial presence of the poor, the oppressed, the rejected, and the disadvantaged has not been neglected. In theological terms they have exhibited a "worldly otherworldliness." Virtually every institution in the black communities committed to racial justice has found a strong, if not indispensable, ally in the churches and in clergy leadership. Church buildings have been meeting halls, worship services have been rallies for social justice, and church members and their leaders have provided an interlocking directorate and leadership cadre for nonreligious social and political change.

Because of their history in this land, black Americans have known that the life of the believer entails the simultaneous experience of light and shadow, suffering and pain, tragedy and celebration, and the admixture of belief and unbelief. They have rejoiced in the grace of God and they have accepted suffering as the concomitant of faithfulness. The suffering of Christ has provided a window through which they have glimpsed the suffering of God and thus were enabled to elevate their own struggle to a place in the divine economy. Thus, there has been hope in the midst of suffering, confidence in the ultimate goodness of God in the face of massive evil, and certainty that his sovereignty over time and eternity is unimpaired by the human misuse of freedom.

America needs to work from and learn from the religious heritage of blacks. It is an experience that has grown out of some three hundred and fifty years of pain and suffering.

Black and white remnant must work together. It has been so before. Harriet Beecher Stowe, author of *Uncle Tom's Cabin*, was a white woman. There were some white federal soldiers who fought and died for the black man's freedom. The Supreme Court abolished segregation, and the nine judges were white. Without blacks the suit would never have been launched and without the white Supreme Court we would not have had the 1954 decision outlawing segregation in the public schools. Without some concerned white Christians, the black private colleges would never have been organized.

Black and white remnant must be the conscience of the nation. The future calls for more than atomic and hydrogen bombs, biological and chemical warfare, and spending $100 billion a year for arms. The bomb is the property of many nations now. It is illogical thinking to believe that these instruments will bring peace or save us. If the nations believe that this is the way to salvation, we are indeed a stupid people. Repentance and not arms, love and not hatred, brotherhood and not racism, plenty of bread for everybody, not plenty for a few—these are the goals God is calling us to seek—black and white together. Blacks and the white remnant must make it clear to the world: "Except the Lord buildeth the house, they labor in vain that build it. Except the Lord keepth the city, the watchman waketh but in vain."

Response

The extent to which black Christianity contributed to the pacification of black Americans has long been a topic of debate. Benjamin Mays's view that from the beginning the black church demonstrated the principle of dignified, nonviolent resistance to white racism, while promoting the affirmation of a truly universal humanity for both blacks and whites represents what has now become the viewpoint of traditionalists of the black churches who were associated with the civil rights movement. But it is not guaranteed to be satisfying to the younger militants who either suspect the black churches to have been the source of Uncle Tomism or else wish to find in their history much more vigorous roots of black nationalism and black revolution.

A study of the Christianization of American slaves shows that the slaveholders at first viewed this process with some alarm. They rightly sensed that Christian community might be incompatible with slave property. A baptized slave might claim to be freed thereby. Moreover, some of the early preachers among the blacks, Baptists and Methodists of the eighteenth century, were vigorous abolitionists. The founder of Methodism, John Wesley in *Thoughts upon Slavery* (1774), was clearly against the slave system. Catholics and Anglicans, among others, followed the traditional viewpoint (founded on Aristotle) that nature ordained some men to lordship and other men (and women) to servility.

But by the end of the eighteenth century even the Protestant sectarians had generally moved to accommodation with slavery as the price of being allowed on the plantations to catechize the slaves. These preachers assured the slaveowners that baptism saved the soul, but had no effect upon the freedom of the body, and that, in fact, the chief effect of Christianization would be to produce docile and obedient slaves. Slaveholders promoted Christianity among their slaves only on this assumption. The approved text for all white plantation preachers, supported by the masters, was: "Slaves, obey your masters as the Lord" (Eph. 6:5–7; cf. 1 Tim. 6:1 and 1 Pet. 2:18ff.). This element has led some movements within the black urban underclass to repudiate Christianity as the white slavemaster's religion and to declare that black identity demands an alternative religion that is truly one's own, that of the black Muslims.

Recently black scholars and theologians have sought to present a more vigorous image of a black Christianity which promoted resistance and revolt. Spirituals are seen as subversive songs of freedom that beckoned the slaves, not to an otherworldly heaven, but to the freedom that lay at the other end of the underground railroad. "Steal away to Jesus" was a code message for escape. The religious element in the Nat Turner and Denmark Vesey revolts are cited as proof that blacks immediately fashioned their own (true) version of a black Christianity that led to black rebellion. Gayraud Wilmore's *Black Religion and Black Radicalism* (1973) and the several writings of James Cone, *The God of the Oppressed* (1975), also *The Spirituals and the Blues* (1972), are examples of this viewpoint.

Eugene Genovese's monumental study of slave life and culture in *Roll, Jordan Roll: The World the Slaves Made* (1974) represents an intermediate view. According to Genovese, black Christianity did indeed promote escape when possible and occasionally even revolt, but to stress these elements is to miss the larger picture of the role of black Christianity in promoting the self-affirmation of blacks. The system created by Southern slavery made escape extremely difficult and revolt all but impossible. This has nothing to do with any supposedly lazy or docile character of blacks as slaves, as the slavemasters preferred to think (although they lived at the same time in constant fear of the opposite). A comparison with black history in Brazil and the Caribbean shows that there large-scale slave revolts, involving many thousands of blacks, were constant, leading finally to blacks states such as Haiti.

But the odds against such revolt in the American South were overwhelming. Unlike the Caribbean system, where hundreds of blacks worked in gangs on plantations, American blacks generally worked in very small units of twenty or less. The ability to communicate or organize among large groups of blacks was extremely difficult, and the few attempts were quickly detected and crushed. The uprising of a small group of blacks could wreak mayhem for a few days, as in the Nat Turner rebellion, but brought such counter-productive results as to convince black preachers that outright confrontation of the system was suicidal. Also, in the South, unlike the Caribbean, blacks were a tightly controlled minority in a white majority. Moreover, black Americans were stripped of African culture and tribal identity, unlike those on the larger plantations of the Caribbean where these elements of cohesion could be retained. These differences suggest why the doors to organized rebellion were closed off for American slaves.

Genovese also suggests an African element in black Christianity that was not conducive to revolution. Black religion was life-affirming, not apocalyptic, in a way that integrated the African into the cosmos and the world system. The messianic element in Christianity, it is true, could always be rediscovered as an apocalyptic religion of world overthrow. Nat Turner is an example of this development. But he is the only well-known example in slavery times. By and large the African element in black Christianity tended to turn it toward the affirmation of the joys and hopes of the life that was, rather than toward a violent repudiation of this present world necessary for the revolutionary spirit.

In any case, the primary drama of black religion does not lie in the occasional escapes and still more occasional rebellions, but in the steady, day-by-day, defense of black humanity and black dignity against slavery and racism within the American system itself. Within this space created by the black preachers and the black church, blacks could build up their own community where they could tell themselves the truth about the white system against the constant lies and mystification of white slave-holders' preaching. Within this space they could affirm their own humanity, dignity, pride, and love of life against the efforts of slavery to reduce them to zombies. Black religion, in a sense quite different from white otherworldliness, saved the *souls* of black people.

The question today for many black Christians is "how is this tradition still usable?" Black religion promoted neither Tomism nor black revolutionary nationalism. What it promoted was the building up of autonomous black institutions within a black community of self-affirmation, but within an overall accommodation to American society. In so doing it also offered a constant challenge to the larger society to be converted to the fuller human vlues promoted by the black church. In a society in which both integration on white terms and black separatism lead to self-contradictory failures, the black community has found no better solution to their problem than this unity of autonomy, resistance, and the call to change traditionally pioneered by the black church. The white community promotes an integrationalism which is really a dissolution of the black community into white institutions. Its chief effects today are to emasculate the black middle class by incorporating them into white institutions and to impoverish the black community, leaving it leaderless. But black nationalism promotes an illusion of creating a black state that has no place to go.

What is needed, paradoxically, is fusion of separatism and integration. This means black institution-building to develop the infra-structures of educational, economic, political, and cultural progress within a black-run community, while still promoting the full incorporation and equality of blacks within the larger American society, but now on black rather than white terms, with black institutions standing behind black development, rather than simply black individuals fragmented within white institutions. The formula of the black church was precisely this. It needs to be reborn in much more extended ways into all the other areas of black community-building. In this way the black community can indeed hold out the hand of common humanity to whites, from the basis of strength rather than weakness, calling white Americans to join them in building a new America.

ROSEMARY RADFORD RUETHER

The Women's
Experience
and Perspective

Introduction

Rosemary Ruether shows again in the essay which follows why she is one of the strongest theological-political minds of our generation. The vision she presents is complex and rich. In addition, she is not afraid to face evidence that tells against a simplified version of her own views; she toughens and complicates her own thought in order to incorporate within it the strongest objections from opposite points of view. Finally, the vision she presents is one that is bound to excite admiration. She sets before us an image of a society we ought to struggle to achieve, a society in which we may "live out the ancient promise that 'in Christ there is neither Jew nor Greek, slave nor free, male nor female.'"

For my part, while sharing the vision and admiring the fiery clarity she gives it, I find myself approaching it from a very different side of the mountain, over very different terrain. It is not so much that I reject what she has to say, whether in whole or in any of its subordinate theses, but rather that I read it in some awe and appreciation, like that of a traveler who has never gone, and will likely never go, that way. My own remarks will not contradict hers. They lie, as it were, on the other side of the mountain—within a different horizon, proceeding by quite different plodding steps, with different loyalties and different reactions to important symbols and signals along the way.

One of the keys to Professor Ruether's interpretation of Christianity is her attachment, made explicit in the early pages of this paper, to the sectarian, as opposed to the church, traditions of the Reformation era. She is fired by the image of a society of universal equality, whether of nation, class, race, sex, or institutional form. It is, as she says, a lower-class vision of the world, a vision as seen from below, and it is full of utopian fervor. In its light, she does not hesitate to see even St. Paul as falling from the highest levels of spiritual perception. In her eyes, even Jesus is to be understood as a socio-political revolutionary, offering a vision for the remaking of human society on earth, a vision that appealed first to the most servile and disenfranchised members both of Palestine and of the empire as a whole. The high point of Christianity in her eyes seems to be that early period in the Reformation in which the left-wing sectarians preached the equality of all—calling back Christianity from centuries of corruption that seem to have reached right back to the beginnings of the apostolic era. In her eyes, true Christianity has appeared but seldom and fitfully in history and has lived most of its history under a "broken covenant." Similarly, in her eyes, the United States also lives under a "broken covenant." She lives in hope, while conscious of betrayal.

My own starting place would be both less visionary and less covenantal. It does not seem to me that Christianity is best understood, as so many Protestant Christians understand it, as a social covenant. It is true that God has bound himself to the human race by a new covenant; it is also true that in our baptismal vows we pledge our acts to his service; and it is, finally, true that our pledges commit us not only to personal but also to social and political efforts to "realize God's kingdom on earth." It has never been part of my faith, however, that this world *will be* transformed economically, politically, and socially into a kingdom worthy of him. We *work toward* that goal. It is not a goal ever to be realized in history, even in a "preliminary" or "proleptic" way. This world remains too heavily under the bondage of irrationality, injustice, absurdity, and lie for that. It is not part of the covenant *I* have with God that God will "act in history" to "realize his kingdom" here; or that my acts, however arduous, must or will or can bring that day closer. Despite my best intentions, I fear that my understanding of politics, economics, and social structures may mislead me; that what I take to be good may turn out, to future generations (not to mention to God), to have been far more evil than I had imagined; in short, that I may have unwittingly served the wrong side. The contemplation of admirable men broken by the ironies of history inspires in me some sober fear of God's judgment. I go forward, but am not willing to confuse my political-social dreams with the Kingdom of God.

Let me take one single idea in order to illustrate the ambiguities that give me pause. "Equality" has many political and social meanings; so does "authority." Some seem to hold that in a truly human and Christian world, all authority would dissolve; decisions would be reached in egalitarian ways, consensually. I reject that as an ideal, because I believe it to be disproportionate to the concrete realities of human individual and corporate life, even under ideal conditions. Wherever corporate activities of many human beings are in question, several conditions arise which make the exercise of authority by one person or by a few not only the most expeditious and economical with respect to finite energy, but also the most practical, wise, and likely of success. Human individuals vary in experience, flexibility of imagination, insight, and capacity to command. It is natural—an ideal to be pursued—that leaders emerge and that they lead. In a word, certain kinds of inequality—of talent, vision, ability, training, temperament, and character—are both inevitable and much to be admired in human affairs. It follows, for me, that institutional structures will always mirror such fundamental inequalities. In an ideal situation, every person will operate at precisely the level suited to that person's talent. In an irrational, unjust, absurd, and wholly typical situation some will be in higher positions than their talents warrant (the "Peter principle") and some great talents will go overlooked.

I do not hold these views because of some preliminary belief in the "great chain of being" mentioned by Professor Ruether. I hold them because of my experiences with many forms of corporate structure, some frustrating and some satisfying; and because of reflection on the basic conditions of human action in history. I hold such views *not* because this world is sinful. Even apart from sin, natural inequalities, wisely and graciously accepted, would mark any perfect human society.

I do not believe that all talent for higher levels of responsibility is to be found in one sex, race, class, ethnic group, or religious community. In God's wisdom, talent appears to be distributed freely and with considerable abandon throughout the human race. Eleanor of Aquitaine, as Henry Adams remarked, was the single most towering person in the twelfth century, ruling as queen for nearly eighty years, while generations came and went. For reasons having at first to do with the necessities of the human race and with differential physical strength as between men and women, no doubt, social systems have systematically granted to men advantages withheld from women; and many women of high talent did not find their rightful place in society. And so with many of the other historic and systemic forms of inequality. These distorting factors have corrupted the natural system of inequality; they have been forms of "oppression"—unnatural force holding persons down where natural talent, left to itself, would have propelled them to rise.

Well, one might say, if you work to remove these sources of oppression, so that everyone, Jew or Greek, male or female, free or slave, has an equal opportunity to rise to the appropriate level of personal responsibility, you join Professor Ruether in a similarly glowing vision. Yes, perhaps the vision is the same. But look again at the contrast in terrain we face in climbing toward it.

In my view, God has *not* promised us that these oppressions will be overcome, not in our lifetime, or in the lifetime of the human race. I read the words in this wise: "*In Christ,* there is neither Jew nor Greek, slave nor free, male nor female—but in real life in this world, you better believe there is." The Christian message is addressed to each of us in the

generation and in the circumstances in which we find ourselves. Life
eternal with God is to me no more pie-in-the-sky than some future utopia
in which society will be organized in justice and in truth. Thus, I do not
believe that Christianity, or the United States, has *broken* its covenant;
there never was any covenant promising anything differently from what
we see. Rather, the covenant, such as it is, still nourishes us. Little by
little, we move closer to realizing parts of it—but only, I think, while
falling away from other parts of it. History, to my eyes, is less a matter of
"progress" than a matter of trade-offs. Progress along one line com-
monly means losses along another. Human society is not so much improved as rearranged. There *is* improvement; there *is* progress—but not
so much, and surely not so unadulterated, as the history-makers would
have us believe. In every age, in every circumstance, God's grace is
sufficient to all who call upon him. In a perfect world, Jesus would not
have been crucified.

Concerning class: There will in every society be different social classes,
variously structured by economic and other relations. Even in a
thoroughly open society, of perfectly equal opportunity, there will be
differential social classes based on talent, taste, character, and other
autonomous factors.

Concerning race: The sacrifices European white society made in the
name of abstract thought, a capacity for saving and capital accumulation,
promotion of the inventive practical mind, and habits of competitive
strife—and these sacrifices have not been without price—have given
them in the last four centuries a decisive advantage over the peoples of
other continents and other races. At present, the other peoples of the
world are imitating the white race on every level: borrowing basic
Western concepts of national identity, liberation, struggle, economic
development, technological sophistication, and the rest. Few of them
even pretend to imitate the democratic political institutions, voluntary
associations, or judicial bills of rights developed in North Atlantic but in
few other national cultures on this planet. These are also decisive long-
term advantages for productivity, originality, and energy. Within the
United States, every group of color, including the blacks of the West
Indies, has leaped above American blacks in average per-capita income
and into the professional occupations. At some moment, American
blacks will have to note that neither their stars, nor others, prevent them
from doing what others, equally poor or even equally black, have been
able to do.

Concerning sex: To speak of women as a caste is misleading in some respects, for upper class women with college educations are in a considerably more potent social, economic, political, and personal situation than either men or women of less privileged classes. That such women today are wearying of a pampered and leisurely life, and embracing new challenges and responsibilities is a sign less of "liberation from oppression" than of an admirable impulse to shoulder their due weight in a society quite capable of demanding far less. Midge Decter's profound analysis of the terrors of responsibility, in *The New Chastity,* diagnoses with appropriate cynicism how pervasive these terrors are among powerful women in America's elites.

It is our vocation as Christians to make the world as fair, just, truthful, and free, both in its personal practices and in its institutions, as we can. This world of ours does not bear much fairness, justice, truth, or liberty. Yet it is marvelous to see, considering how flawed an animal is humankind, how much grace shines through Christian history and, in America, from sea to sea. Having fewer utopian expectations, one rejoices even in flawed achievements, never before equaled in human history, and perhaps not forever to endure.

MICHAEL NOVAK

The Women's Experience and Perspective

ROSEMARY RADFORD RUETHER

Both Christian and American foundations represent "new covenants" that promised to free humankind from various powers and principalities that had previously oppressed it. Both made their claims, not in terms of a particular sociological group, but in the name of universal humanity. Both speak a universal language that purports to be valid for all kinds and conditions of human beings. Yet both of these covenants were in the process of being betrayed at the very moment when their foundational texts were being canonized. Hierarchies of sex, race, and class were again allowed, even justifying themselves by reference to the authorities of these new foundations. It is the purpose of this essay to make a small comparative excursus into the ways in which the universalism of these two covenantal languages was betrayed. I wish to show the way the languages that justified this betrayal, theologically on the one hand, and socially on the other, intermingled in ongoing American ideology. Yet I wish to show also the way the universalism of the Christian and the constitutional languages, in their peculiar American mix, continually provided the basis for new criticisms and revolts against these betrayals by the betrayed.

Rosemary Radford Ruether is Georgia Harkness Professor of Applied Theology at the Garrett Evangelical Theological Seminary, Evanston, Illinois. She holds a B.A. (Religion and Philosophy) from Scripps College, Claremont, California, and an M.A. (Ancient History) and Ph.D. (Classics and Patristics) from the Claremont Graduate School. She is a member of the editorial board of the *Journal of Religious Thought* and is a contributing editor to *Christianity and Crisis* and *The Ecumenist*. Among her books are *The Church against Itself, The Radical Kingdom: The Western Experience of Messianic Hope, Liberation Theology: Human Hope Confronts Christian History and American Power, Religion and Sexism: The Image of Women in the Judeo-Christian Tradition, Faith and Fratricide: The Image of the Jews in Early Christianity, From Machismo to Mutuality: Essays on Sexism and Woman-Man Liberation* (co-authored with Eugene Bianchi), and *The New Woman and the New Earth: Sexist Ideologies and Human Liberation*.

Sexism and Redemption in
the New Testament

The New Testament was written during a transition between two frameworks of thought or two world views. The messianic hope of Old Testament prophetism was essentially a this-worldly futurism. It was a hope for the realization of the blessed era for humanity and creation when every injustice will be overcome. It is in this spirit that Jesus, in the Gospel of Luke, declared the inauguration of his mission by proclaiming:

> The Spirit of the Lord is upon me,
> because He has anointed me to preach good news to the poor.
> He has sent me to proclaim release to the captives,
> and recovering of sight to the blind,
> to set at liberty those who are oppressed,
> to proclaim the acceptable Year of the Lord.
> —Luke 4:18, from Isa. 61:1

But in the two hundred years before the birth of Jesus, Jewish messianism was in the process of transition to another world view. In the apocalyptic perspective finite creation came to be seen as an inadequate framework for human realization. Not merely injustice, but the finitude of creation itself must be brought to an end. The present mortal, material creation must end and a new immortal, immaterial creation arise, in order to fulfill the human longing for transcendence over evil. The present finite, created world comes to be seen as an alien nature that does not represent our "true home." Persian and Greek dualisms were imported into Jewish apocalyptic to express this growing world alienation and the longing for an immortal world. Gnosticism provided the cosmogony for this world alienation. Yet Christianity could not accept the gnostic rationale of evil located in the very act of finite creation itself. It insisted on retaining the earlier biblical view of the goodness of creation. But the inconsistencies in Christian theology and spirituality are rooted in this gap between a this-worldly creationalism and an anti-worldly eschatology.

The truncation of the social message of the Christian gospel is related to this eschatologizing of messianic hope. Christianity took its rise as a charismatic movement that called people out of their accustomed social structures and appealed to those scorned as the 'am ha'aretz' or unwashed of Israel or as the slaves of the empire. On every level, from the family, to the political and religious leadership of Israel, to the Roman Empire, the good news called for an exodus and a judgment upon social structures that incarnate unbelief and antagonism to the coming Kingdom of God. The language of the Gospels makes it clear that the call of repentance sets one in tension, not only with the macrostructures of temple and empire, but, more immediately, with the microstructures of the family and the "home town folks." One must be ready to "hate" one's mother and faith, leave spouse and children, in order to follow the Lord. One's brothers by blood will betray you, just as they betrayed Jesus. A certain unconventional mingling of men and women outside the structures of family roles may have been one result of this opposition of the messianic movement to the family and the kinship group. Later, slave and free, Jew and Greek also mingled in the expanding church in a way that broke down the traditional social barriers. These facts impressed at least some sectors of the early church with the idea that the messianic age was to be realized in a new universalism where men and women, slave and free, Jew and Greek meet in a new equality and the barriers of enmity built by society are overcome in Christ. This is expressed theologically in Paul's famous declaration that in Christ "there is neither Jew nor Greek, there is neither slave nor free, there is neither male nor female" (Gal. 3:28).

But the social radicalism implied by such statements was quickly nipped in the bud in "orthodox" Christianity. Within the period of the ministry of Jesus the potential connection of messianic expectation and a zealot revolt against the empire was avoided or suppressed, even though Jesus himself was probably crucified because, in the minds of the Jewish and Roman authorities, the two continued to be linked together. Active struggle against the empire is deleted from the foundations of the New Testament, although it survives in a passive form in an acute alienation from "Babylon" and a hope for its quick demise, along with the whole realm of the Beast which it represents. The political framework for this hope surfaces most clearly in the Christian book of Revelation. But even this political alienation is covered over by temporal accommodation, especially in Luke and Paul, so that apologists can represent Christians as the best citizens of the empire, even though, paradoxically, they regard its titular deities as "demons" and hope for its rapid demise in a Kingdom soon to come. No wonder the empire continued to regard Christians as hidden subversives, until under Constantine it finally succeeded in coopting them into the imperial ideology!

Socially, Christians made no radical departures from conventional use of slaves in economic life and, by the time of the Pastoral epistles, the church models its ministry clearly on the traditional patriarchal family. Gradually the inequities of rich and poor, even among Christians, cease to be regarded as scandalous. The traditional subservience of women to men, slaves to masters, is reaffirmed. The message of a new equality in Christ is repeated, but its meaning is spiritualized. It is seen as referring to an equality of spiritual condition, not a mandate for a transformation of social conditions. Its realization is for heaven, not for earth.

The split between creation and eschatology allows a dualism of "two orders" to be maintained. This means that the messianic order of equality in Christ is not taken to be the goal and mandate of the present creation. Rather, it becomes a separate sphere, to be realized only inwardly, ideally, eschatologically. The created reality then asserts its own present reality, no longer propelled or judged by these messianic goals. The concept of the "order of creation" reifies the present injustices in society and allows them to be identified with "nature." In the name of this order of creation all the hierarchies of class, race, and sex, even slavery, are reaffirmed. The order of creation becomes the way of sanctifying the social structure as it is and identifying it as the order divinely established by God at creation.

In Paul there is also implied this two-leveled thinking, which commands continued subservience to the "laws" as the order of creation, while declaring equality in Christ to be the spiritual identity of the church. Thus Paul insists on the continued observance of the subordination of wives to husbands, slaves to masters, and even acquiescence to evil government. Equality in Christ is a spiritual and eschatological reality, presumably to be realized in heaven. But meanwhile the external order of creation persists and with it these social structures of subservience which Paul identifies with it. The new equality in Christ is not allowed to become a social mandate that points back to society, judging its injustices. Instead the church and Christian society are allowed to acquiesce in these structures of subordination as the "nature" of the present order of creation which has not yet been overcome. This treatment of slavery and female subordination is very different from Paul's treatment of the third category of Jew and Greek. Here the new equality in Christ is not merely "eschatological," but an immediate social mandate for the church to negate all the barriers of custom that separate the two groups. The difference is doubtless that this division touches Paul personally, whereas the other subjections of women and slaves do not.

Christianity and Revolution

In the society built by Christendom no fundamental objection was made to social hierarchy. On the contrary the great "chain of being" built on the hierarchy of soul over body suggested a new way of reifying the social hierarchies of class, race, and sex, and the ranks of the angels, as a mirror of the "created order." The dominance of master over serf, male over female, was assumed to be fundamental to this order. Only in the left-wing messianic sects that flowered briefly in peasant revolutions did the messianic ideals of heaven become social ideals which judged the contemporary class system as demonic; not as an order created by God's will, but by human evil. When slavery again arose as an institution with European colonialism, the churches, Protestant and Catholic, were prepared to accept it as a relationship in no way incompatible with Christian identity. Proponents of slavery noted that, both in the Old and New Testaments, slavery and the subjugation of wives to husbands and children to parents are closely woven together in the fabric of the patriarchal family. The only autonomous person in the patriarchal family is the male head of the family. Women, children, servants, or slaves belong together as subservient persons. These subordinations are all deemed equally natural. Patriarchy is thus the master image for all such inferior categories of persons throughout Christian history to the present time.

However, beginning in the peasant revolutions, growing in the Puritan struggles of the seventeenth century into explicit form in liberal and socialist revolutionary ideology in the nineteenth century, a new world view began to be shaped that broke down the wall between messianic equality and the order of creation. In these movements Christendom ceases to be the legitimate order established by Christ "until the Kingdom comes." It is reevaluated as a demonic order, as a representative of Babylon and the Beast. This viewpoint, born in the sectaries, grows into a general attitude of all who come to see the old feudal church and society as the *ancien régime* vis-à-vis the new "Age of the Spirit" or, in secular terms, the age of Enlightenment informed by reason and science, freed from the oppressions of the nobility and the "superstitious priestcraft" of the clergy. Equality of persons ceases to be a messianic ideal fulfilled only in heaven. It is the true identity of every human being, stolen from them by the fallen reign of kings and priests, to be restored in the new age of rationality.

Liberalism and socialism reject the identification of social hierarchy with nature. The subordination of bourgeoisie to nobility, the subordination of worker to owner, these do not express a design of nature, but an alien human distortion contrary to that equal personhood which is everyone's "God-given nature." The messianic ideals of Christianity are de-eschatologized and become the social mandate of the human historical future. The Kingdom of God is brought back to earth and established as the future horizon of the aspirations of the world.

Revolutionary ideologies of modern Western society are all informed by this appropriation of the ideal of the messianic future as the aspiration and mandate of human history.[1]

American ideology is a special blend of the secular rationalist translation of messianic futurism into the language of the Enlightenment and the earlier religious reformism of English Puritanism. The language of the Enlightenment provided the legal and constitutional language for the statement of the American ideals. But its fire and power were always fueled by the deeper resources of the biblical religious vision, as Robert Bellah shows in his recent book, *The Broken Covenant*.[2]

The language of equality forged in the English and French revolutionary struggles expressed mainly the aspirations of a rising bourgeoisie for political equality with the old nobility. It was not seriously assumed that the "lower orders," the newly colonized dark-skinned peoples, much less *women,* were intended to share in these "inalienable rights" with which "all men" were endowed by their Creator. Sweeping statements were made by the revolutionaries in the name of "all mankind" without noticing that the only mankind actually in view was white, male, and propertied. When these same slogans were taken up by peasant and proletariat and even feminist revolutionaries, bent on more sweeping changes, the middle-class leaders quickly grew conservative and turned back to the church and to restorations of monarchy or established class structure, now allied with their commercial power.

This same contradiction between sweeping statements of human rights and actual social conservativism, lodged in an established planter and merchant class, characterized the American Revolution. The difference was perhaps that the formation of American society by immigration gave a more lasting illusion of having already become a "classless society," lacking the trappings of the old nobility, a place where all could rise according to their ability, where no fixed rank existed. No full-scale social revolution emerged out of the depths of the American revolt to challenge the right of the local ruling classes to assume the mantle of power. Yet, even from its beginnings, with the bringing of the first slaves and the first indentured servants, the basis of a class and racial caste society was being laid.

1. See Rosemary Ruether, *The Radical Kingdom: The Western Experience of Messianic Hope* (New York: Harper & Row, 1970), pp. 16–17 and *passim*.

2. Robert Bellah, *The Broken Covenant* (New York: Seabury, 1974).

In the French revolutionary struggles the peasants and urban proletariat were quick to realize the way the new Declaration of Rights and Constitution reflected the class interests of the bourgeoisie. New revolutionary movements were touched off which intended to complete, on behalf of those still held in subjection, the revolt begun by the bourgeoisie. After a generation of reaction these movements again arose under the banner of socialism. Feminism also arose during the French Revolution, in the appeals of women to be included in the franchise, although the later Napoleonic Code nailed them as firmly as ever into the house of patriarchal society. Certain strains of early socialism also regarded themselves as espousing the cause of the liberation of women, along with the dissolution of the relation of private property to the family. This line was inherited by Marxism, which taught that women were the first proletariat and the male-female relation the first class relation. Women too, with the proletariat, would be freed for a new equality in the classless society.[3] Socialists were convinced that the civil rights of the liberal state could not establish the equality they desired, either for the worker or for women. Civil rights in the liberal state presuppose power and leisure built on a structure of property and the low or unpaid labor of others. Neither women nor workers could win their place as self-actualizing persons without a fundamental reorganization of property, work, and the family. Feminism and socialism continue the doctrine of equal rights built on equal "natures" of the Enlightenment. But they go beyond liberal revolutions by demanding a socio-economic revolution as the foundation of the promise of equality.

Contradictions of the American Covenant

America, at the Revolution, was a class and patriarchal society, but also a slave society. The failure to deal with slavery in the constitutional provision for civil rights is the most glaring instance of that implicitly limited view of "man" in the name of which the planter and merchant classes made their revolution. Many blacks participated in the Revolution in expectation that its success would strike the manacles from their hands as well. That women, even of the ruling classes, should be included among the citizenry was not considered. But that does not mean that some women were not beginning to reflect on the anomaly.

On March 31, 1776, Abigail Adams, wife of John Adams, addressed a

3. Frederick Engels, *The Origin and History of the Family, Private Property and the State* (Zurich, 1884).

letter to her husband, then attending the Continental Congress. She appealed to him to see to it that women were included in the liberties which the Congress was seeking to safeguard.

> . . . in the new code of laws which I suppose it will be necessary for you to make, I desire you would remember the ladies and be more generous and favorable to them than your ancestors. Do not put such unlimited power into the hands of the husbands. Remember, all men would be tyrants if they could. If particular care and attention is not paid to the ladies, we are determined to foment a rebellion and will not hold ourselves bound by any laws in which we have no voice or representation.
>
> That your sex is naturally tyrannical is a truth so thoroughly established as to admit of no dispute; but such of you as wish to be happy willingly give up the harsh title of master for the more tender and endearing one of friend. Why then not put it out of the power of the vicious and the lawless to use us with cruelty and indignity with impunity. Men of sense in all ages abhor those customs which treat us only as the vassals of your sex.[4]

In this letter Abigail Adams appeals to the fundamental principles of the American Revolution. Against the paternalism of feudalism, she asserts that the rights of those in servitude cannot be secured by trusting to the virtue and magnanimity of the masters. This relationship must be replaced by the relationship of equal citizens before the law. Secondly, she appeals to the principle that laws are binding only upon those recognized as partners in the "social contract." If women are left out of the American definition of the parties of the social contract and the rights of citizens, then they too, like their husbands in revolt against their colonized relation to the English king, would have to foment a revolution against their subjugation to laws in which they have no representation.

John Adams's reply to this letter is instructive. It illustrates the humorous contempt with which the women's issue is typically dealt with by males. But it also clearly recognizes the links between sexism and the subjugation of children, servants, lower classes, and conquered races in the patriarchal order which the American leaders still represented. The determination to limit the "rights of man" to whites, males, and the propertied is evident, as well as the assumption that any enlargement of this view will undermine the fundamental bonds of society that are held together by the relations of mastery and service.

> As to your extraordinary code of laws, I cannot but laugh. We have been told that our struggle has loosened the bonds of government everywhere;

4. *Feminism: The Essential Historical Writings,* ed. Miriam Schneir (New York: Vintage, 1972), pp. 3–4.

that children and apprentices were disobedient; that schools and colleges were grown turbulent; that Indians slighted their guardians and Negroes grew insolent to their masters. But your letter was the first intimation that another tribe, more numerous and more powerful than all the rest, were grown discontent.

April 14, 1776[5]

The failure of the American Constitution and Bill of Rights to address the inequalities of class, race, and sex would become all too evident in the turmoil of our subsequent history. Yet, at the same time, the very language of natural rights and the right to rebellion of the unrepresented was to be used for an ongoing revolutionary struggle to include in the American covenant those categories of persons at first ignored. It is not accidental that, when the Black Panthers declared their intention to hold a Second American Constitutional Convention in the late 1960s to remedy the inequities of the first, they did not choose the *Communist Manifesto* as their text, but repeated the words of the Declaration of Independence as their statement.

In the 1830s the great struggle against the most obvious violation of these principles—slavery—began in earnest. Women from the North and South soon made themselves prominent among the abolitionists' ranks. The abolitionists cited not only the secular language of natural rights, but also appealed to the religious traditions of repentance and conversion and the expectation of an era of millennial blessedness awaiting the American people of God once purged of their evils. In so doing they presumed that the redemptive language had a social, historical reference and not simply a personal and eschatological one. The meetings of the abolitionists, such as Theodore Dwight Weld, later to marry the feminist abolitionist Angelina Grimké, were modeled, in preaching style and in calls to witness, on revivalism.[6] The ideology and style of abolitionism vividly illustrated the intertwining of civil and evangelical traditions in American culture.

However, women in the antislavery movement soon discovered that they were not treated as equals with their male colleagues. When Lucretia Mott and Elizabeth Cady Stanton attended the World Anti-Slavery Convention in London in 1840, as members of the American delegation, their rights to be seated in the convention were denied on the grounds that only males could be delegates. The two women spent the ten days

5. Ibid., p. 4.

6. Gerda Lerner, *The Grimké Sisters from South Carolina* (Boston: Houghton Mifflin, 1967), p. 219 and *passim*.

watching the convention from the gallery and planning how they should bring the cause of women before the American public and before the abolitionist movement in particular. In 1848 these discussions were to bear fruit in the first women's rights convention in Seneca Falls, New York.

The Declaration of Women's Rights of Seneca Falls repeats the opening paragraphs of the American Declaration of Independence, but now makes clear that women too are included in those laws of nature which recognize all humans equal. They too, like Abigail Adams, declare that women should withhold allegiance to such government as "through a long train of abuses and usurpations" evinces a design to "reduce them under absolute despotism." The Women's Declaration then goes on to detail the specific abuses of patriarchal legal codes which allow unjust domination of men over women:

1. Withholding of the franchise.
2. Nonrepresentation in the laws to which she is called to submit.
3. Denial of basic civil rights.
4. The status of "civil death" of the married woman.
5. Withholding of property rights, even to her own wages.
6. The subjugation to a state of servitude to her husband, even to the extent of giving him the right of corporal punishment.
7. Neglect of female interests and rights of children in divorce laws.
8. Taxation without representation.
9. Withholding of profitable employment and giving of unjust wages in those jobs which women are allowed to pursue.
10. Denial of higher education.
11. The subordinate position of women in the church, including the denial of the ministry.
12. The double-standard in sexual morality.
13. The usurpation by men of the role of God as lawgiver, sanctifying unjust laws by religion.
14. The promotion of a culture and social conditioning designed to lessen in every way woman's self-confidence in her own powers and to make her dependent on men.

All laws that deny women's full humanity and equality as citizens are declared null and void before the bar of the higher law of nature and nature's God. The women pledged themselves to struggle in every way to abrogate such denial of legal and social status in fact.[7]

7. *Feminism*, pp. 77–82.

The abolitionist movement split over the question of including the women's issue in its purview. Many took the position that the issue should not be raised at all in their ranks, either because women had no just cause for protest, or else because it was inexpedient to link one controversial issue with another (this argument often being a cover for an antifeminist attitude). However the Garrison wing of the movement insisted that all forms of oppression must be opposed. The great black abolitionist Frederick Douglass concurred in principle in this union of all forms of oppression with the struggle to overcome the enslavement of the Negro. Commenting on the Declaration of Rights recently issued from Seneca Falls, Frederick Douglass wrote:

> We should not do justice to our convictions, or to the excellent persons connected with this infant movement, if we did not in this connection offer a few remarks on the general subject which the Convention met to consider and the objects they seek to attain. In so doing, we are not insensible that the bare mention of this truly important subject, in any other than terms of contemptuous ridicule and scornful disfavor, is likely to excite against us the fury of bigotry and the folly of prejudice. A discussion of the rights of animals would be regarded with far more complacency by many of what are called the *wise* and the *good* of our land, than would be a discussion of the rights of women. It is, in their estimation, to be guilty of evil thoughts to think that woman is entitled to equal rights with man. Many who have at last made the discovery that Negroes have some rights as well as other members of the human family have yet to be convinced that women are entitled to any.
>
> Eight years ago a number of persons of this description actually abandoned the anti-slavery cause, lest by giving their influence in that direction they might possibly be giving countenance to the dangerous heresy that woman, in respect to rights, stands on an equal footing with man. In the judgment of such persons the American slave system, with all its concomitant horrors, is less to be deplored than this *wicked* idea. It is perhaps needless to say that we cherish little sympathy for such sentiments or respect such prejudices. Standing as we do upon the watch-tower of human freedom, we can not be deterred from an expression of our approbation of any movement, however humble, to improve and elevate the character of any member of the human family.
>
> *The North Star*, July 28, 1848[8]

But the women soon recognized that their most formidable foes were among the Christian clergy who gave to the subjugation of women the hallowed status of divine writ and will. In this period of nineteenth century America, St. Paul's injunction that women should keep silent

8. Ibid., pp. 83–85.

was not taken merely as an objection to the ordination of women, but was read as a general social mandate against women's vocal participation in public gatherings, civil as well as ecclesiastical. When women sought to speak at public gatherings, especially those held in churches or church halls, but even in secular halls or legislative bodies, they met with this generalized use of the apostolic injunction.

The battle for civil rights, for the Negro and for women, in the context of nineteenth century American culture, inevitably became a theological and exegetical battle. The proponents of equality were quite sure that this was the true divine intention, written in Scripture, however obscured by later interpretation. They had the responsibility of clearing away the scriptural statements seemingly to the contrary, either by arguing for a different meaning for those statements, or else by demoting them to secondary rank as merely the reflection of past historical conditions and time-bound human opinion, to be set aside by more fundamental scriptural tenets. In an era of biblical literalism, little accustomed to historical criticism, this latter view was far more dangerous. Only a few, such as Elizabeth Cady Stanton, and even she only in her old age in the 1880s, dared to assail Scripture itself as a document that reflected many inferior prejudices against women that must be rejected for more fundamental doctrines of faith in equal human personhood.

The appeal to Scripture as the basis of the doctrine of equal rights as the original and "natural" human condition can be illustrated from the tracts of Sarah and Angelina Grimké. These two women grew up in a South Carolina plantation owner family, but fled to Philadelphia and turned to Quakerism over their dismay at the slavery system and the tacit support of it by the main body of institutional churches. When the two women were confronted on scriptural grounds by the clergy's denial of their rights as women to speak in public against slavery, they added the woman's cause to that of the slave. In Angelina Grimké's "Appeal to the Christian Women of the South" (1836), and in Sarah Grimké's "Epistle to the Clergy of the South" (1836) and her "Letters on the Equality of the Sexes and the Condition of Women," published in the *New England Spectator* the following year, we see in the scriptural argument a definite parallelism of the two causes of Negro and female emancipation.

The key text for equal human rights is taken to be Gen. 1:26–27. This text establishes the unity of humanity, male and female, in the image of God. The subsequent verses establish the dominion of the human pair over the animals, but in no way suggest that men are given similar dominion over women or over any other group of humans. The fundamental differentiation of all humans beings from animals is established as being one of equality in personhood in the image of God, all enjoying dominion over the earth and its "lower" forms of life. But this basic human situation also rules out the possibility that any group of human beings be regarded as sharing the subjugation of the animal world to human beings. In the realm of "dominion over the earth" no humans can be included in the lower status of animals. Therefore when any dominion of humans over other humans arises it is a contravening of the very nature of human beings in distinction from lower creation. All subjugation of humans to other humans is a denial of their humanity and a ranking of some humans with beasts. All human traditions that create such dominion must therefore be regarded as an attack on the original created nature of humanity and an expression of a sinful perversion of nature contrary to the divine will.

The sisters were anxious to exempt the Bible itself from any falling away from the standard of "nature." On the issue of slavery they made the standard arguments of the abolitionists that slavery in biblical times is in no way comparable to American chattel slavery. It was a bonded servitude from which a person could work free. The American brand of slavery, originating in the theft of the blacks from Africa, would fall under the biblical injunction against man-stealing condemned by the apostle (1 Tim. 1:10) and punishable in the old covenant by death (Exod. 21:16). As for statements in the Bible, especially in St. Paul, which apparently sanction the subordination of women, Sarah Grimké was quite sure that when women are allowed to learn Hebrew and Greek and to participate in biblical studies, they will be able to discover "various readings of the Bible a little different from those we now have." That God created woman and man equal, according to the first creation account of Genesis, is something equally certain, in the sisters' opinion. That both women and men are included equally in the image of God and the dominion over the lower world also indicates that God intended for woman to move in the same sphere as man. Therefore her present inferior position must be ascribed, not to her nature or the divine intent, but to the sinful works of fallen men who have thrown the divine plan of creation into disarray.

> The lust of dominion was probably the first effect of the fall, and as there was no other intelligent being over whom to exercise it, woman was the first victim of this unhallowed passion. . . . All history attests that man has subjected woman to his will, used her as a means to promote his selfish gratification, to minister to his sensual pleasures, to be instrumental in

promoting his comfort, but never has he desired to elevate her to that rank she was created to fill. He has done all he could to debase and enslave her mind, and now he looks triumphantly on the ruin he has wrought and says that the being he has thus deeply injured is his inferior. . . .[9]

Replying to a letter of the Massachusetts clergy warning that the promotion of woman's rights threatens to debase the female character, Sarah retorted that there is indeed such a danger of debasement of female character, but it comes from quite a different source than the clergy imagine:

danger from those who, having long held the reins of usurped authority, are unwilling to permit us to fill that sphere which God created us to move in, and who have entered into league to crush the immortal mind of woman. . . . No one can desire more earnestly than I do that woman may move exactly in the sphere which her Creator has assigned her, and I believe her having been displaced from that sphere has introduced confusion into the world.[10]

The defenders of slavery appealed equally to the Bible as their authority. The patriarchal subjugation of women is, in their opinion, so firmly established that it need not even be discussed. This assumption of the divinely given character of the patriarchal family is one of the proslavery camp's chief biblical defenses of the "peculiar institution." The slave, like the woman, is basically an immature, childlike being whose protection and cultivation in virtue demand a state of dependency upon a fatherly master. The proslavery advocates could appeal with good effect to ample evidence in both the Old and the New Testaments that slavery is taken for granted as an acceptable social institution. They were also quick to point out the integral relationship of slavery to the patriarchal family in the biblical record.

Frederick Ross, in his treatise *Slavery Ordained of God* (1857), declares it self-evident

that the relation of master and slave is sanctioned by the Bible, that it is a relation belonging to the same category as those of husband and wife, parent and child, master and apprentice. . . . that the relations of husband and wife, parent and child were ordained in Eden for man, as man, and modified after the fall.[11]

9. Ibid., p. 38.

10. Ibid., p. 39.

11. Frederick Ross, *Slavery Ordained of God* (Philadelphia: Lippincott, 1857), p. 99; see also pp. 52–68.

Slavery, according to Ross, is fundamentally based on these same family dependencies. But it is a more temporary historical arrangement on the part of God. It exists only until such time as the wise nurture and protection of the slave provided by the slave master will have elevated the character of such degraded, ignorant, and helpless types of sunken humanity to the point where they can stand on their own feet. Slavery is, by its nature, both a proof that the Negro presently exists in such a degraded and helpless condition and is also the perfect instrument designed by God to elevate and bless the Negro. But if Ross hints that the Negro may eventually be elevated out of slavery by the pedagogic effects of slavery itself, he offers no such hope for the state of woman's dependency. Woman having been created in her very being as a dependent and helpmate "for man, as man," the original state of dependency created before the fall is intended to last "forever."

George Armstrong, a pastor of Norfolk, Virginia, in a treatise also published in 1857 titled *The Christian Doctrine of Slavery,* draws primarily on St. Paul as the apostle who disturbs not the conscience of the slaveholder. Armstrong argues that nowhere in the Christian gospel is slavery or slaveholding condemned or slaveholders excluded from the membership of the church. On the contrary, in numerous places (Eph. 6:5–9; Col. 3:22–25; 4:1; 1 Tim. 6:1–2; Titus 2:9–10; 1 Pet. 2:19) slavery is upheld. The slave is admonished to obey the master and not to try to alter his enslaved condition, while the master, in turn, is admonished only to be a just and kind master. Slavery and slaveholding are nowhere included by Paul among the sins which Christians must overcome. On the contrary, the Scriptures are all addressed to Christians "in slaveholding states" in a way that upholds that institution for Christians.

Armstrong also notes the close relationship of slavery and the condition of women and children in the patriarchal family in these scriptural passages. He makes this his strongest defense of the beneficent and divinely ordained character of slavery. He asserts that the new covenant seeks only to overcome the abuses of these relationships of servitude, not to alter them. Rather these institutions are designed to protect and elevate the character of those in servitude. Just as, in his opinion, the effect of Christianity through the ages has gradually done away with the abuses of wives and children and has revealed the wholly salutary character of their dependency in its fundamental nature, so in a similar way, although "there are incidental evils attaching to the system, . . . all that has ever been done for the slave has been done through this agency."[12] The position of women in the patriarchal family provided the proslavery argument with its basic analogy, since, despite the outcries of women, such as the Grimké sisters, the completely "natural," divinely ordained, and beneficent character of patriarchy was regarded as unassailable.

The struggle against slavery finally issued in the Civil War. The Fourteenth Amendment completed Lincoln's Emancipation Proclamation by declaring that the full rights of American citizenship shall not be abridged by reason of race or previous condition of servitude. Women lost their bid, however, to have sex included in this extension of citizenship. Indeed the Fourteenth Amendment for the first time explicitly excluded women from its constitutional provisions by using the word "male" as a qualification for citizenship. The more militant wing of the women's movement was furious and opposed the amendment until it would include sex as well as race. The passage of this amendment had the effect of bringing out the latent class and race antagonism between the women's movement and black advancement. Thereafter feminism, which has arisen in such a close relationship with abolitionism, drifted into increasing indifference or negativity toward the racial issue.

As the women's movement became a mass movement in the 1880s, it was influenced by a racist and classist social Darwinism and generally abandoned a liberal creed. Even the Social Gospel movement, which preached against the exploitation of labor, acquiesced in most cases to the leading scientific dogma of Negro "evolutionary" inferiority.[13] The movement's paternalistic concept of reform, moreover, little disposed its leaders to criticize the role of women in the family. In this period feminism began to accept a rationale for the enfranchisement of women that was tacitly racist and elitist. No longer did they stress that universal rights be shared equally by all human beings. Victorian feminists often accepted the leading romantic dogma of woman's different and superior moral nature to men. They tried to turn this doctrine from its rationalization of woman's domestication to a mandate for a distinctive social and political role for women as guardians of morals in society. At the same time, the women's movement acquiesced to the Jim Crow and literacy laws that were *de facto* disenfranchising the Negro and the im-

12. George Dodd Armstrong, *The Christian Doctrine of Slavery* (New York: Scribner's, 1857; reprinted: New York: Negro Universities Press, 1969), pp. 59–60.

13. Richard Hofstadter, *Social Darwinism in American Thought* (Boston: Beacon, 1944, 1955), pp. 105–10; also Thomas F. Gossett, *Race: The History of an Idea in America* (New York: Schocken, 1965), pp. 144–75.

migrant. Increasingly they argued that, not women *per se,* but a certain kind of woman, the wives, mothers, and sisters of the white Protestant ruling class, should be enfranchised in order to double the vote of this group and assure the beneficent guidance of the superior classes over the inferior. This point was made in a resolution passed at the National Women's Suffrage Convention in 1893:

> *Resolved:* that without expressing any opinion on the proper qualifications for voting, we call attention to the significant facts that in every state there are more women that can read and write than all the negro voters, more white women who can read and write than all the negro voters, more American women that can read and write than all the foreign voters, so that the enfranchisement of such women would settle the vexed question of rule by illiteracy, whether of the homegrown or the foreign-born production.[14]

The same paternalism that had argued that dependency and denial of civil rights protected and elevated the inferior, guarding the moral tone of all of society, so often urged against rights for women, was now adopted by bourgeois white Protestant women against civil rights for blacks and Irish Catholics. The drift of the feminist ideology into this camp at the turn of the century reveals an essential danger of a women's movement that does not analyze the relations of sexism to racial and class hierarchies; namely, that it can become diverted into a crusade on the side of the status quo. A concept of "rights for women" in the context of the class privileges of the ruling class and race can become a means by which that ruling group doubles its own political power, through the vote, or its own economic power, through doubled income, while shifting new inequities onto lower classes and races, male and female.

The women's movement of the nineteenth and early twentieth centuries made enormous gains, however, which would ultimately benefit all women and social groups. Fundamentally it broke apart the millennial caste status of women which had excluded them from being regarded as autonomous civil persons. Through the vote, property rights, rights to control their own income, manage their own businesses, women acquired a civil existence and civil rights and ceased to be what they had been for almost the entire history of patriarchy, permanent dependents upon fathers or husbands. The early women's movement also opened up higher education for women, thus ending the equally long practice of

14. Aileen Kraditor, *The Idea of the Woman Suffrage Movement, 1890–1920* (Garden City, N.Y.: Doubleday Anchor, 1971), p. 110.

excluding women from learning and participation in the public processes of culture. The right to enter the professions and the schools which prepared and licensed these professions was closely tied to this winning of the right to higher education.

Many loose ends in this winning of civil rights and professional and educational equality still remain to be completed, but the victory resulted from the one-hundred-year feminist struggle from the first quarter of the nineteenth to the first quarter of the twentieth centuries. This victory still remains to be won in many other societies around the world. What liberal feminism did not touch is the basic economic relations between home and work that still tie most women to traditional roles. Without systemically changing this economic relation of home and work, liberal feminism remains token feminism, opening new avenues to "exceptional" women by virtue of wealth, unmarried or childless status, or exceptional energy to carry the "second shift" of homework along with a job. Since the basic economic caste status of women remains unchanged, the basic stereotypes of "female nature" and such "roles" as full-time mother and wife also continue as though unaffected by the fact that these stereotypes no longer describe the actual lives of large numbers of women.

In the mid-1960s a new feminist movement was born to complete the work left undone by the grandmothers. Once again the participation of women in a struggle for black rights was a catalyst for a new awareness of sexual discrimination. The famous phrase attributed to Stokely Carmichael that "the only position for women in the movement is prone" summed up, for a generation of women, radicalized by the sexism of the civil rights and peace movements, the unanalyzed attitudes toward women still typical, not only of conventional society, but also of the men they had taken to be their allies in the struggle for human dignity. Angered by this experience, radical feminists more and more tended to separate out into their own groups. They began to insist that sexism is a much more primordial social ill than capitalism or even racism (at least the racism that arose through European colonialism of dark-skinned people). Sexism cannot be subsumed automatically under the banner of any other movement. Neither socialism nor overcoming racism will automatically remove male domination unless there is specific attention to the special stereotypes and status of women.

Once again, too, a feminism that began in alliance with the black struggle began to become alienated from blacks, this time because of the lack of reciprocity of black men in recognizing the claims of feminism.

Neither black men nor white women find it easy to really understand the other's experience of oppression. The reasons for this are in large part endemic to the system of domination itself, which does not have one simple division, but multiple divisions of servitude by class, race, and sex, and, in the immediate situation, sets the various groups of subjugated people in tension with each other. The racial domination of a group also involves the sexual use of its women and the humiliation of its men personally and socially, as well as economically. White women may appear the immediate benefactors of this, so it is hard to recognize their struggle against an ornamental and trivialized status.

Black women could provide an important key to the links between the two oppressions, but it is seldom easy for them to sort out their own distinctive types of experience of both racial and sexual contradictions. They are falsely imagined to be "dominant" because they are the breadwinners of last resort for their families and are told to "step back" so normative patriarchal culture can be reestablished in their communities. The division of women and, increasingly also, blacks by class allows token middle-class members of each group to benefit through an adjustment of the structural oppression of the whole group. The black community as a whole grows poorer and is unable to build up infrastructures of development of its own, such as schools and businesses, while token members of its elite are drawn off into white institutions as display cases of "integration." One could make similar analyses of other minorities.

The white male ruling class adjusts but does not basically change its domination of all these systems of power, while it holds out token places of advancement to blacks, browns, and women in a way that makes them the immediate competitors with each other. All these enlargements of "rights" function from the excess profits of the system. "Liberalism" quickly fades from all the dominant institutions, including the churches, during a recession, when the basic determination of the present white male ruling elite to retain its position becomes evident.

What are the prospects for the American covenant; for a new commitment to the society of equal opportunity for all citizens in a country which, from the first, was divided by class, racial, and sexual contradictions of this ideal? In Detroit in August of 1975 a conference on Liberation Theology was gathered that brought together feminists, black theologians, native Americans and Hispanics, representatives of militant labor unions, and Latin American Liberation theologians, together with a few sympathizers from the white male theological establishment. There emerged from this conference, at least on paper, an analysis of American society in terms of the interstructuring of race, sex, and class, and the imperial, neocolonialist relations between the United States and the Third World. For the participants, the solution that must be envisioned is not an expansion of existing capitalism, but a "new economic order" based on quite different priorities. This commitment to a "new covenant" intertwines biblical faith and modern revolutionary faith. For all those gathered at this conference the struggle for such a new society means to live out the ancient promise that in Christ "there is neither Jew nor Greek, there is neither slave nor free, there is neither male nor female." It also means today to believe in "liberty and justice for all."

Response

Drawing upon the thought of Max Weber, Michael Hill, in a passage on which I frequently draw, distinguished between two types of change in relation to tradition. On the one hand, change is called for by the charismatic leader who takes a tradition and moves beyond and outside it. "The typical statement of a charismatic leader can be given as "It is written, but I say unto you. . . .' " On the other hand, Weber's virtuoso "follows what he takes to be a pure and rigorous interpretation of normative obligations which already exist in a religious tradition," and as a kind of extremist, works to use it for change. "The characteristic statement of a virtuoso is 'It is written, and I insist. . . .' "[1] Most of the way, Rosemary Radford Ruether analyzes the American traditions and then makes her prescriptions on the grounds familiar to the virtuoso. Then, suddenly, near the end she shifts field and makes the charismatic claim and appeal. She reads the tradition and finds that most of it is not acceptable to those who would work for human liberation, particularly of sexes, races, and classes. But at the core of the tradition, as in the Declaration of Independence, there is a never yet lived up to impulse for liberation. The same Jefferson who wrote that all men are created *equal* did not free his slaves, and by writing that all *men* were created equal denied full validity to half the citizens, the women. But, better than he knew, he wrote the correct theme. "It is written, and I insist. . . ." Here is virtuoso use of what Benjamin Franklin in 1749 had called for as "a *Publick Religion.*"

Dr. Ruether treats America's major "private religion" in similar fashion. Christianity, and in particular the religion of America's other set of "founding *fathers,*" Protestantism, comes in for searching and indicting inquiry because of its patent and rather consistent patriarchalism—although she might as well have extended her probe to race and class where, as it is well known, the patriarchs did little better. They used the Bible and especially the Pauline teachings to try to keep women in a position of silence in the church and, by analogy, in the society. Bad things were written into the tradition. But again, at its core, in the midst of some eschatological trackings and trajectories even in and especially in Paul there is an ultimately liberating message. That language of "will be" becomes the language of "is" in Gal. 3:28: "There is neither Jew nor Greek, there is neither slave nor free, there is neither male nor

1. Michael Hill, *The Religious Order* (New York: Crane, Russak and Company, 1973), p. 2.

female; for you are all one in Christ Jesus." The virtuoso again says, "It is written, and I insist. . . ."

Her analysis of the world of the Puritans and of Adams and Jefferson is sufficiently accurate for these purposes. Not all the ambiguities of their positions or all the contradictions within them need a fresh historical accounting. The main point is clear. Emancipation of slaves did not come until 1863, and a full recognition of equality in society is still in the distance. The extension of liberties to women was by no means a completed project with woman suffrage and would not be fulfilled with the passage of an Equal Rights Amendment. Discrimination and repression are written into too many practices, habits, laws, and literatures for us to expect a single constitutional fiat to achieve this work any more than did emancipation for blacks. And limits to such rights are connected, according to Professor Ruether, with class discriminations that perdure in America. Written into our covenant is a charter for change, "and I insist."

In a small religious order, the kind of movement that Michael Hill studies, virtuoso extremism can occasion sudden and sweeping change. In a complex pluralistic society with so many entrenched and overlapping styles of self-interest, it is much more difficult to expect a revolution on virtuoso grounds. Only evolution, development, and gradualism could ordinarily be expected, "all things being equal."

It is evidently with this kind of recognition in mind that Ruether shifts ground on the closing pages or, better, lets us know what she had in mind all along—for she has made no secret in her other writings that she calls for more drastic change than mere extensions and adjustments in liberation would allow. Referring to the Detroit conference on Liberation Theology, she reports with evident agreement that the emergence of "an analysis of American society in terms of the interstructuring of race, sex, and class, and the imperial, neocolonialist relations between the United States and the Third World" led to a conclusion. "The solution that must be envisioned is not an expansion of existing capitalism, but a 'new economic order' based on quite different priorities. This commitment to a 'new covenant' intertwines biblical faith and modern revolutionary faith."

It is not likely that the struggles for and the declaration of independence in America could truly be seen as part of a "modern revolutionary faith" except in such accidental and partial ways that they would be of little use. She means instead the more searching and sweeping Marxian-style revolutions, which are of quite a different order from the American adjustment with the British background, in which private property was so explicitly affirmed.

Biblical faith? It is part of the old covenant in America. In the heyday of the New Left in the 1960s William Appleman Williams and other historians in his train reread colonial documents and reexplored colonial existence. They found that far from being purely individualist, as the American myth would have it, there was a sense of an organic community with a controlled economy. One could resurrect this sense and say, "It is written, and I insist . . ." and Ruether's appeal would gain some power if she would reassure her clienteles that there is some precedent. But the context and corollaries of such a biblical appeal would be so alien and confusing to agents of radical change today that it would be almost futile to invoke them.

Lacking a base in either of the national covenants, the biblical or the contractual, she must call for a "new covenant." This is easy and logical in what is a prerevolutionary circumstance. The experience of the 1960s tells us that America is not near such a context. On most substantive societal issues about 80 percent or more of the American people express faith in the old covenant and consensus, mingled with mild regret for the way they are left out of some of its benefits. This is much different from a society that does not take pains to coopt peasants and proletariats, that does not "buy off discontent" with color television, and the like. It is precisely in what would be peasant and proletariat classes that the revolutionary instinct has both been neglected and killed off. People in these classes would see the Detroit conference, should they ever hear of it, as an elitist liberal gathering of academically tenured people who have a heavy investment in "what is" and an intellectual empathy for Christians and Marxists in truly prerevolutionary societies.

A risk is there for either type. The virtuoso can be muffled, reduced to impotence by gradualist forces. The charismatic, by misreading the signs of the times, may be dismissed as utopian and irrelevant. Yet who can know when change might come on gradual and evolutionary lines? And who can know at what moment vague societal discontent can be stirred to true revolutionary fervor? Calculation and faith are implied in both commitments to these competing futures. I see nothing that makes her kind of straight-out socialist resolution feasible or capable of being envisaged in today's America. Some days I would like to be wrong, when I see what she sees so far as unfinished revolutions of sex, race, and class are concerned.

MARTIN E. MARTY

A Concluding
Perspective on
American
Religious Values
and the
Future of America

Introduction

That America has its "Catholic fourth" is a proposition with which most of us can agree. One need only open his or her eyes to the environment or to the books of statistics. That the size and shape of this fourth have not always been discerned or reckoned with by both non-Catholic and Catholic America is almost equally obvious, although much of the anti-Catholic literature of the past did treat the Catholic people as a homogeneous whole, a kind of "half" of American power. Where it has been discerned, stereotypes have often led to injustices. For example, in recent decades the Catholic fourth has often been regarded as especially illiberal and prejudiced, whereas polls show that not to be the case. And there is great potential for this Catholic people and the rest of America if Catholics get their heads and hearts and selves together.

These, I take it, are Michael Novak's main points in the essay which follows, and I find not only little reason to disagree with them but much reason to assent. How do we account for the neglects and misperceptions? Here he implies some answers that can easily be supplemented by non-Catholic historians and general citizens alike. Despite the Catholic headstart from 1492–1607, once the Anglos began to come to the thirteen colonies, Protestant and other non-Catholic forces and sources had the field almost to themselves until the mid-nineteenth century. During that time non-Catholics did the naming of things in America, and names have enduring power. They set the terms for textbooks and theses, for history books and power relations. More than a century after Catholicism became the largest single religious grouping in America, three-and-a-half-century-old customs and habits linger. On a selective basis, non-Catholic and especially Protestant America continues to hold many kinds of power. Whether this Protestant power is as mobilizable as Novak thinks it is is another question, but that such power is latent and that it can lead to some false generalizing about Catholic people is clear.

Having stated these areas of agreement with his theses and having tried to account for the perception gaps, I now share three questions from within the context of the essay which follows, that will stimulate its author and its readers to further questioning and inquiry.

(1) *How Catholic is "Catholic"* in this essay? Clearly Professor Novak is not restricting the concept of Catholicism to the churchgoing, responsive, obedient, faithful, mass-going, active members. Lest he suggest that his respondent is applying Protestant norms for measuring another people—since Protestantism is voluntaristic and thus trained to drawing sharp

borders around its flocks—let me hasten to say that in social analysis such dogmatic line-drawing means little. I am and can regularly be as messy about Protestant borders as any observers of America can be—although I must confess it takes some stretching to see Protestantism to be as pervasive as does Mr. Novak. He almost equates Protestant with all non-Catholic in American life; were it not for the lurking presence of some Jews in the urban Northeast, one would think we have only two Americas.

The Catholic people for Novak are the people who came from lands that in the sixteenth century did not basically turn toward the Protestant Reformation. They are Irish, southern and eastern European, or central European from the territories that remained Catholic. Their Catholicism seems to be transmitted through the genes, much as Puritanism was supposed to have been passed on "through the loins of godly parents," and as Judaism is genetically inescapable. It is virtually impossible to be non-Catholic or ex-Catholic if one is from such stock, although Michael Novak does recognize that one can cease being an overt practicing ecclesiastical Catholic.

There is nothing wrong with such a broad and extensive definition of Catholicism, since in most of the people about whom he speaks there is a lingering if attenuating sense that Catholicism once meant something to one's ancestors and might to one's self. I suppose at the swimming pools around the "swingers' singles" high-rise apartments or the campuses or the more remote suburbs there are memories of the days when only a decade or a generation ago one was expected to have spent the Sunday morning at mass. But such a sense of Catholicism is not really very mobilizable; it gives little shape to Christianity, the church, or American patterning. Most of all, such Catholicism will thin out progressively in each generation. Surely, some few will affirm grandfather's world and come back. But mobility, media, mixed marriage—all these increasingly make the Catholic reminiscence dim and the Catholic substance thin.

Insofar as such latent Catholicism should be called Catholic, much of what Novak says about it is no doubt true, although one might question some of his assertions. Recalling how most of the world's Catholics—he and I met their leaders at Vatican II—look at American Catholics, I find it hard to see how he thinks the latter are so free to place morality on a second level in political determination. I then dined with Spanish bishops—the kind of people who, in Protestant eyes, were heirs of the Inquisition!—who mildly derided American Catholics for their moralism, their puritanism, their squeamishness about religious observance for themselves, and their standards for the society. No word comes up more frequently than the sneer "Jansenism." American Catholicism was not seen as sunnily Mediterranean, but grimly "Calvinist" in outlook. D. W. Brogan noted wryly many years ago that as Puritanism died out among rural Protestants, it moved to urban Catholicism. Witness all the Catholic efforts, long ago and even now, against pornography and for high moral standards in conduct. While it is true that urban political Catholicism tolerates a measure of moral corruption in some of its voting patterns, has Mr. Novak listened to the Catholic griping and sulking about politicians being "on the take"? I live in the late Mayor Daley's city—and have not been a rabid anti-Daleyite—where Daley held great appeal because in politics he was "moral." He went to mass daily and seemed to profit little monetarily from his power.

(2) *How Protestant is the Protestantism* in this essay? Now I can be more brief, for the same spectacles can now be turned on the Protestant phenomenon. Where does one stop being Protestant, if one's ancestors were neither from Africa or Asia (and there are many Protestants there!), or from Catholic and Jewish Europe? Only a very small percentage of America's immigrants from Protestant domains brought any kind of reflective or articulated Protestantism with them. It was part of an old habit that died soon. And among those who did bring it, there were millions who came from the continent, for example, where many of the moralisms of which Mr. Novak speaks never were present—nor did they develop in America. The ten million Lutherans and their ancestors always observed "the continental sabbath" and looked Catholic to the Anglos. If few became Protestant in any determining and defining sense, it is true that many more "got religion" here. He and I are in perfect agreement about the depth and scope of the Protestant "empire" that was set up here in the nineteenth century.

Protestantism thins out as does Catholicism among "the Protestant people" through the generations. Much of what he calls Protestant today I would call "plastic." He sometimes writes as if all American norms are generated from either Catholic, Protestant, or Jewish sources. But the colonial Protestants were often laggards, the early nationals were "enlightened," the national period had its pagans—how Protestant are the Thoreaus and the Whitmans?—and for a century there have been both merely and utterly secular tendencies that receive little attention here. Has not modernity itself, have not technology and inter-nationalization and science, generated an America that is non-

Protestant *and* non-Catholic? Professor Novak has always done American politics a service by pointing to the religiosity that many political scientists easily overlook. But it would be a disservice to carry the Protestant label too far.

(3) *How political is the American polis?* The *polis* is "the human city" in its many dimensions, the sphere in which Christ's church expresses itself beyond the ecclesiastical. For Michael Novak the political metaphor is encompassing; it seems to be a be-all and end-all of definition at many times. I share his view that politicization is extensive; we are a political society, and our lives are determined in countless ways by what goes on in politics. But we also have withheld consent from its order. Apathy rages. Creative foot-dragging is its own voting pattern. American church people for the most part spend their lives drawing few connections between their religion, their spiritual values, and political awareness. They live by their Sunday church bulletins; if they vote, they vote AFL or Republican party or pocketbook more than they vote Swedish *versus* Norwegian Lutheran, Baptist *versus* Methodist, Catholic *versus* Protestant. But most of the time they do not vote at all. An astonishingly small percentage attends even the most basic kind of political gathering, and an even smaller percentage welcomes any political reference in their churchly gatherings. So far as Protestantism is concerned, we now have data on that recent putatively most volatile decade since colonial or pre-Civil War times, so far as religion-and-politics mixtures are concerned. The evidence is clear: a few clerics and a few lay leaders were involved in the storms of the sixties. Most were uncomprehending or resistant compartmentalizers of life.

These three questions and the partial answers I have provided, answers that suggest measures of disagreement, should not be interpreted as a dismissal of Novak's viewpoint. He has done much to help the sectarian-minded enlarge their definitions of Catholicism and Protestantism. He has a fine eye for the inevitable political expression that goes with deep personal convictions in the religious sphere. He is patient to watch the social behavior of the American people. It is not likely that we are going to have too many people perform such services so persistently or so well.

MARTIN E. MARTY

A Concluding Perspective on American Religious Values and the Future of America

MICHAEL NOVAK

Just over ten years have elapsed since the concluding ceremonies of the Second Vatican Council, December 8, 1965, in St. Peter's Basilica. Those of us who were young then, participants of a sort, remember from the four council years the rise and fall of crystal waters in the fountains of Piazza San Pietro, the scent of the evening air, the traces of sunset in the evening sky, the exhilaration of having witnessed momentous historical events. Those who were not there, those then too young to remember, may never recognize how dramatically their lives were altered by those meetings in distant Rome.

For Catholics in America, the experience of growing up Catholic was changed for all time. What the American Catholic Church was before 1965, and what it became after 1965, are psychologically and culturally two different symbol systems. The Eucharist is now a dramatically different sort of event—in language, mood, tone, style, emphasis, design, and attitude. So also with the daily administration of every ceremony, instruction, and organizational necessity. Not everything has changed, of course. But few institutions have ever changed their symbolic character so thoroughly and in so short a time.

Shall we call it a revolution? It was, in any case, a very rapid evolution.

Michael Novak has written two novels and several influential books, including *The Rise of the Unmeltable Ethnics, Choosing Our King, The Experience of Nothingness, A New Generation,* and *Ascent of the Mountain, Flight of the Dove.* His books and articles have been published in nine languages. In two of his three years on the faculty at Stanford, 1967 and 1968, the Senior Class elected him "most influential professor." He has served as a judge for the National Book Awards, and a juror for the Dupont Awards in Broadcast Journalism. He is Executive Director of EMPAC! (Ethnic Millions Political Action Committee), a consulting firm and membership organization supporting aspirations for equality and justice on the part of the one in four Americans of white ethnic background. A nationally syndicated columnist with the *Washington Star* syndicate, he is the Ledden-Watson Distinguished Professor at Syracuse University.

It was so dramatic that almost one-quarter of all American sisters and lay brothers left their vocations, and their gross numbers fell by one-third. The numbers of diocesan priests fell by 15 percent. Millions of American Catholics began to practice contraception with greater public approval. Daily attitudes toward sex and marriage were affected. Catholics became far more visible in social and political activities, not least in various forms of protest and social action. The traditional anti-Catholicism of the news media softened considerably; Catholic themes or stories were handled with far greater frequency, fairness, and even generous good spirit than had earlier been the case. At every level of Catholic culture in America the changes have been cumulative, deep, and rapid.

I was among those who helped to articulate this rapid change and to promote it. Yet I do not like all of its consequences. In execution it was not what I had imagined it would be. Many of its thrusts need now, I believe, to be opposed. Others need to be deepened and altered. The general situation of Catholics in America at this point needs to be reconsidered.

The Catholic people are not where they were ten years ago. Their relative position in the American religious community, and in American society generally, has shifted. New issues have emerged. To be a "pilgrim people" is to have to change direction often, to address circumstances ever changing and ever new, and to have to shift priorities and emphases all along the line. In the phrase of Cardinal Newman, one does not ascend a mountain in a straight line but, rather, by zigzagging back and forth, and sometimes even by giving up a height previously gained in order to get around a fresh obstacle in another place.

It is part of my assignment here to attempt to achieve some unity encompassing the preceding essays; or at least to draw threads from each of them and weave a single cord. Yet it would be a weak conclusion to a set of strong chapters to offer a watered-down overview of all the forms of religious life in America. Better, it seems, to treat more fully one significant part of the American religious family, especially if that one may be interpreted in such a way as to shed light on the whole. Of those traditions assuming a new role in American life, the Catholic stands out, both for its size and for the potential depth of its influences upon other traditions. A change among Catholics portends answering changes in the self-conception of Protestants. Shifts in those two far larger families suggest shifts, as well, among Jews. For this and other reasons, I limit myself to the Catholic case. Cultural changes among Catholics since Vatican II have dramatically altered the public possibilities of all religious bodies in America; it is not implausible that the next stage in the transformation of Catholicism will have similar effect.

I wrote in 1964, in *A New Generation: American and Catholic:* "No moral issue facing the people of the United States will be unaffected by the changes occurring among the new generation of Catholics growing up in America. . . . The time in which we live is germinative; it is the beginning of an era; small efforts now will have effects for many generations. . . . There is a heaviness in the air as before a rain." Just at that time, several young Catholics in the Boston area established a national journal for Catholic college students. They called their journal *New Generation.* Today, a dozen years later, after a rush of events, cultural currents, and cataclysms, there is a gathering of breath. There is, once again, a hesitation. There is again "uncertainty regarding the future . . . dissatisfaction, restlessness, energy, trial and error. . . ."[1] During these dozen years, many experiments have been made. It is in the nature of experiments that some fail. Now is a suitable hour for assessment.

The Relative Position of Catholics in America

The first point to note is the present relative position of Catholics in America. In official figures, Catholics number almost one in four Americans—48 million out of 210 million.[2] Yet official figures count only about 3 million Spanish Catholics. The more plausible figure is four or five times that high. The Spanish-origin Catholics are probably the largest single body of Catholics, approximately 12 million—including about 2 million Puerto Ricans, about 1 million Cubans, and almost 10 million Chicanos and other Latinos. In addition, there are many millions of Americans who are Catholic in culture and tradition although no longer so in practice. One would expect that their attitudes, behaviors, and biographical trajectories share in the statistical profiles of other Catholics to a significant degree, distinguishable from the statistical profiles of Jews, Protestants, and others. There is, then, "a Catholic quarter" in the American population. It is one-quarter demographically. It is also, although distributed nationally, a "Catholic quarter"

1. Michael Novak, *A New Generation: American and Catholic* (New York: Herder and Herder, 1964), pp. 9 and 11.

2. See Harold Abramson, *Ethnic Diversity in Catholic America* (New York: Wiley, 1973), pp. 18–19.

geographically, concentrated largely in the Northeastern quadrant, from Maine to Maryland to Missouri and Minnesota. (Florida, Texas, and California are also just a little less than one-quarter Catholic.)

The history, sociology, and even basic demographics of the Catholic people have not been studied with one-quarter of the resources of the American universities and intellectual centers. Catholics number one-fourth; but they do not yet occupy, so to speak, one quarter of the intellectual consciousness of Americans. They are vastly understudied, relatively unknown. In part, the fault is that of Catholics. They have neither produced their own studies in sufficient volume, nor insisted that other scholars and research institutes treat them with one-quarter of the nation's intellectual resources. The result is that myths, stereotypes, and distortions about Catholics abound in the minds even of highly educated people, including Catholics. Social engineering and political strategies that fly in the face of hard sociological realities enjoy great currency—and do much damage. The largely Catholic neighborhoods of many of our great cities (Boston, Philadelphia, Cleveland, Detroit, Chicago, and many others) often look today like war-torn areas, abandoned to urban decay and divisive institutional racism. National ignorance has been devastating to Catholic peoples.

Moreover, the language of politics is dominated by a rhetoric and a way of thinking hostile to many interests of ordinary Catholic people. In the Republican party of 1976, neither the faction led by President Ford, nor the faction led by Ronald Reagan, nor the faction symbolized by Nelson Rockefeller and Elliot Richardson had its base in the needs, aspirations, symbols, or economic realities of the Catholic people. In the Democratic party as well, the rhetoric and programs of the left wing were rooted rather in Protestant (or Jewish) liberalism, on the one hand, and in Protestant populism, on the other. One seldom encounters a political leader in our decade who understands, speaks for, and has a socio-political strategy rooted in the daily realities of the lives of most American Catholics. Catholics tend to vote with greater regularity than any others, save the Jews.[3] They tend to call themselves "independent" more frequently than either Protestants or Jews. They tend also to be more "progressive" than the mainstream. In states like Pennsylvania, New York, Illinois, and Michigan—bastions of a progressive national

3. Cf. Mark R. Levy and Michael S. Kramer, *The Ethnic Factor* (New York: Simon and Schuster, 1973); also Andrew Greeley, *Ethnicity in the United States: A Preliminary Reconnaissance* (New York: Wiley, 1975), pp. 121–55. On related issues, see Richard Hamilton, *Restraining Myths* (New York: Wiley, 1975), esp. pp. 147–218.

politics—progressive candidates cannot win unless they come out of Catholic wards in the major cities with overwhelming majorities. Small majorities would not be sufficient to overcome the considerably more conservative Protestant vote.

Many commentators and strategists, both in the academy and in the media, systematically imagine Catholics to be far more conservative, hawkish, racist, and backward, than their actual behavior shows them to be. Catholics are, it might be shown, with their fellow immigrants, the Jews, the most potent and successful component of progressive politics in the twentieth century. The advent of their grandparents to these shores changed the entire political climate of America. They made the urban victories, and later the national victories, of the Democratic party possible. They made possible, as well, the victories of progressive economic legislation and civil rights legislation. The Catholic people, Archie Bunker-like in image, have in reality supplied the electoral majorities for virtually every type of progressive legislation enacted these last fifty years. The presumption of sociologists since Gerhard Lenski's *The Religious Factor* (1961, 1963) has been that the growth of the Catholic population would bring a conservative pressure on American politics.[4] As Mary Hanna has shown in a magnificent doctoral dissertation at Cornell (1975), the reverse has proved to be the case.[5] By virtually every index Catholics are considerably more "liberal" than Protestants, or than the mainstream as a whole. The same can be said of Catholic legislators, taken as a whole.

This is not to say that Catholic liberalism is the same as Protestant or Jewish liberalism. Quite the reverse. It *is* to say that Protestant and Jewish liberals (and many Catholics, as well) have an *image* of the Catholic voter at variance with the reality. A cultural distortion seems to be at work. Protestant and Jewish liberals have often been the traditional adversaries of Catholic populism. (In an essay, "Bosses and Reformers," Daniel Patrick Moynihan has given a classic portrait of this adversary relation with respect to the Democratic party in New York.)[6] "Catholic-baiting," Peter Viereck wrote, "is the anti-Semitism of the liberals."[7] Intellectual

---

4. Gerhard Lenski, *The Religious Factor* (Garden City, N.Y.: Doubleday, 1961, 1963).

5. Mary Hanna, "Religion and Politics: The Influence of Catholicism on American Politics in the Past Decade" (Ph.D. dissertation, 1975, Cornell University).

6. Daniel Patrick Moynihan, "Bosses and Reformers," in *Coping* (New York: Random House Vintage Books, 1975), pp. 53–68.

7. Peter Viereck, *Shame and Glory of the Intellectuals* (Boston: Beacon, 1953), p. 45.

observers have been far more kindly to Catholics since 1965 than formerly; but a quite profound ignorance and distortion still hold sway.

In the 1970s the American Catholic people, as never before, find themselves politically, culturally, and economically poised for a new assertion. For the first time, Catholic young people are now going to college in proportionate numbers. The household median income of Catholics is equal to, or above, the national average.[8] In the cinema, in poetry, in professional life, and in a number of fields in the universities, significant talents are beginning to make a new sort of impact. There *is* such a thing as the Catholic tradition, and a Catholic culture, and a Catholic experience. Catholics—in their statistical profile—are not like Presbyterians, or Methodists, or Baptists, or Jews. The imagery alive in their heads, the attitudes they have toward family, the experiences they have of God and sin and grace, the historical memory they carry of economic systems and political struggles, are not the same as those of other Americans. It is true that the common culture of America—the English language, the curriculum of English literature and Anglo-Saxon pragmatism, and the experience of the same mass media—has deprived many Catholics (and other Americans) of a public voice, of words, of concepts, and of images that well articulate what is hidden in their hearts. One of the prices of migration into a foreign culture is to have lost for a while the means of expressing one's own inmost feelings—or even to have lost one's own conscious access to them. For two generations, or three, or four, immigrants and their children had to "put on" a foreign culture. They had to assimilate. They were "Americanized." And so many children of immigrants have put on, from outside-in, as it were, an American identity. They look like other Americans. They dress like them. They talk like them. Yet there is always a music in their blood, experiences in their memory, unconscious yearnings in their heart, which have not yet found here an objective correlative in public expression.

To be the children of immigrants is to be, in part, spiritually disconfirmed. The music of America is still, by and large, Protestant, watered down to various "common denominators." Only in the creation of works of art outside the self, and works of intellect, and political movements, and strong institutions, does the heart find ways of finding

8. A stream of studies, bulletins, and reports on these matters has been generated by Andrew Greeley and his associates at the National Opinion Research Center, the University of Chicago. Those issued before 1975 are cited in *Ethnicity*. Cf. also Greeley's *The American Catholic: A Social Portrait* (New York: Basic Books, 1977).

itself mirrored in public reality. Many Catholics are still pilgrims in a strange land. Many are still, even in the fourth or fifth generation, immigrants whose psychic voyage has not reached its term. America is not yet representative of them. Yet their energies boil up. They have sharpened their talents. They have built a solid economic base. That is why one can, with quiet confidence, predict a great Catholic assertion in the final years of this century, a "second spring."

Two Prejudices

Two prejudices stand in the way of such a resurgence, however. On the one hand, many commentators are so committed to the "assimilationist thesis"—viz., that all Americans are, or are becoming, alike—that they even unconsciously neglect to note salient differences between Catholics and, say, Methodists. Some have an interest in seeing "middle America" in undifferentiated ways. Necessarily, the drift of the national media is in that direction. The national media try to exorcise as much particularity as possible. They aim at a "national" audience. *Time* and *Newsweek,* for example, reach at most one in ten Americans, a kind of national superculture of "opinion leaders." The audience for cinema has also shrunk to about one in ten Americans, of the same professional, mobile type. So also with the audience for "public affairs" television, the documentaries and shows like *Meet the Press* and *Face the Nation:* audiences for the latter are believed to represent eleven million viewers and are believed to be composed of "opinion leaders." The makers of mass television aim for the more affluent adults, ages twenty-one to forty-nine, on the assumption that such "demographics" promise the largest proportion of the high consumers. In a word, it is in the interest of several national elites, both political and commercial, to bring about a kind of standardization.

In addition, classic prejudices of region, religion, and class tend to concentrate the interests of scholars on certain elite cultures in America, with less proportionate consideration of cultures of lower status. For example, although fundamentalist and evangelical peoples form easily the largest segment of American Protestantism, the number of studies of their way of life, experiences, and beliefs is far smaller than that of the minority Protestant traditions of higher social status: the more "liberal" Protestants of the Northeastern upper class. Catholics are not alone in suffering from relative scholarly neglect.

The second prejudice arises among Catholics themselves. Emerging from the relative segregation of the Catholic ghetto so often described in

the literature of the 1950s and early 1960s, many educated and influential Catholics have been busy in the process of "Americanization."
Vatican II gave them an explicit directive to "enter the modern world."
Many eagerly looked beyond church reform and the needs of the Catholic
community to enter upon the more general American struggle for justice,
peace, and social reform. "Out of the chancery into city hall." "Away
from the Vatican to concern over the Pentagon." These might have been
the mottoes of the time. (I would characterize my own work of the 1960s
as aiming, in general, in this direction.) One may trace this movement of
interest in the pages of *The Commonweal* and the *National Catholic
Reporter,* and in the careers of such disparate symbolic persons as Daniel
Callahan, Garry Wills, Wilfrid Sheed, Daniel and Philip Berrigan,
Jacqueline Grennan, Corita Kent, and countless others.[9] In every
religious community, in every college setting, in every diocese, one may
trace the movement of interest, passion, and career choice from a focus
within the church to a focus on the world. Many, indeed, left their
religious vocations; many, too, left the church. Among the thousands
who gave leadership in the struggles of the world while remaining
Catholics, moreover, one may also trace a remarkable change in basic
symbolism, in the sources of their intellectual nourishment, and in their
style of life. It would not be too much, I think, to choose a word for this
spiritual movement, and to refer to it as the "Protestantizing" of
Catholic consciousness.

Reinhold Niebuhr[10] and other Protestant writers frequently noted that
the Catholic tradition had a much stronger sense of social justice than did
the Protestant tradition. The Protestant tradition excelled by virtue of its
exceedingly high emphasis on the individual. The movement of "the
Social Gospel" was directed toward compensating for this weakness (and
this excellence) among American Protestants. Protestants did, however,
have very high traditions of social "reform," of appeal to "conscience,"

9. For a critical view, see James Hitchcock, *The Decline and Fall of Radical Catholicism*
(New York: Herder and Herder, 1971). For a partisan account, see Garry Wills, *Bare Ruined
Choirs* (New York: Doubleday, 1971). For a sympathetic historical overview, see David
O'Brien, *The Renewal of American Catholicism* (New York: Oxford, 1972). Two bench-
marks for measuring the later mood are Daniel Callahan's *The Mind of the Catholic Lay-
man* (New York: Scribner's, 1963), and *Honesty in the Church* (New York: Scribner's,
1965).

10. See Reinhold Niebuhr, *Man's Nature and His Communities* (New York: Scribner's,
1965). This book is an account of how Niebuhr fared "in adjusting the original Protestant
heritage of individualism and perfectionism," and how he changed "from a purely
Protestant viewpoint to an increasing sympathy for the two other great traditions of Western
culture, Jewish and Catholic," pp. 15–16.

and of commitment to the "the Protestant principle" of protest against all finite powers.

In America, these Protestant traditions had an ironic side. For the true powers of America, both in symbolic status and in institutional supremacy, were unchallengeably Protestant. Thus the role of Protestant social protest was often, in effect, a way of "legitimating" existing Protestant power and giving it a strongly moralistic rhetoric. The "enlightened" Protestant upper class was traditionally rather quick to adopt, after a period of initial resistance, the moral appeals of its reformers. One can look at the magnificent structures of Union Theological Seminary, and the divinity schools at Harvard, Yale, Princeton, and Chicago and see how this ironic double thrust functioned. The architecture of such places announced considerable social, cultural, and political power—virtually unchallengeable power. Meanwhile, the voices of many who worked within them were "radical" voices. Such radicalism seemed to challenge Protestant power, but in its latent function was to give Protestant power a moral legitimacy, a moral direction, even, but above all a highly moral tone. By comparison, the Jewish Theological Seminary and the local Catholic seminaries lacked all status and any semblance of comparable social, political, or cultural power. (And when they try to compete—as in the awe-inspiring St. Charles Seminary in Philadelphia—there is a hint of vulgarity and unreality.)

Catholics and Jews were at a double disadvantage. From the Protestant moralists, they learned of their own lesser moral vision and less high-minded instinct for reform. From the real powers of the Protestant establishment, local and national, they learned of their true position on the rungs of decision-making. In an ironic way, Protestant moralists have been, and remain, even in their protests and even when they purport to "speak the truth to power," agents of Protestant social power. We are lucky, of course, that Protestant power has had so deep a concern for moral legitimacy; not all elites in this world do.

Meanwhile, however, Catholics who leaped into the general social activism of the late sixties and seventies were soon drawn out into a social process they could scarcely control (or even recognize). Increasingly, the texts they read and the leadership cadres they joined were governed by Protestant rhetoric and Protestant styles. Clergy and Laymen Concerned about Vietnam, for example, like so many other ecumenical programs of social action, while seeking out Catholic and Jewish participation, and being nourished by new traditions of insight and articulation, remained transparently and predominantly "Protestant" in style. We are all so close to the Protestant style—we swim in it as fish in a sea—that it is difficult to express it in words. We cannot hold it at a distance.

Protestant writers themselves have been exceedingly critical of the national atmosphere, at once civil and religious, which Protestant America and American Protestantism had together created.[11] In a manifesto prepared in 1935, *The Church against the World*, Francis P. Miller wrote: "The domestication of the Protestant community in the United States within the framework of the national culture has progressed as far as any western land. The degradation of the American Protestant church is as complete as the degradation of any other national Protestant church." In the same book, Reinhold Niebuhr warned that God could choose another community, outside the Anglo-American community, if the latter failed him. Philip Schaff had written in 1855: "I doubt whether the moral influence of Christianity and of Protestantism has more deeply and widely affected any nation, than it has the Anglo-Saxon." Horace Bushnell wrote after the Civil War: "We are the grand experiment of Protestantism! Yes, we—it is our most peculiar destiny—we are set to show, by a new and unheard of career of national greatness and felicity, the moral capabilities and all the beneficent fruits of Christianity and the Protestant faith."

In the twentieth century, Protestant writers have been concerned to teach Protestant America a sense of tragedy, irony, and realism. Reinhold Niebuhr could upbraid "the foolish children of light" and his students could agree; yet the century-old temptations would arise again and again. In America's relation with the Third World, for example, Niebuhr explicitly warned against the Marxist view that all disparity of wealth between nations is due to exploitation.[12] His view is current now; it was voiced often, even by leading American Protestants and students of Niebuhr, at the World Council of Churches meeting in Nairobi in 1975. Ironically, too, protests against the "domestication" of Protestantism are couched in a highly Protestant language. Both left-wing and right-wing political theologians appeal to specifically Protestant values, in specifically Protestant ways.

There is great diversity within Protestantism, as Martin Marty and

---

11. I am indebted to Martin Marty, *Righteous Empire: The Protestant Experience in America* (New York: Dial, 1970), for the citations in this paragraph. See his pp. 16, 88, and 234–35. Marty's discussion of the American Protestant character, in its varieties, is a classic.

12. Reinhold Niebuhr, *The Irony of American History* (New York: Scribner's, 1952), pp. 115–16. See also his *The Children of Light and the Children of Darkness* (New York: Scribner's, 1944), p. 11.

Sidney Ahlstrom have made plain.[13] To define a style of vision as "Protestant" is, then, to designate an ideal type on a high level of generality—a set of perceptions that strikes an outsider as distinctively Protestant, indeed, distinctively *American* Protestant. Protestant critics frequently single out some such perceptions in self-reproach; so these cannot be solely figments of Catholic or Jewish misperception. There is a way of perceiving things that is distinctively Protestant; even those Protestants who try to transcend their own particularity nonetheless exhibit it. Each of us, in each religion and culture, is similarly particular. It is entirely human to be so; no apologies are in order. "Here I stand," Martin Luther said, "I can do no other." Since all agree that Protestant Christianity is the single most determinative cultural force on the American character, it may be useful to describe how that force is felt by those to whom it is not native. Here, then, are the three components I distinguish as "the Protestant way."

(1) The American Protestant style places an extraordinary degree of weight upon "moral" factors in social situations. No doubt, moral factors are always present and must always be respected. Still, it is one thing to begin with the moral impulse, to concentrate initially and throughout upon the moral issues, and to govern one's actions more or less solely by moral imperatives. It is another thing to try to grasp the structures of community interests, powers, histories, and entanglements, and then try to reach a compromise that moves actual events a little closer to the moral ideal. There is a difference between holding a "moral" protest against the war in Vietnam because it is "immoral," and trying to bring the war to an end with the widest possible participation and the least social damage to America and to Vietnam. There is a difference between hating the war because one doesn't understand it and doesn't want one's sons to go, and calling the war "immoral." Catholic politics is called "machine politics." Protestants try as often as possible to work under the flag of "reform" and "morality." The Protestant style in America is to use the word "moral" as a club by which to undermine the standing of others. By presenting one's own interests as "moral," one realizes them as effortlessly as possible. (Whenever I hear the word "moral" from a Protestant, I can't help feeling that he's out to get me, even if I don't immediately see how.)

(2) The American Protestant style also has a manifest anti-institutional

13. For my own discussion of five versions of the Protestant civil religions in America, see *Choosing Our King* (New York: Macmillan, 1973), pp. 103–59. See Marty's and Ahlstrom's essays in this volume.

bias. (Its latent function is less anti-institutional than appearances suggest.) The genius of the British is never to abandon an institution, even if its purposes must be altered in time. But the British who came to America were the dissidents, the enthusiasts, the puritans, the saints ("the children of light.") The British distrust the individual and respect institutions. Many Anglo-Americans, by contrast, tend to believe that the individual left to himself is virtuous; they find institutions burdensome, corrupt, and inadequate. Outside the South, Protestants tend to be Republican, and as Republicans they are accustomed to a fiercely antigovernment, anti-Washington, and even antipolitics rhetoric. The Protestant tendency, as Rollo May has put it, is to desire a world innocent of power and politics. Even as Democrats, Northern Protestants inherit a rhetoric that flays institutions and idealizes individuals—that attacks the party, the city machines, the organization, the labor unions. Recent public targets for this traditional animus have been the Congress, the Presidency, the Pentagon, the FBI, the CIA, and large corporations. The American public suffers orgies of purification, which the more sober British regard with a kind of horror. A quest for moral purity hardly appropriate for individuals is here applied to institutions. Tolerance for a certain amount of corruption and inadequacy, elsewhere a principle of wisdom and maturity, is here taken as a sign of weakness and dishonesty. In this country, as other nations (even the British) note with trepidation, the itch for purity knows no bounds. Anti-institutional perfectionism nourishes this itch.

(3) The American Protestant style is, finally, a style of revival—of moral spasm. Intense moral outrage leads to hurried rituals of reformation, ends in quick forgetfulness. Our national lust for moral purity, combined with immaturity with respect to institutions, is based on such unrealistic expectations of the human race that it is not supportable, over the long run. For this reason, American popular concern runs in spurts. Great excitement, great ballyhoo, then boredom. In many of our cycles of "reform," very little is actually changed. So much energy is spent on moral feelings that attention cannot be sustained. Laws of power, self-interest, and institutional necessity require practical and lasting compromises. Striving for purity, the children of light often reject those modest compromises that might bring small but real and long-term relief.

In *Moral Man and Immoral Society* (1932), Reinhold Niebuhr summed up his objections to the prevailing spirit, emphasizing in his foreword to the paperback edition (1960): "The central thesis was, and is, that the

Liberal Movement both religious and secular seemed to be unconscious of the basic difference between the morality of collectives, whether races, classes or nations. This difference . . . refutes many still prevalent moralistic approaches to the political order.''[14]

Sometimes, definitions are best drawn by facing their opposites. One opposite to the Protestant style would be the wit and wisdom of Mister Dooley, or the sage advice of New York's Mr. George W. Plunkitt:[15] "When a fellow tells you, Mr. Dooley says, 'Tain't the money, it's the principle,' it's the money."

Thus, to assert that many Catholics entering the struggles for social justice in our society are rapidly becoming "Americanized" or, more precisely, "Protestantized," is to assert something specific; viz., that one sees in their attitudes, speech, and behavior: (a) a single-minded focus on moral factors in complex matters, (b) an anti-institutional bias, and (c) dependence on evanescent emotions of moral outrage. For this reason, "apathy" and "gradualism" are their great spiritual enemies. They depend on rapid changes wrested in the heat of moral passion. Such attitudes run quite counter to the historical experience of the Eastern Europeans, the Italians, the Irish, the Germans, the Spanish-speaking, and the other major Catholic ethnic groups. Yet such attitudes need to be learned in this country. They have been learned, chiefly, from high Protestant role models. Entering into the secular world in great numbers from about 1965 onward, Catholic activists took their cues from Harvey Cox, William Stringfellow, William Coffin, and others. Abandoning much from their own traditions, they won high status in the competition to be counted as "moral."

To be sure, certain Catholic predispositions made this transition both easy and (almost) inevitable. Not wishing to identify with less highly educated or less Americanized Catholics, many of our best and brightest were all too willing to find a new moralism, a new orthodoxy, as simple and clear as the moral theology they had known in their youth. Their long struggles against authoritarianism and bureaucracy in the church gave them a wealth of metaphor to transpose into a fresh anti-institutional bias in their struggles against the powers of state. And, finally, their own traditions of saintly authenticity, witness, and even

14. Reinhold Niebuhr, *Moral Man and Immoral Society* (New York: Scribner's, 1932, 1960), p. ix.

15. See, e.g., William L. Riordon, *Plunkitt of Tammany Hall* (New York: McClure, 1905).

martyrdom were all too easily transposed into the categories of moral outrage and moral protest. "Taking a moral stand" became a fashionable way of behaving, almost everywhere.

On some issues, it is true, Catholics also have been moralistic in politics, as in the banning of certain motion pictures, protests against abortion, and other "moral issues." Such "moralism," however, has three distinctive differences: (a) Its origin lies in ecclesiastical positions, (b) enunciated on the basis of *specific "moral teachings,"* and (c) applied to *particular kinds of acts.* The parallel here is with the Protestant effort to prohibit the production or use of alcoholic beverages. In such cases, the moral teachings of one or more ecclesiastical traditions are imposed on a pluralistic society. Two kinds of "moralism" are involved: first, the imposition of a particular moral view on all others; and, second, the interpretation of certain kinds of acts in a way that gives salience to certain of their aspects, without equal concern to other of their aspects. For example, the destructive possibilities of alcoholism are stressed, or the degrading aspects of pornography, or the destructive aspects of abortion. Focusing on these, opponents try to ban liquor, or pornography, or abortion. By contrast, proponents of alcohol use, access to pornography, or the practice of abortions do not usually deny the destructive aspects; they give other aspects greater salience.

When John F. Kennedy first went to the White House, an aide was pleased to note that there was nothing Catholic about him at all. By contrast, Sargent Shriver is an intense and self-conscious Catholic. Yet, in an odd way, Shriver is not perceived by the public as Catholic; he seems almost "Protestant" in his speech and way of defining issues. Why is this? Shriver is an upbeat, cheerful, optimistic, idealistic public figure. In his way of perceiving, the world is an intensely moral place, a realm in which idealism and voluntarism and moral concern have weight. Here is a moralism of a different sort. It infuses one's whole attitude toward life. This is the sort of moralism that seems to outsiders specifically Protestant. (Obviously, it is not limited to Protestants.) The common accusation against Cardinal Spellman, Mayor Daley, or even John Kennedy (until posthumously idealized) has been that they were pragmatists, who dealt in "hardball" and "clout," and to whom straight moral considerations were secondary. This indeed is the traditional—and, I would hold, proper—attitude toward politics. Politics is mainly concerned with judgments about power and interests; secondarily, it is concerned with moving power and interests in a moral direction (or, more modestly, in such a way as to diminish the number of immoral consequences). It is quite "Catholic," not in an ecclesiastical but in a cultural sense, to be uncomfortable with the word "moral" too early in political discourse. It is quite "Protestant" to give the word "moral" high salience in such discourse.[16]

Analogous pressures are felt by American Jews in the process of Americanizing. For many Jews, socialism on the one hand and the Enlightenment doctrine of the perfectibility of man on the other have been carriers of a special passion for sainthood. Glorious battles for losing causes, in the name of grand universal principles, are the very stuff of a certain vein of Jewish moral and political life. Let Irving Howe, Howard Zinn, Arthur Waskow, Richard Barnet, and others stand for the traditions I am here sketching: traditions of the secular saint. Other Jews worry about the unreality and ultimate self-destructiveness of unchecked moral passion; they worry about the "Americanizing" and "Protestantizing" of Jewish realism. They worry about "moralism" and "utopianism" run wild. One thinks here of Nathan Glazer, David Riesman, Daniel Bell, Norman Podhoretz, Irving Kristol, Emil Fackenheim, Ben Wattenberg, and many others of the Right and Left.

Among American Protestants, too, a vigorous tradition opposes the dominant tendencies of Protestant culture; Edward Banfield, David Armor, Robert Nisbet, the late Richard Hofstadter, and others are among its leading figures. Reinhold Niebuhr built a major part of his career on an effort to chasten the three characteristics of the national Protestant psyche mentioned above. It was the misfortune of the recent Catholic explosion into American public life in the last ten years, however, that the work of Reinhold Niebuhr had gone into eclipse, and that blown by the winds both of black rhetoric and antiwar fervor, the weakest features of Protestant social criticism were once again in full sail. Martin Marty's classic history of the American Protestant temper is called *Righteous Empire;* the motif has been changed only slightly in the new formulation: *Righteous Opposition to Empire.*

An excess of righteousness sooner or later stimulates the return of realism. Three realities enforce present discontent. First, the Protestantizing spirit is out of tune with human nature and social reality; the latter assert themselves. Second, the times have become more dangerous, both internationally and domestically; mere righteousness can no longer be indulged. Third, the latent function of moralism is to strengthen certain elites; moralism always masks a power struggle between elites. Let me elaborate. The partisans of "the new politics" want

16. For a larger discussion of moralism, see Novak, *Choosing Our King,* pp. 57–102.

to regain the presidency and to control both domestic and foreign policy. Michael Harrington calls them "the constituency of conscience." When a fella says, "Tain't the power, it's conscience," it's the power. A rigorous analysis of who will pay the costs—and for which programs—is now powerful in public opinion. Many recognize that those out of power righteously attack the ins; the ins, too, cover themselves with righteousness. The politics of righteousness is a smokescreen. Many Americans are learning this the hard way. A case from my own experience may be illuminating.

In 1969, I published *A Theology for Radical Politics*[17] and said that I wished "to bring a radical Christian theology to the support of the student movement of the present generation." I still hold to the values I held in that book; its analyses of person, community, wisdom-in-act, evil, humanism, etc., are deeply Catholic and deeply traditional. Its explicit polemical target is the same as that of the present essay, there expressed as "The Myth of the Pure Protester" (pp. 49–51). The worst fears I had as I wrote came to pass: that the mood of that time might pass (p. 79), that the fuse of activism might be unconscionably short (p. 81), that "the moral pretension and class snobbery in the purity which many of the young try to maintain in themselves" (p. 124) might prevent them from overcoming their "class prejudice" and coming "to sympathetic understanding with the lower middle class, with firemen, gas station attendants, meter men" (p. 125). I would today revise many opinions about American society I expressed in that book. In particular, I no longer trust the moral integrity of the Left. I should have seen earlier how deep the class snobbery was, how rooted in power and wealth, and how self-serving its use of moral language was. I should have been more cynical, and even more Catholic than I was trying to be. Above all, I failed to see how useful the "youth culture" would be both to the media and to the traditional establishment. Soon, *The New Yorker* was to run "The Greening of America." "Radical chic" was in full swing. John D. Rockefeller III was writing about "The Second American Revolution," and every bank in America was making its new international theme "interdependence." The moral language of the counterculture was a perfect mirror of traditional Protestant values: "Do your thing," high moral outrage as a cover for self-interest, and contempt for the less moral "pigs" of the lower classes.

The net impact of the student movement of the sixties was, I did note,

17. Michael Novak, *A Theology for Radical Politics* (New York: Herder and Herder, 1969).

to reintroduce the word "moral" back into politics (p. 32), after a brief pragmatic-realistic interlude (1950–65) in our national history. It did not seem to me then that the pragmatic-realistic center of American politics would collapse so swiftly. It seemed to me that the new moral vision would fuse with the well-established realism, giving a new direction and new energy to basic American traditions and institutions, carrying them closer to their always unfulfilled promise. Instead, many leaders in fashionable industries—from journalism and social action to television and cinema, from advertising and publishing to academic life—began to be "greened." There began an orgy of condemnation of our institutions and way of life; there began fashions in hedonism and ideological conformity such as I had not had in mind at all. It was as though Reinhold Niebuhr had never vanquished the moralistic streak in American politics; it burst back in full fever.[18]

What begins as a minority vision in American life can, abetted by the media, soon become a rage. What begins as critical thought ends as fashionable and subtly coercive ideology. What began, often enough, among Catholics like Tom Hayden and Mario Savio, and Jews like Michael Rossman and Mark Rudd, ended by reinstalling the moralism that is the nation's most corrupting and persistent vice.

I now see a second fault in *A Theology for Radical Politics*. "The enemy in America, then," I wrote, "is the tyrannical and indifferent majority: the good people, the churchgoers, the typical Americans . . ." (p. 79). The intention of that sentence was not so harsh as it now appears. For example, I described white working class people as "the most neglected Americans, scorned by the intellectuals, scorned by the mass media, frightened of the rising blacks and the unemployed" (p. 125). "We will have to look for men of politics, and for political parties," I wrote, "that can speak to them as well as to ourselves." Still, I did not then sufficiently mark out the differences among the many Americans in this "majority"—regional differences, ethnic differences, differences in income, and education, and suffering, and need. They may be the "enemies" of an elite, but in a democracy they cannot be enemies: they are us. In the years that followed, those last pages of that book moved into the center of my thought.

The Catholic People

An important part of this majority is "the Catholic quarter." Most Catholics are urban. They vote in proportionally high numbers. They are

---

18. See my "Needing Niebuhr Again," *Commentary* 54 (September 1972), pp. 52–62.

concentrated in key electoral states. Tending to be independent in their voting, they constitute a huge swing vote. The representatives they send to Congress and to the Senate usually are among the nation's most progressive—senators like McCarthy, Hart, Kennedy, Mansfield, Biden, Muskie, Tunney, and others. The Catholic quarter is not liberal in the way that Northeastern Protestants are liberal, or in the ways that Jews are liberal. On issues of life-style and "social" questions—like marijuana use, the treatment of criminals, abortion, and environmental protection—Catholics are seldom eager to be leaders; but opinion polls show them surprisingly tolerant and open to the values of others, generous and enlightened. Such issues as these, however, are not *their* priorities. Their families are hurting. Their values are ignored or scorned. Even so, their profile both in public opinion polls and in voting behavior is more liberal, by far, than those of Protestants or of the nation as a whole.[19]

Still, a discouraging split has opened up between Catholic intellectual elites, especially those on the more liberal side of the spectrum, and the Catholic people. In Massachusetts, Senator Edward Kennedy appears to care more about his support at Harvard than about his support in South Boston. The *National Catholic Reporter* and *The Commonweal* seem to accept the definition of issues as it is forged by opinion leaders whose roots are Protestant or Jewish; seldom do they add to national debates a fresh Catholic wisdom not to be heard elsewhere. They follow; they do not lead. The perspective and the rhetoric of many Catholic social activists owe far more to paperback books and magazines of the general culture than to a distinctively Catholic realism. They imitate; they do not innovate. The project of becoming "American and Catholic," it seems, has become altogether one-sided. Catholic intellectual elites are giving much evidence of their ability as "Americans," but they show too little differentiation as Catholics. In particular, they tend to treat the ordinary Catholic people as their enemy. Many seem to want to dissociate themselves from the mass of the Catholic people. There do not seem to be many efforts to work from within the people, articulating a new voice and direction for the nation's politics.

There seem to be three reasons. First, in the long struggle between "conservatives" and "liberals" in the church, the latter, in winning at the Council, seemed to weary of the conflict and to seek new allies and interests outside Catholic circles. Second, a number of Catholic leaders have studied at Protestant divinity schools, in such a way that they have had little or no advanced training directly in their own traditions. Even in

19. Cf. Hanna, "Religion and Politics: The Influence of Catholicism on American Politics."

studying Catholic materials, they have done so from a Protestant perspective (Rosemary Ruether's thought, for example, owes much to left-wing traditions of the Reformation). Thirdly, in ecumenical alliances with Protestants in social action, Protestant perspectives, language, and styles have generally prevailed. Even in breaking from ecumenical groups like Clergy and Laymen Concerned about Vietnam, as Daniel Berrigan did, many on the Catholic left found themselves competing for attention in the media according to symbolic rules fairly well established in the Protestant style. There were, of course, distinctive Catholic touches—a sense of ritual and liturgy, for example, and a rhetoric of almost sacramental witness. For a while, the Catholic left was even more "radical" and more "colorful" than the usual forms of Protestant protest. But the symbolic language was Barthian, stark, absolutist. The traditional Irish Catholic antagonism toward American Protestant establishments was transmuted into a highly moral protest against War, Death, Evil.[20] It was almost if Catholics had suddenly become Quakers. The traditional Catholic sense of social texture, its realism, its tolerance of ambiguity, and even its prudence were held in some disdain. The Catholic left saw itself not so much as an organizer of a Catholic majority against the war, but rather as a voice of condemnation, a judgment, a prophetic witness. The Protestant spirit had triumphed in the bosom of Catholicism.

Issues of the Near Future

Suppose for a moment now that the strongest massive constituency for progressive politics awaits without leadership in a place in which the Catholic liberal leadership seldom looks—among the masses of the Catholic people. What, then, might be done to bring Catholic elite and Catholic people back together again?

Politics in a democracy is essentially and in the long term a process of building an electoral majority. Such majorities, when well and deeply based, have a massive daily influence on every aspect of democratic politics. They affect the decisions of city councils, state legislators, the Congress, and the administration in Washington. They affect long lists of appointed officers in the military, the justice department, and the agencies of health and welfare. It seems to some that progress through the

20. See my essay on the Berrigans in John Raines (ed.), *Conspiracy* (New York: Harper & Row, 1975). See also Francine du Plessix Gray, *Divine Disobedience* (New York: Knopf, 1970) and William O'Rourke *The Harrisburg 7 and the New Catholic Left* (New York: Thomas Y. Crowell, 1972) for sympathetic but revealing accounts.

mechanisms of democracy is too slow and too partial. The politics of witness and outrage (and of crisis management) is always tempting and sometimes necessary. Yet in the long haul it is those moral forces that marshal an electoral majority that most affect the millions of decisions made by government officials every day. Government is a creature of habit and routine; it moves rather like a huge aircraft carrier in the ocean, hardly able to make rapid, sharp turns, not capable of great speed. (Indeed, this is one plausible argument for minimizing the size and role of government in human affairs.) For large-scale and national movement, nonetheless, control of the government can mean a difference of significant degree both in direction and in pace.

The experiences of the Catholic people, both in America and preceding their coming to America, make them an especially valuable resource for progressive politics. Most of them have been underdogs; most have been poor; most have experienced various forms of social disdain and discrimination. In addition, many have a taste for the rough-and-tumble of politics. Catholics tend to be tough, reasonably cynical, down-to-earth people. Economic issues matter to many of them. By hard work and thrifty habits, they have raised their median income a few points above the national average.[21] Indeed, their statistical profile is of a people heavily bunched near the median—not too many, it appears, burst high above the median. They might be called "middle class." But this term is deceptive. There is a great difference between those with high education and professional status, and those who have solid incomes but few pretensions: between, say, readers of the *New York Times* and readers of the *Daily News*. Many are in the predicament of earning, say, $18,000 a year (from salaries of both husband and wife), which is too much to qualify their children for college scholarships but not enough to pay tuition for three or four children. They are not alone in this condition, of course.

On opposition to the war in Vietnam, working people in general, and Catholics in particular, were *more opposed* than persons in the more affluent and educated classes.[22] This stands to reason. Their sons were not in college, and not eligible for deferment.

On racial matters, Catholics are *more* supportive of various black causes, including busing, than the population as a whole.[23] On the other

21. See Andrew Greeley, Report to the Ford Foundation, 1975.
22. See Hamilton, *Restraining Myths;* also Greeley, *Ethnicity,* and *American Catholics: A Social Portrait.*
23. Cf. Greeley, *Ethnicity.*

hand, when pressed unfairly by an affluent and moralistic upper class that does not share the burden, as in Boston and also in Detroit, specific groups of Catholics are defiant, tough, and resistant to what they perceive as vast injustice.

In political terms, the Democratic left tends to talk about issues in a language redolent of the interests and symbols of the academic suburbs— towns like Lexington and Concord near Boston, and like Evanston near Chicago. The Republican right tends to talk about issues in a language redolent of the interests and symbols of *laissez-faire* corporate barons. In this sense, the interests and symbols of most Catholics seldom find a perceptive and accurate political voice. The terms "liberal" and "conservative" apply most accurately to the conflict between the two wings of the upper 10 percent of Americans by education, status, and income. The political dialogue seldom seems wholly relevant to most working people, or to those within those elites who do not define themselves in the traditional Anglo-American terms. A distinctive Catholic voice in politics is seldom heard today from those who define the issues and symbols of national politics.

Until recently, American Catholicism has had a claim on its laity hardly matched in any nation in the world. No group of Catholics in the world has built an equal to the American Catholic school system. Few can match the fidelity of the American Catholic laity to mass and the sacraments. Often this extraordinary church attendance is attributed to imitation of the churchgoing of the Protestants; but since Catholic churchgoing has exceeded Protestant by a considerable margin, this interpretation is weak. A far more plausible explanation seems to be the *anti*-Catholicism of Protestants, on the one hand, and, on the other, the genuine social, political, and economic services centered around the Catholic parish. Such services were not organized by the clergy or the parish *per se,* but in common speech Catholics usually identified even their neighborhoods by their parishes: "In Gate of Heaven," they would reply, when asked where in the city they lived. The city "machines" were organized on a local base.

In this way, so to put it, the earthy symbolism of the Catholic sacramental system found its objective correlative in political fact. It took sacrifice to put up the churches in which the liturgy was celebrated. Participation in the rites was in itself an almost political statement. Thus the strong sacramental system—the "eating" of the Body of Christ, the novenas, the parish missions, the processions, the confessions, baptisms, marriages, and funerals—these embodied not only personal piety but also, as it were, political and social solidarity. There was in the American Catholic immigrant experience—and there still is—a most potent "political theology." Thus, to emphasize the cultural and political dimensions of Catholic life, so often neglected in theological reflection, is not to slight the power and effectiveness of the sacramental system. Rather, it is merely to stress that system's operative effects; it *was* realized, as it is supposed to be, in the daily fabric of the people's lives. It is one more measure of the "Protestantizing" of American Catholicism that Catholic parishes, bishops, and theologians have neglected in recent years the concrete political and economic needs of the people they serve: so many parishes abandoned, so many schools closed, so many neighborhoods devastated by economic and social forces. This neglect may be as responsible as any other factor in the widely noted falling off in church attendance among American Catholics. When the church is "merely" a system of piety, it is unfaithful to its own sacramental realism.

For three generations, however, Catholic political elites (Mary Hanna describes the condition) have faced the need to find acceptance among Protestants and others. Often, they have had to define themselves in ways that set them apart from the Catholic people. Such pressures, while subtle, are very strong. The impulse to do so is, in part, healthy and creative. It is by responding to new cultural milieux and to new challenges that a tradition grows, expands, and incorporates new enlivening materials. In part, however, the process tends to create a class of "Uncle Toms" and "Aunt Tomasinas," acceptable to the larger world, detached from their communities of origin.

The nation needs a politics that grows out of the experiences of ordinary people, including the Catholic people, who are so urban. The advent of such a politics depends upon a greater fund of historical and sociological knowledge than we now have. The experiences of the American Catholic people are diverse, powerful, and full of political significance. That they are so poorly known, even to ourselves, is an enormous political disadvantage. Take, for example, the Catholics of the Philadelphia region. Who are they? What have their family histories been? How do their present situation and their past experiences compare with those of what E. Digby Baltzell has called "the Protestant establishment" of the Main Line?[24] With those of the Philadelphia Jews? With those of the Philadelphia blacks, studied in 1944 by E. Franklin Frazier and by others since? How do Catholics stand in the local

24. E. Digby Baltzell, *The Protestant Establishment* (New York: Random House Vintage Books, 1966).

law schools, the medical schools, and at the prestigious universities? How do they stand in the corporate world? In civic institutions? In the Philadelphia media? Who best articulates what lies in their hearts, whether in literature, or in religion, or in politics?

It is impossible for a progressive politician in Pennsylvania to carry this state without coming out of Philadelphia's Catholic wards with huge majorities; how do progressive politicians treat Philadelphia's Catholics? Approximately 33 percent of the population of Pennsylvania is Slavic or Eastern European. Are the Slavs represented in comparable proportion at every level of decision-making, visibility, and power in this state? And if not, why not? Is an Italian name worth as much as an Anglo-Saxon name?

There is an assumption that ethnicity no longer matters in American society. Then why are positions of influence distributed so unequally? Why are some misrepresented groups championed by "human rights commissions," while others are not? Is this due to a conscious desire to be divisive?

Issues of deep concern to many Catholic people include, perhaps above all, (1) the condition of the *family*.[25] Among Catholics, morality and ethics are not so much individualist as they are familial. Who analyzes morality in familial terms? What study groups or research centers try to work out governmental and corporate programs that would strengthen families?

(2) *Neighborhoods* are a second major concern. Some neighborhoods are stable, strong, mutually supportive, and happy; others are deteriorating, broken, and entangled in various pathologies.[26] What makes the difference? What are the conditions that differentiate them? Outside the family, the freedom and peace and prosperity of the neighborhood are the conditions that most give sense to one's life. If physical safety is not guaranteed, elementary civil rights—mobility, safety of life and limb—have been taken away.

(3) *Jobs* are a third concern. Without a reliable and dependable economic base, families cannot long survive. Without jobs, the elemental dignity of economic independence is not available.

(4) A social system that rewards *integration of the races*, rather than a

---

25. See my "The Family out of Favor," *Harper's Magazine* (April 1976), pp. 37–46.

26. Two study groups that gather and disseminate useful information on neighborhoods are the National Center for Urban Ethnic Affairs, Washington, D.C., and the Institute on Pluralism and Group Identity, the American Jewish Committee, New York, New York.

system that (as at present) punishes it, is essential in multiracial cities like Philadelphia. Where are the study groups at federal, state, and regional levels that are devising a healthy, nonpunitive system of integration?

(5) Finally, in *foreign policy,* I believe that most Catholics have a distinctive outlook seldom tapped by intellectual commentators or political leaders. Many Catholics—from Eastern Europe, from Latin America, from Ireland, and elsewhere—have families trapped in real, concrete suffering. They are not partisans of "cold war." Neither are they partisans of isolationism. They do have a sense that the world is a dangerous, corrupt, and even evil place, where armies do indeed "clash by night." They recognize that the dreams of the nineteenth century—of a rising tide of democracy in the world—have not been realized. Nations that have since 1945 ceased to be colonies are now, by and large, economically insecure tyrannies. The circle of nations in which civil rights obtain is very small, even shrinking. The United States is the shield of whatever freedoms do exist in the world; many Catholics come from nations in which their families overseas experience far fewer liberties than their relatives here. So it is difficult for many Catholics to side glibly with the prevailing liberal-radical assaults on the CIA, the FBI, and other institutions of this land. The revulsion against Vietnam seems to have led many on the left to swing to the other end of the pendulum's arc: to become anti-American, and to see in America only militarism, counterrevolution, and imperialism. That America can be evil—can make mistakes and, more than that, be implicated in cruel and evil deeds— Catholics have no doubt. Such falls sadden them. They do not make them lose their grip on hard realities. Most of the regimes of the world, socialist or antisocialist, are tyrannous, corrupt, and unjust. To deal with them is to dirty one's hands. There is no way to purify the world. The United States must deal with the world as it is.

That is why Daniel Patrick Moynihan as ambassador to the United Nations made such a deep impression on the national consciousness. Moynihan grasped essentials clearly. Whatever the faults of the United States, faults he never denied, this nation does represent in world affairs the best hope of the world's material and spiritual well-being. No economic system is so well organized, or draws on more highly developed skills and productive habits. We consume a large share of the world's resources; we produce far more than we consume. Even if India's growth rate would be double ours from now until the end of the century, by the year 2000 India's position would be even further distant from ours than it is at present.[27] So it is naive to believe that other parts of the world can catch up to the dynamic headstart of the North Atlantic nations even in the lifetimes of our children. It is not even certain that our nation and other free nations will survive the worldwide trend toward tyranny and subversion. "Liberation" movements in the world seldom liberate. "Revolutions" habitually result in changes in tyrannical elites.

The Catholic people are a great reservoir of concern for the rest of the world. Most Catholics have families elsewhere. Catholics also have traditions of cynicism, tragedy, and irony that make them skeptical of a merely moral language in international affairs. The rhetoric of this nation's liberal elites awakens traditional suspicions in the Catholic public. The recent rhetoric about interdependence, justice, peace, and liberation, accordingly, has a hollow ring. Beautiful words, which do not match what is happening on this very sinful planet. A rhetoric more chastened by irony, tragedy, and cynicism cleaves closer to the truth.

It is not certain that this nation and its experiment with self-government can survive for another century. We know now that it runs against the tides of history. The first task of the United States, it appears, is survival. Its second, in the words of Camus, is a modest task: to diminish "at least by a little the number of those who suffer." The peoples of the world are members of America's family not only metaphorically, but also in flesh and blood; Americans are their migrant cousins. The destiny of Americans is not isolated from theirs. In a corrupt world, there is not much, often, Americans can do to help them. Yet the survival of the United States is indispensable to millions, as a vision of possibility. Every step this nation can take beyond that—in wisdom, justice, and equity—is a great gain both for them and for the fulfillment of America's aspirations.

The Catholic people did not come to this new nation solely for selfish and material reasons. They came here to increase the quantum of justice, liberty, equality, and self-government in the world. Having received much from America, the Catholic quarter has now the destiny to give back to the nation special Catholic gifts. High among these is a new and progressive realism in domestic and international affairs. May the days ahead find the Catholic people better known, better led, and better organized in the fulfillment of their high destiny than they find themselves today. Such an outcome will be beneficial, as well, to Protestants, to Jews, and to the nation.

27. Cf. Irving Kristol, *On the Democratic Idea in America* (New York: Harper Torch-books, 1973), p. 136.

Response

In 1654, twenty-three Jewish refugees fled the Portugese Inquisition in Recife, Brazil, and embarked on the French privateer *Saint Charles* to New Amsterdam where they petitioned for asylum and residence. At the wharf of the ostensibly "liberal" Dutch colony, the twenty-three Jewish "illegal aliens" were greeted by Governor Peter Stuyvesant and his Council who promptly ordered them to depart.

Jewish merchants in Holland, among them some major shareholders in the Dutch West India Company, supported their co-religionists' right to remain in New Netherlands, which was in fact seeking immigrants to help build the Dutch colony in the New World. Governor Stuyvesant pleaded vigorously against extending rights to the Jews. In October 1655, he wrote to the directors of the Dutch West India Company in Amsterdam, "Giving them (the Jews) liberty, we cannot refuse the Lutherans and the Papists."[1]

After repeated petitions and pressure from affluent Dutch Jews in Holland, this hapless group of Jewish men, women, and children were finally allowed to remain—the first Jewish immigrants to America. But they had to wage a continuous struggle for the minimal rights to engage in trade, to own property, to serve in the militia, and to gain citizenship. The rights to work at crafts, to hold public office, to build a synagogue, or to engage in public religious services were never won in New Amsterdam. These were to come later, after incessant struggle over decades by Jews in New York and then in every colony of the new nation.[2]

As Michael Novak demonstrates persuasively in his essay, nativist prejudices of anti-Catholicism and anti-Semitism run very deep in American culture. A Jew as well as a Catholic utters such a judgment, with evident ambivalences. On the one hand, it is a manifest truth that, despite the deep-seated intolerances, bigotries, and discriminations against non-Anglo-Saxon Protestant minorities throughout much of our nation's two-hundred-year history, both Catholic and Jewish communities have achieved what the Rev. Andrew Greeley has characterized in his latest book as "an ethnic miracle."[3]

1. Abraham J. Karp, *Golden Door to America—The Jewish Immigrant Experience* (New York: Penguin Books, 1976).

2. Rufus Learsi, *The Jews in America* (Cleveland: World, 1954).

3. Andrew Greeley, *An Ugly Little Secret: Anti-Catholicism in North America* (Kansas City: Sheed, Andrews and McMeel, 1977).

Contrary to the popular images promoted in the academic and media worlds that "the blue-collar ethnics" are illiterate, second-rate, and impoverished, the Reverend Greeley writes (as corroborated by Michael Novak in this essay):

> The eastern and southern European immigrants now have a higher college attendance rate than the national average for young people of college age. . . . In the space of a single generation, between 1945 and 1975, Poles and Italians have surpassed the national average in college attendance. (The Irish, incidentally, also surpassed the national average, and they did it in 1910.)
>
> Eastern and southern European immigrants not only earn more money than the national average for whites but also more than British Protestants. Those who could not assimilate have become successful. . . . Irish Catholics, for example, are the richest, the best educated, and the most occupationally successful of any Gentile group in American society. And in terms of income at least, the Italian Catholics are right behind them—and moving up fast.

Greeley concludes, "Reformers didn't manage to Americanize us in the public schools and . . . there is substantial evidence that it is precisely the strong values of home, family, and neighborhood that facilitated the educational, economic, and occupational success of the ethnics."[4]

As anyone conversant with the sociological literature knows, similar empirical evidence documents "the ethnic miracle" of American Jewry whose socio-economic status is at least comparable to that of Episcopalians and Presbyterians. The academic achievement of the Jewish community, which is the "secret" of Jewish mobility and attainment, is probably the highest of any religious-ethnic group in America.

In the face of such unparalleled historic achievement for Catholic and Jewish ethnics—both of whom are authentic embodiments of the "rags-to-riches" mythos of America—the most appropriate human responses are those of deep gratitude and appreciation for the opportunities which American society made possible. Gratitude not only for opportunities for realizing material abundance and security, but as well for the authentic and equally unparalleled experiences of religious, political, and civic freedoms in which both communities have flourished spiritually and intellectually.

But the negative, destructive horn of the ambivalence remains, and cannot be ignored. There is underrepresentation of Catholics in the elite,

4. Ibid., pp. 72–75.

decision-making centers of American life, which by and large are WASP preserves—the foundations, the universities, the media, the board rooms of major corporations and banks. When General George Brown and the discredited former vice-president, Spiro Agnew, blithely hurl anti-Semitic stereotypes across the nation's media of "Jewish control of America," they are in fact diverting attention from the scandalous reality that the leadership and control of the real centers of American financial and industrial power, the *Fortune* 500 corporations, are virtually *"Judenrein"* in their "executive suites" and their "social clubs" where the business contracts of heavy industry and multinational corporations are negotiated. All our "executive suite" studies continue to demonstrate that Jews—as well as Catholic ethnics, blacks, and Hispanics—are excluded from the management levels of the major banks, the public utilities, the insurance companies, the *sanctum sanctorum* of Protestant power and domination of America's wealth.

It is critical for the future self-understanding and democratic well-being of America that the nation faces up in a wholly conscious way to Michael Novak's major thesis; namely, that "Protestant Christianity is the single most determinative cultural force on the American character." It is not my interest to do unto Protestants what Protestants have frequently done unto Catholics, Jews, blacks, and "foreigners," that is, engage in the latest form of bigotry and scapegoating, "anti-Waspism."

But Novak's analysis of the formative influences of the constituent elements of "the Protestant way"—or more accurately, "the several Protestant ways"—is not simply nostalgic reflections on a past heritage, but a statement about clear and present forces that continue to impact on the lives of non-Protestants and on the domestic and foreign policy-making of American society.

With candor and courage, Novak lays out the elements in this threefold pattern:

(1) "The American Protestant style places an extraordinary degree of weight upon 'moral' factors in social situations. . . . The Protestant style in America is to use the word 'moral' as a club by which to undermine the standing of others. By presenting one's own interests as 'moral,' one realizes them as effortlessly as possible."

(2) "The American Protestant style also has a manifest anti-institutional bias. . . . The Protestant tendency, as Rollo May has put it, is to desire a world innocent of power and politics."

(3) "The American Protestant style is, finally, a style of revival—of moral spasm. Intense moral outrage leads to hurried rituals of refor-

mation, ends in quick forgetfulness. . . . Laws of power, self-interest, and institutional necessity require practical and lasting compromises. Striving for purity, the children of light often reject those modest compromises that might bring small but real and long-term relief."

Let me illustrate how real and potentially serious that style of Protestant moralizing can be. As is generally known, the safety and security, the very existence of the State of Israel and its three million inhabitants, are supreme issues of moral, spiritual, and human concern to the Jewish people everywhere. After the loss of one-third of the Jewish family to the murder-machine of the Nazi Holocaust, it is simply unendurable psychologically to any Jewish conscience that any credence whatsoever could be given to Article 15 of the Palestine Liberation Organization's Covenant which calls for the destruction of the State of Israel, its replacement by a so-called secular democratic Palestinian state (what the PLO wrought in Lebanon, especially to its Christian Maronite community whose power has been fatally destroyed, is a paradigm of what the PLO means by pluralism and coexistence in a "secular, democratic state"), and the use of terror and violence as justifiable means for realizing the PLO's "self-determination."

The following are true accounts of what I actually experienced with liberal Protestant church officials:

(1) Two years ago, the director of overseas missions of one of the major liberal Protestant denominations, in a face-to-face "dialogue," told me in exactly these words, "The right of the State of Israel to exist is by no means a closed issue. Israel may have to be dismantled for the sake of world peace." (Some months later, the WASP president of one of our nation's leading banks declared, "Israel is standing in the way of increased trade with the Arab nations. I hate to say it, but Israel may just have to go down the tube in our national interest.")

(2) In recent years, liberal Protestant church officials have joined with Arab propagandists and American oil companies in attacking "the Israel lobby" or "the Jewish lobby" in Washington as being somehow "un-American." What is not generally known is that in April 1977 and again in October 1977, these same liberal Protestant moralists met with Arabist members of the State Department and drafted a strategy for producing a series of resolutions for adoption by liberal Protestant church assemblies that would recognize "the PLO as the sole, legitimate representative of the Palestinian people," as well as bring "one-sided leverage" on Israel.

In September 1977, the Arab missions people of the United Presbyterian Church drafted exactly such a resolution, had it printed and

placed in the kit of all the delegates to the General Assembly of the
United Presbyterian Church meeting in Philadelphia. The delegates—
local pastors and lay delegates from across the country—declared
spontaneously on the Assembly floor that they refused "to baptize the
PLO and terrorism as legitimate." They voted down the pro-PLO
resolution by a 75 to 25 percent vote, and adopted instead a balanced
resolution that recognized Israel's right to security as well as the
legitimate rights of Palestinians—which the majority of the Jewish people
support. (What form of nationhood these rights will take is to be worked
out by the hard negotiation of political compromise.)

(3) In November 1977, the Division of Overseas Ministries of the
National Council of Churches drafted a similar initial text that was anti-
Israel and pro-PLO. The text went through several reformulations, but
even the final version was filled with moralistic, pietistic jargon.
Quintessential example: "Righteousness among men is prior to their
security and peace, for these latter depend ultimately upon relationships
which men recognize to be at least tolerably just." For my part, I would
not trust the security of my children to such "righteousness."

The mentality and rhetoric of these liberal Protestant church
bureaucrats toward Israel, the Palestinians, and the Middle East are a
classic illustration of the "Protestant moralism" that Novak describes.
Beneath the high-sounding, moralistic phrases, with all their suggestion
of altruism and perfectionism, are obscured the naked power and
financial interests of these elements within liberal Protestantism. If you
will read the *Handbook of Missions,* you will find a fascinating statistic
which these moralistic churchmen never acknowledge in any of these
discussions: American liberal Protestantism provides 70 percent of the
finances of their missionary installations in Arab countries as well as in
other overseas areas. They also provide close to 70 percent of the
missionary personnel in these countries.

I happen to hold to a Jewish theology of Christianity which looks
favorably upon constructive missionary enterprises as instruments which
have brought the covenant of Israel to the farthest reaches of the earth. If
not for Christian missions, millions of people might never have been ex-
posed to the Torah and its redemptive message of love of God and love of
fellowman. But I am appalled by the hypocrisy and the double standards.
When Catholic ethnics engage in political action that is specifically
Catholic their action is sneered at as "machine politics"; when Jews
engage in political action designed to secure the lives of millions of their
brothers and sisters, their action is "the Jewish lobby" which is somehow

to be disdained as conspiratorial and "un-American" and smacks of "double loyalty." When liberal Protestant church bureaucrats engage in identical behavior with their friends in the State Department and in the U.S. Congress or the White House, that is the work of salvation.

Reinhold Niebuhr earned the reverence of Jews and Catholics as well as Protestants because he refused to play such moral shell-games with himself as well as with others. He wrote (with Alan Heimert) in *A Nation So Conceived*:

> Our pressure on all previous sovereignties who shared the hemisphere with us and the tenacity of our land hunger under the moral sanction of what our patriots called "manifest destiny" may have given the first intimation of the formation of a unique national characteristic or trait of character, namely, the expression of a vital impulse in the name of an ideal. For we began our history by claiming the sanction of a democratic ideal for an imperial impulse, which was ostensibly disavowed and overcome by these same democratic principles.[5]

Professor Niebuhr concluded with advice for coping with such dangerous moralism that is as appropriate today as when he wrote in 1963:

> Democracy [this great Protestant prophet asserted] is an ultimate norm of political organization in the sense that no better way has been found to check the inordinacy of the powerful on the one hand and the confusion of the multitude on the other than by making every center of power responsible to the people whom it affects; by balancing subordinate centers with other centers of power to prevent injustice; and by denying immunity from criticism to any organ or mouthpiece of prestige and authority.[6]

In the third century of America's unfolding, the tolerated ethnics may well bear the providential task of prophetically checking "the inordinacy of the powerful" and of "denying immunity from criticism to any organ or mouthpiece of prestige and authority."

MARC H. TANENBAUM

5. Reinhold Niebuhr and Alan Heimert, *A Nation So Conceived* (New York: Scribner's, 1963), p. 10.

6. Ibid., p. 127.

Index